W9-BBC-110

The
Victorian
Temper

The
Victorian
Temper

A Study in Literary Culture

BY JEROME HAMILTON BUCKLEY

HARVARD UNIVERSITY PRESS
CAMBRIDGE, MASSACHUSETTS

FOR ELIZABETH

Preface
to the Reissue

WHEN I began work on *The Victorian Temper* some twenty
years ago, I was already aware of a considerable quickening of interest in Victorian literature. New biographies of the principal poets
and novelists were appearing, or about to appear, far more complete
and definitive than the older standard lives; new techniques of analysis were being tentatively turned to both the verse and the prose;
important new editions were in preparation. But I had no notion
that the revival would be so spirited and sustained as it has proven
since that time. Especially in the past decade the Victorian period has
become one of the major areas of research and criticism, one that now
commands a half-dozen journals exclusively devoted to its poetry or
fiction, its periodicals or bibliography or general cultural history. Innumerable monographs on major and minor figures, studies in rhetoric and prosody, psychological appraisals of books and authors, all
these testify each year to the wealth of materials still awaiting re-
assessment. Though the prejudice against a vague "Victorianism"
that my first chapter calls into question has not disappeared, the
epithet "Victorian" has acquired increasingly positive connotations
until it may now frequently designate an exuberance and amplitude
scarcely to be recovered yet devoutly to be wished for.

If I were now to rewrite this book, I see clearly that recent scholarship might alter some of my judgments or shift certain emphases. More attention might perhaps be accorded the novelists, though the poets would remain most accessible and most relevant to my purposes; Hopkins should be given closer consideration; Swinburne's early rebellions might be taken somewhat more seriously. I know, too, that my own further readings of primary sources would leave their mark on some of the following chapters. My study of Tennyson, for example, has given me a rather different perspective on his development and on the real function of such poems as *The Princess;* and my continuing interest in the history of ideas has convinced me that more might to advantage be said of the idea of social as well as literary decadence. On the other hand, by an extensive revision I might well lose more than I could expect to gain, for I had originally to reject much illustrative detail, and I now fear that I should be quite overwhelmed by the multitudinousness of the evidence that recent Victorianists have made available. In any case I should not be inclined to discard the central design of my argument. I should not wish to attempt a more categorical analysis of Victorian ideas and beliefs, nor should I care to introduce, at the expense of larger themes, more detailed discussion of specific works. This book was intended as a sort of literary biography of the Victorian period, early, middle and late, a relatively brief life history of its aesthetic moods and tensions and particularly of the shifts through the years of the way in which its writers conceived their responsibility to their public; and my notions of the essential character of the age, its temper, have not greatly changed since first publication. In preparing this reissue, I have therefore contented myself with the correction of a few errors of fact and dating and with several slight verbal emendations.

J.H.B.

Cambridge, Massachusetts
April 1969

Preface
to the First Printing

"TASTE," said John Ruskin, "is not only a part and an index of morality; — it is the *only* morality. The first, and last, and closest trial question to any living creature is, 'What do you like?' Tell me what you like, and I'll tell you what you are." Now, however a post-Victorian world may have chosen to regard other Ruskinian dogmas, many a "moral" indictment brought by the twentieth century against the Victorian character has rested squarely upon some generalized impression of Victorian taste. Such generalizations are, as the first chapter of this book seeks to suggest, seldom quite accurate or especially useful. For Victorian taste is intelligible only in a context of thought and feeling which defies easy definition. If Victorian literature — which remains perhaps the truest reflection of that taste — was in part the work of its individual authors, it was also in large measure, necessarily, the product of a diverse culture, of attitudes social and moral which helped condition its values, of the background, in short, that it is my present purpose to describe.

The chapters that follow constitute neither an intellectual history of Victorian England nor an ordered survey of Victorian letters. They strive neither to trace in detail the growth, for example, of scientific or religious thought nor to examine the specific development of dominant literary genres like the novel or the personal lyric. They are devoted rather to a charting of the impulses that prompted and the forces that shaped a manifold creative expression, to a study in particular of the "moral aesthetic," its rise and decline, and its relation always to a variable climate of opinion and emotion. Though

I have tried to indicate, where possible, parallel motifs in Victorian painting and in the plastic arts, I have drawn most freely upon literary sources, including a good many minor writers whose work, whatever its subsequent fate, was in its day broadly representative. Insofar as I have sought an interpretation of what might be called the Victorian temper rather than a reappraisal of Victorian talents, I have attempted no detailed analysis of the major artists as such, no close criticism of such doughty figures as Arnold or George Eliot, Meredith or Hardy. Instead, I have chosen a relatively few centers of literary influence — Carlyle, for instance, Tennyson, Kingsley, Ruskin, Oscar Wilde — and from these I have repeatedly widened the focus of discussion to embrace a number of the "schools" and the movements, the leagues and the coteries, that lent a tension and a vitality to the whole Victorian background.

I should like to acknowledge my deep indebtedness to the John Simon Guggenheim Memorial Foundation, without whose generous support this project could scarcely have been undertaken, and to the Graduate School of the University of Wisconsin for material help in carrying my research through to completion. I wish to thank Professor Hill Shine, editor, for permission to reprint certain parts of the tenth chapter which appeared in *Booker Memorial Studies* honoring Professor J. M. Booker, published by the University of North Carolina Press in 1950. I appreciate the encouragement and assistance of many friends and colleagues, particularly of Howard Mumford Jones, Ricardo Quintana, Ruth Wallerstein, Paul Fulcher, and Helen C. White. I am grateful to Edgar Lacy who followed with patience and good counsel the development of my manuscript, chapter by chapter. And I owe more to the endurance, the humor, and the sympathy of my wife, Elizabeth, than any mere dedication may record.

J. H. B.

Madison, Wisconsin
May 1951

Contents

Illustrations

The Victorian
Temper

I

"Victorianism"

Oh, so, when modern things are thrust
By death below the coffin lid,
Our liberal sons will spurn our dust
And wonder what it was we did.

— TENNYSON

B<small>Y</small> the time of Prince Albert's death in 1861, many of the Manchester liberals had come to regard the monarchy as merely the relic of an unprogressive age which had not yet learned the advantages of a complete *laissez faire*. Five years later, when Victoria had long since retired from public life, John Bright addressed a great rally of British reformers, some of whom were prepared to demand the queen's abdication. As suggested president of the new republic, Bright was earnestly confident of his cause. Still, he felt it only right during the course of his remarks to repudiate the libels that his more zealous followers had passed upon their widowed sovereign. But the mere mention of Victoria's name brought an immediate and not altogether expected response: of one accord the republican audience arose to sing with fervent heart and voice,

> *God save our gracious Queen,*
> *Long live our noble Queen,*
> *God save the Queen!* [1]

Victoria indeed outlived most of Bright's republicans by many years. She lived long — long enough to see her name indissolubly

linked to a remarkable century's culture. Yet if "Victoria" had once
been able to awaken a distinct and uniform impression in the minds
of one assembly, the age which bears her name has since been subject to diverse and divided judgment. Already by the 1890's "Victorian" had become a favorite derogatory epithet to a generation
which, ironically enough, was spending lavishly of its pounds and
poetry to celebrate Victoria's Diamond Jubilee. And into the twentieth century "Victorianism," defined ambiguously if at all, persisted,
a shield for the conservative and a target for the modernist.

Any cultural period suffers distortion from a generalized indictment, however speciously formulated. But the outlines of the Victorian era blur beyond recognition in the confusion of contradictory
charges. The Victorians, we are told, were "a poor, blind, complacent
people";[2] yet they were torn by doubt, spiritually bewildered,[3] lost
in a troubled universe. They were crass materialists, wholly absorbed
in the present, quite unconcerned "with abstract verities and eternal
values";[4] but they were also excessively religious, lamentably idealistic, nostalgic for the past,[5] and ready to forego present delights
for the vision of a world beyond. Despite their slavish "conformity," [6]
their purblind respect for convention, they were, we learn, "rugged
individualists," given to "doing as one likes," [7] heedless of culture,
careless of a great tradition; they were iconoclasts who worshiped
the idols of authority. They were, besides, at once sentimental humanitarians and hard-boiled proponents of free enterprise. Politically, they were governed by narrow insular prejudice, but swayed
by dark imperialistic designs. Intellectually and emotionally, they
believed in progress, denied original sin, and affirmed the death of
the Devil; yet by temperament they were patently Manichaeans to
whom living was a desperate struggle between the force of good and
the power of darkness.[8] While they professed "manliness," they
yielded to feminine standards; if they emancipated woman from age-
old bondage, they also robbed her of a vital place in society.[9] Though
they were sexually inhibited [10] and even failed to consider the existence of physical love, they begat incredibly large families and
flaunted in their verses a morbidly overdeveloped erotic sensibility.[11]

Their art constitutes a shameless record of both hypocrisy and in-genuousness. And their literature remains too purposeful, propa-gandistic, didactic, with too palpable a design upon the reader; yet it is clearly so romantic, aesthetic, "escapist," that it carries to posterity but a tale of little meaning.

Since most of such charges represent personal reaction rather than objective analysis, the terms "Victorian" and "Victorianism" have acquired the vaguest of emotional connotations. They have become what Ruskin chose to call "masked words droning and skulking about us." While the social historian[12] of the Victorian age who is able to withhold opinion is forever aware of intrinsic complexities, the critic intent upon cultural evaluation is constantly betrayed into premature judgment. And it is the aggregate of these judgments that obscures definition. Many are agreed that in Victorianism inheres a single tragic flaw which vitiates all its sounder impulses. But to one it is a moral hypocrisy,[13] to another a deliberate sentimentalism,[14] to a third a social snobbery.[15] An eminent debunker[16] laments the total failure of the critical faculty. And a sensitive student of abnor-mal psychology detects in all Victorian life "a manifestation of the anal complex[17] operating upon the group psyche." Yet all the sub-tleties of oversimplification merely confuse; "Victorianism" remains obscure; we approach no nearer the Victorian essence.

But whatever its central defect, the age, we gather, must in some hidden way have been deeply pernicious. Apparently so persuaded, not a few essayists have attempted to salvage their favorite Victorian authors from the contamination of an unfortunate background. Lewis Carroll has been recently depicted as a frustrated professor attacking "those jungles of nonsense which were merely the daily life" of cultured adults "in the now legendary reign of Victoria"; and his biographer advises us that we may safely "call the *Alice* books art, and the entire Victorian age a neurosis." [18] From a similar point of view, the Brownings may be commended for having reared their son Pen with intelligence and sympathy, for "neither Robert nor Elizabeth Browning were in any way typical Victorian parents." [19] Even Tennyson, who is somewhat more difficult to dissociate from his milieu, finds an apologist who contends that the Laureate, having resisted the "rigid dogma" of his time, may speak to an inquiring modernity, "in spite of all his Victorianism." [20]

It has been possible to recognize the manifold dissatisfactions and rebellions of Carlyle, Dickens, Ruskin, Morris, Samuel Butler, and at the same time to insist that "the note of revolt is not characteristic of the Victorian Age." [21] By definition, the cultural leader must advance beyond his less gifted contemporaries in grasping the problem of his time, but he can scarcely be considered a leader at all if he stands entirely out of relation to those who lag behind. It is, therefore, by no means clear how reasonably we may dogmatize about the acquiescence of the Victorian era, when many of its most representative and influential writers appear restive or refractory. At any rate, we are hardly to be convinced by criticism like that of the British scholar who, writing in the year of the Munich appeasement, condemns Victorian smugness, with the conviction that Englishmen of 1938 have "scarcely a trace of complacency left." [22]

Whether or not, then, their entire age was spiritually apathetic, the most articulate Victorians were, like wakeful minds in any generation, quite prepared to assail omnipresent stupidity and vicious self-satisfaction. Often, to reinforce their assault on the forts of folly, they resorted to the same sort of oversimplified indictment that has since been turned against them. Almost always, they were able to muster their attack with a vigor of statement compared to which latter-day polemics pale into gentle censure. John Morley, for instance, could ally impassioned eloquence to reasoned principle in his denunciation of Victorian England as "a community where political forms, from the monarchy down to the popular chamber, are mainly hollow shams disguising the coarse supremacy of wealth, where religion is mainly official and political, and is ever ready to dissever itself alike from the spirit of justice, the spirit of charity, and the spirit of truth, and where literature does not as a rule permit itself to discuss serious subjects frankly and worthily — a community, in short, where the great aim of all classes and orders with power is by dint of rigorous silence, fast shutting of the eyes, and stern stopping of the ears, somehow to keep the social pyramid on its apex, with the fatal result of preserving for England its glorious fame as a paradise for the well-to-do, a purgatory for the able, and a hell for the poor." [23]

If Morley, by reason of his relationship to the positivist radicals of the seventies, seems too clearly biased a witness, we may turn to a comparatively calm early Victorian chronicler who makes no claim to peculiar insight. Reporting with statistical exactitude on the industrial advance of his generation, George Richardson Porter paused to caution a complacent reader against undue optimism. "It must be owned," he wrote, "that our multiplied abodes of want, of wretchedness, and of crime — our town populations huddled together in ill-ventilated and undrained courts and cellars — our numerous workhouses filled to overflowing with the children of want — and our prisons (scarcely less numerous) overloaded with the votaries of crime, do indeed but too sadly and too strongly attest that all is not as it should be with us as regards this most important branch of human progress." [24] Beside strictures so disillusioned and so vehement, twentieth-century anti-Victorianism seems imaginatively stale and rhetorically flabby. The Victorians are still their own severest critics, possessed of an amazing capacity for detachment, a singular command of invective, and, as we shall see, an unequaled talent for parody. "Victorianism" was undoubtedly, at least in part, a monster created by rebellious spirits and bequeathed to a posterity which all too frequently is content to regard the spirits as the monster's children.

Violent and vituperative as it frequently was, Victorian self-criticism found direction in the implicit sense that the faults it assailed were remediable by individual and collective reform. For the Victorians were quite unable to view their long era as a static entity, a unique whole to be described by a single sweeping formula. The doctrine of organic development was so thoroughly diffused throughout nineteenth-century science and philosophy that no serious thinker could escape its implications. Whether or not the thoughts of men were widening with the process of the suns, there were everywhere evidences of continual growth and decay. Wistfully Frederic Harrison looked to the joys of a vanished past; early Victorian life, he felt sure, must have been pleasanter than existence in the seventies, for certainly Dickens and Thackeray "tell us of a livelier, jollier age than that recorded in *Middlemarch* and *Fors Clavigera*." [25] In a more sanguine mood, Walter Besant chronicled the incalculable changes between the accession of Victoria and the Golden Jubilee. He lingered over quaint customs long outmoded, as if contemplating the strangeness of a remote antiquity; for in 1887 he could find scant similarity to early Victorian tastes, no parallel, for instance, to the rules of etiquette acceptable fifty years before:

> Never ask a lady any questions about anything whatever.
>
> If you have drunk wine with every one at the table and wish for more, wait till the cloth is removed.
>
> Never permit the sanctity of the drawing-room to be violated by a boot.[26]

If many changes were wrought by deliberate reformers fighting old prejudices, many also, like the shift in standards of deportment, resulted from the gradual operation of hidden social forces.

All in all, the Victorian period achieved little of the stability we have learned to associate with a semimythical neoclassic culture. It moved from form to form, and nothing stood. Almost every Victorian thesis produced its own antithesis, as a ceaseless dialectic worked out its designs. Throughout the period there were vast differences between rural and urban society; the fields of the agrarian South were, as Mrs. Gaskell suggested, a far cry from the smoky cities of the industrial North. And between the towns themselves sharp distinctions could be drawn; the London of Oscar Wilde had little in common with the Birmingham of Joseph Chamberlain. Besides, the "climate of opinion" varied from year to year, from decade to decade; the seventies was perhaps as distant from the eighties as we imagine the twenties of our own century remote from the thirties. The Victorian age as a whole was forced to adapt itself to new values as old traditions crumbled; and the term "Victorian" is, therefore, egregiously abused when invoked to describe attitudes that the Victorians inherited, modified, or discarded.

Viewed in its long perspective, nineteenth-century culture appears entirely relative to the manifold developments of a changing society. Yet within the Victorian period itself, "Victorianism" may well have been a necessary postulate, a distinct absolute deduced from a vague composite of social and aesthetic values which creative thinkers felt compelled to dismiss, in order to clear the way for radical innovation. And to the Edwardians the fiction may have served an essential purpose in assisting towards fresh objectives, until such a time as those objectives were attained and the generation of Virginia Woolf and James Joyce might devise the myth of "Edwardianism." Ultimately the debunking of things Victorian became an amusing pastime rather than a meaningful criticism; the distortion of a past culture represented little more than the evasion of a present problem. Havelock Ellis, who in 1890 had attacked all that seemed to him false within the Victorian world, lived to find "the gesture that was once a vital reaction to real things" becoming at last "a stale and empty trick." [27]

Now that half a century has elapsed since Victoria's death, facile repudiation of the Victorian era seems, in truth, quite as outmoded as the attitudes we can no longer recapture. But the sentimentalization that in some quarters has replaced it is scarcely more constructive. The interests of modern design are not appreciably furthered by the self-conscious revival of baroque styles or the rediscovery of bric-a-brac which has acquired the charm of the antique. We can understand the significant backgrounds of contemporary thought only by transcending indiscriminate praise or blame. Collective guilt, we have learned, is never easy to determine; and value-judgments are best confined to specific creeds and individual works of art.

Working inductively, distrustful of "masked words" and slanted evidence, the historian might discover the sources of the precise concepts upon which less objective interpreters have based their general indictment. The idea of progress, for instance, an idea which admittedly had considerable currency during the Victorian period, might be related to a broader cultural context. It might be seen as an outgrowth of Cartesian philosophy, receiving its major extension among the *philosophes* of eighteenth-century France, passing with

variations through the anarchism of Godwin and the poetry of
Shelley towards the socialism of Saint-Simon and the positivism of
Comte, until with Herbert Spencer came the assumption that progress and evolution moved consistently in the same direction. Or
within the age alone, it might be linked to the Victorian's awareness
of his very real social advance. The notion of perfectibility would
seem to have some immediate sanction at a time when men were
devising a system of education on a broad democratic basis, establishing the rights of free speech and trade unionism, progressively extending the franchise, reshaping their entire legal code, and discovering the principles of a medical science by which the sum of human
suffering might be immeasurably reduced.

It might then be debated whether the idea of progress was not as
much an incentive to further reform as a cause of stupefying satisfaction with the advances already achieved. Yet a cursory review of
Victorian opinion indicates that the idea, whatever its effect upon
those who embraced it, was much less widely accepted than we have
been led to believe. Huxley, who was at least as articulate as Spencer,
insisted that evolutionary change not seldom ran counter to ethical
improvement. And Tennyson, whose early visions of the future have
too readily convicted his generation of blind optimism, attained by
1886 a thoroughly disillusioned view of the "glooming alleys" where
"Progress halts on palsied feet" and a sense of the disaster involved
in the failure of social adaptation to keep pace with scientific discovery; if Tennyson held to a modified faith in evolution, he recognized the possibility of regression:

Forward then, but still remember how the course of time will swerve,
Crook and turn upon itself in many a backward-streaming curve.[28]

The Victorian temper is thus not to be adequately gauged in terms
of a concept which flourished long before 1837 and was subject to
important qualification from 1850 onwards.

Many of the specific values associated with the anomaly known
as "Victorianism" have, like the idea of progress, partial basis in objective evidence; and the inconsistency of the generalizations itself

testifies to the bewildering complexity of the era. It is almost impossible to reduce a culture so various to a common denominator; and conflict, indeed, may emerge as the only unity in a great diversity. Yet it is not difficult to find certain doctrines perhaps opposing each other but recurring with an insistency which suggests the breadth of their influence. Probably the most prominent of these, in the early Victorian period at any rate, are Evangelical religion and Benthamite philosophy,[29] both pre-Victorian in origin and both vigorously questioned throughout the nineteenth century. To the one has been ascribed the sententious hypocrisy of Mr. Podsnap; to the other, the uncompromising factualism of Mr. Gradgrind. But apart from their baneful effects, which are to some extent problematical, each encouraged a sense of social responsibility which did much to mitigate the miseries of an expanding industrialism; each contributed, even to its bitterest enemies, something of its earnestness and fixity of vision.

If hardheaded Benthamism was ultimately undermined by the reservations and subtleties of the greatest utilitarian, its zeal for practical reform infected many who found Mill's hedonistic paradox more ingenious than convincing. And if Evangelical restraints and dogmas slowly dissolved under the scrutiny of critical intelligence, the old thirst for righteousness animated so reluctant a heretic as George Eliot, so willful an agnostic as John Morley. Whether actuated by self-interest or Christian principle, moral duty remained for most a categorical imperative. With all the assurance of his brother's orthodoxy, F. W. Newman the freethinker could insist that "all social action, all national cohesion, all reverence for law, all sanctity in rule, is founded upon man's moral conscience."[30] For a few social purpose seemed at one time effectively to coalesce with ethical premise in the short-lived Religion of Humanity. But even to fervent atheists like Charles Bradlaugh the demand for moral sanction and the claims of social justice seemed inescapable. Craving adjustment amid the peril of change, representative Victorians, at least until the seventies, sought either in the radiance of God or in the dim consciousness of man some spiritual absolute by which to interpret and control their material advance; whatever misdirections they may frequently have followed, their impulse was in essence deeply religious.[31]

Prince Albert, we are told, was much concerned with art, though unfortunately he felt it to lie "somewhere between religion and hygiene." [32] Now, if for "hygiene" we might substitute "the general health of the body politic," Prince Albert's view of art would differ little from the first principles of any considerable mid-Victorian aesthetician. The "morality of art" — its religious content — lay in its relationship to the full experience and its power to speak to mankind in the language of universal emotion. For it was the artist's first duty to communicate, and the substance of his message was necessarily of social and, therefore, moral significance. To Ruskin it was clear that the student of art gained the deepest insight into the totality of human affairs. And to Arnold it seemed natural that the critic of books should be first and last a critic of society. The "moral aesthetic" was by no means a Victorian invention; it rested on the major premises of almost every classical aesthetic theory. Yet it bore special relevance to Victorian needs. Confronted with the unprecedented developments of nineteenth-century culture, an emerging middle class with the meagerest intellectual traditions behind it strove desperately to achieve standards of judgment. The early Victorian poet, sometimes no more certain than his contemporaries, was expected to furnish instruction as well as amusement. He could fulfill his vital function in society only by passing dramatic commentary upon the conflicts of his time. Often like Tennyson he had first to relinquish a personal prejudice for a more disinterested aesthetic. But usually he came in the end to feel his renunciation morally — and socially — essential. At all events, out of his sacrifice was born a considerable didactic literature.

In its many-sided concern with manners and morals, the Victorian era was not unlike the Elizabethan age, when conduct-books, pamphlets, plays, sermons, poems explored the problems of degree in an expanding economy. Both periods brought to the present a deep sense of the national past, based upon high scholarship and eager research. Both shared the excitement of vital education. Far from sinking beneath the weight of its "moral," their art at its best followed new experience beyond the bounds of thought. In the years after 1850 novelists and poets exploited the forgotten "local color" of every English county to produce a kind of nineteenth-century *Poly-Olbion*.[33] Like the Elizabethans, the Victorians embarked on their own voyages of discovery. To the far corners of the unknown traveled "manly" adventurers — Layard to buried Nineveh, Livingstone to the dark heart of Africa, Richard Burton to Brazil and Tanganyika and the Great Salt Lake in a valiant effort to live his unexpurgated Arabian nights.

But whether at home or abroad, many a Victorian captured the almost Elizabethan exuberance that led Hurrell Froude to exclaim on the launching of the Oxford Movement in 1833: "What fun it is living in such times as these! How could one now go back to the times of old Tory humbug!" [34] A tireless emotional energy carried Carlyle through continents of passionate prose, just as a physical stamina impelled the somewhat calmer Leslie Stephen to tramp the fifty miles from Cambridge to London on a hot day.[35] Like the Elizabethans, the high Victorians valued a manifold competence; Ruskin like Bacon took all knowledge to be his province, and whether or not, as Whistler suggested, he failed to master his specific subject, he left his mark on many others. Not without some reason, then, did John Addington Symonds conclude that "the English Renaissance of the sixteenth century became renascent in the nineteenth." [36]

Yet it will not do to press the parallel too far. Symonds himself detected in the Victorian period, whatever its buoyancy and promise, elements of "world fatigue" which were, he felt, quite alien to the Elizabethan temper. Certainly the desperate unbelief that permeates so much of Arnold's verse and wracks so little of his prose arises from distinctly Victorian cultural conditions, a sad contemplation of withering faith and an unprecedented fear of encroaching materialism. The paralysis of doubt that is said to have gripped Arnold's generation is far removed from the divided aims of a disillusioned Hamlet. Even if, as seems likely, both conflicts have been overstated, the very real crosscurrents of Victorian assent and denial are scarcely "Elizabethan" in source or direction.

Victorian society was forever subject to tensions which militated against complete spontaneity and singleness of purpose. It experienced in various forms the self-consciousness that is at once the strange disease of modern life and the genesis of analytic science. It learned to fear its own ardors, to distrust the falsehood of extremes. Whenever artist or philosopher was betrayed by the intensity of his conviction, Victorian parody served to restore a lost perspective; laughter prodded eccentric genius into an awareness of common reality. Despite the resounding clash of individual wills, there was until late in Victoria's reign a desire for cultural synthesis urgent enough to inspire from even the most rebellious many a concession to an established social morality. It was often as if the discords were hushed by a half-heard imperious command, "Hark, the dominant's persistence till it must be answered to!" Again and again the poet dreamed of a remote harmony which might catch up diverse themes into a larger pattern, a meaningful Victorian counterpoint. Tennyson prayed for his whole generation a prayer which might be echoed by Victorians of vastly different intellectual persuasion:

> Let knowledge grow from more to more,
> But more of reverence in us dwell;
> That mind and soul according well,
> May make one music as before.

For all his sharp censure of Victorian culture, even John Morley came to feel that the prayer had been at times richly fulfilled; in the best effort of his age he saw "mind and soul according well." In 1921, nearly fifty years after the first appearance of his essay *On Compromise,* he added a few words by way of epilogue, a Victorian's final answer to a skeptical posterity. "Whatever we may say of Europe between Waterloo and Sedan," he wrote, "in our country at least it was an epoch of hearts uplifted with hope, and brains active with sober and manly reason for the common good. Some ages are marked as sentimental, others stand conspicuous as rational. The

Victorian age was happier than most in the flow of both these currents into a common stream of vigorous and effective talent. New truths were welcomed in free minds, and free minds make brave men." Though later critics might charge the Victorians with divorcing intellect and feeling, the liaison was in fact well sustained into the 1870's, and the process of separation was, as we shall see, prolonged and painful. By 1884, when Ruskin sensed a great "storm cloud of the nineteenth century" blotting out the sun and breaking an old "harmony," English culture, heedless of his mid-Victorian warnings, was entering upon a new phase of its development.

The Anti-Romantics

See! on the cumbered plain
Clearing a stage,
Scattering the past about,
Comes the new age!
Bards make new poems,
Thinkers new schools,
Statesmen new systems,
Critics new rules!
All things begin again;
Life is their prize;
Earth with their deeds they fill,
Fill with their cries!

— MATTHEW ARNOLD

IF "Victorianism" on analysis proves increasingly elusive, romanticism has already passed into the realm of the unknowable. The so-called "romantic movement" in England, we discover, subscribed to no common aesthetic capable of general definition. Far more than its Continental parallels, it was eclectic in its tastes, distrustful of systematized creeds, disinclined to issue aesthetic manifestoes. Though poets might attack the artificialities of eighteenth-century diction, none set out self-consciously to challenge the tenets of "neoclassicism." While Victor Hugo could drive an audience at the Comédie-Française to physical violence by his deliberate flouting of the *bienséances* of French classical drama, English romantics were at a loss to find any literary conventions so staunchly maintained, for the Augustan aestheticians had left no rigid rules to cramp rebellious talents. A romantic revolt could scarcely gather head if there were no organized tyranny to overthrow. Nor could a crusade be launched if there were no evangel to inspire its campaign. In Germany Novalis could adjust his dithyrambic verses to the requirements of a newly articulated "romantic idealism." But in Britain no new philosophy became sufficiently entrenched to provide the basis for a new aesthetic theory. However open to European influences they may have been, English artists of the Regency period owed far less to the metaphysics of Kant and Fichte than to the empirical relativism of the British tradition, which they inherited from the eighteenth century and adapted to their own purposes.[1] Intellectually, then, the romantic movement in England was less a sudden revolution than a remarkable development in the long organic process of cultural history. And the Victorians most ready to question its achievements were quite unable to regard "romanticism" as a fixed unit beginning arbitrarily with the first *Lyrical Ballads* and ending climactically with the death of Lord Byron.

Linked together by strange coincidence of genius rather than common loyalty to a single aesthetic, two generations of English romantic poets produced an impressive literature — so various that it escaped classification, so beautiful that it evoked a renascence of wonder, so new that it carried with it both the malaise of modernity and the freshness of an early world. Wordsworth, Coleridge, Byron, Shelley, Keats, each in his own way extended the emotional and technical range of English verse. Each, drawing freely upon an associationist psychology, arrived at a vital concept of the sympathetic imagination by which he might grasp the essence of an integrated whole. Yet each avoided the extremes of the doctrine, not unpopular among other "romantic" groups, that beauty is ultimately irrational and basically beyond intellectual perception.[2] Perhaps their greatest weakness lay in their greatest power. So marked was their gift of tongues that they seemed at times more intent upon self-expression for its own sake than upon communication of an objective reality.

Too frequently they appeared to regard art as an excrescence of mind rather than an imitation of life, as a product of personal impression and private mood rather than a deduction from general experience.[3] Goethe's dictum that the classic was the healthy and the romantic the diseased applied less cogently to English "romanticism" than to German. Yet Ruskin's more guarded distinction was not without meaning in his own country; romantic art, he suggested, lacked the authority of classic art, since the classic writer set down only what was "known to be true," while the romantic expressed himself "under the impulse of passions," which might or might not lead to new truths.[4]

During their most productive years the romantics endured censure as scathing as any the neo-humanist has since heaped upon them.[5] Yet they were scarcely to be intimidated by reviewers who ignored their artistry to decry their radical politics or unorthodox morals. For they kept alive, to their own inestimable advantage, a truer capacity for "aesthetic" criticism. All of the major poets, except perhaps Wordsworth, had some sense of the ridiculous in his own work and some talent for satire. None was quite so serious or sentimental as Lamartine in nourishing his own emotions. And none was blind to the limitations of his fellow craftsmen. Romantic critics like Hazlitt or Coleridge could discern what was false in any romantic theory of art; and Byron as well as Peacock could turn what was once romantic to burlesque.

Yet, for all their critical awareness, the major romantics preserved a sharp individuality of tone, a strongly personal accent. And it was their intense mannerism that inspired lesser writers who were unable to recapture the critical intelligence that had curbed facile sentiment and checked undue fluency. By the time Wordsworth and Coleridge had declined in creative power and Keats, Shelley, and Byron had met premature death, the romantic movement had visibly decayed. A new generation which would reach maturity in the early years of Victoria's reign might still derive much from romantic technique and subject matter, but it could no longer imitate the practices of artists who had developed their individual talents in a different intellectual milieu. If the early Victorians were to realize their own vitality, they had to strike out in new directions; they had to discover their own styles, forms, and critical standards. Though they prepared no indictment of romantic art comparable to the Edwardian myth of Victorianism, they nonetheless were forced to reject certain romantic values, to repudiate specific attitudes and gestures, in order to secure their own orientation. The Victorian era rapidly recognized its proper spokesmen in writers who were strenuously conscious of Victorian problems; and the reputations of the romantics suffered accordingly a far-reaching shift in taste.

Of all the romantics, Wordsworth might appear best able to resist the change of literary fashion. And indeed among cultivated readers of the thirties and forties, his work commanded increasing respect. The young Darwin read *The Excursion* twice through with high enthusiasm;[6] and the disillusioned John Mill, though convinced that "the poet of unpoetical natures" could be a writer of no great preeminence, sought from the shorter poems a guide to the "permanent happiness" that abides in "tranquil contemplation."[7] In 1839 Wordsworth received an honorary degree from Oxford for having "shed a celestial light upon the affections, the occupations and the piety of the poor."[8] Four years later when he succeeded Southey as Poet Laureate, few would deny his services to literature. Yet to many younger artists who could recognize his genius, his style and message seemed already remote and irrelevant. Browning, who had himself evaded political realities, decried the quiescence, the reactionary conservatism, of a lost leader:

> *Just for a handful of silver he left us,*
> *Just for a riband to stick in his coat.*

And Tennyson, who felt Wordsworth "at his best on the whole the greatest English poet since Milton," lamented a deficiency in form: "He is often too diffuse and didactic for me."[9] Macaulay found in *The Prelude* of 1850 "the old raptures about mountains and cataracts; the old flimsy philosophy about the effect of scenery upon the mind; the old crazy, mystical metaphysics."[10] Carlyle admired Wordsworth's sincerity, simplicity, and composure, but saw little to be said for his speculations, which merely "translated Teutonic thought into a poor, disjointed, whitey-brown sort of English"; and in his verse he heard only "a fine limpid vein of melody . . . as of an honest rustic *fiddle,* good, and well handled, but *wanting* two or more of the *strings,* and not capable of much!" [11] If Wordsworth's devotion to the poor was commendable, his "naturalism" was suspect; a dichotomy between man and nature could lead to an unproductive misanthropy,[12] and a philosophic aloofness might provide too ready an escape from social conflict. Wordsworth's great intellectual limitation, said Arnold, was somehow a failure of culture: "he should have read more books"; he too hastily dismissed the critical faculty.[13]

Yet Coleridge, who most certainly cherished the critical faculty, seemed to the first Victorians vitiated by his own quite different "romantic" bias. The impact of his thought, to be sure, was apparent and pervasive. And Mill rightly recognized in him one of the great seminal minds of the nineteenth century. As philosopher he anticipated Carlyle in opening the English intellect to the mysteries of the transcendental Germans. As political theorist he developed in Burkean terms a concept of "Tory democracy" which before long would help shape the creed of Disraeli and the policy of all the new Conservatives. And as theologian he foreshadowed, on the one hand, the Tractarian emphasis upon the organic growth of Anglicanism and, on the other, the Broad-Church concern for a "liberalized" Christianity. But, however wide his influence, he was scarcely immune from attack. For to many it was clear that Coleridge had sinned against the realities of earth. To Carlyle, who might in some respects have been his disciple, he was "flabby and irresolute, . . . terribly deficient in goal or aim," muddled and metaphysical; "in general he seemed deficient in laughter; or indeed in sympathy for concrete human things either on the sunny or on the stormy side. One right peal of concrete laughter at some convicted flesh-and-blood absurdity, one burst of noble indignation at some injustice or depravity, rubbing elbows with us on this solid earth, how strange would it have been in that Kantean haze-world, and how infinitely cheering amid its vacant air-castles and dim-melting ghosts and shadows!" [14] Carlyle's censure is, of course, characteristically turgid. But it indicates quite clearly a Victorian preference, shared by other and more temperate critics, for "realism" and sociological purpose. Eneas Sweetland Dallas, for instance, probably the sanest of Victorian aestheticians, joined Carlyle in assailing Coleridge's nebulosity; Coleridge, he said, "rather prided himself on his anatomy of thought and expression, but he hardly ever made a clean dissection." And Coleridge's definition of imagination reminded him "of a splendid definition of art which I once heard. When the infinite I AM beheld his work of creation, he said Thou ART, and ART was. The philosopher of Highgate never explained himself." [15]

Byron was neither abstruse nor metaphysical, and his rhetoric could hold a public which would not linger long to hear a troubled mariner's tale, much less a philosophic critic's discourse. Indeed, his eloquence and rant, his demonic dreams and heroic aspirations sank far into the consciousness of the common reader, and his dread sentiments deeply infected the imagination of a whole school of lively minor Victorians.[16] Yet like the fallen archangel to whom he was often compared, he suffered a gradual loss of brightness; his literary fame among serious writers of the new age visibly declined. Tennyson was almost alone in preferring the robust realism of *Don Juan* to the rhapsodic *Pilgrimage*.[17] To others, who ignored the genuine vitality of the satire, the pageant of the bleeding heart became a dreary spectacle. Though Ruskin might find in Byron's "steadiness of bitter melancholy" a powerful grasp of tragic fact,[18] and Kingsley might see in his tortured soul "the most intense and awful sense of moral law," [19] Carlyle could announce a weakness only too obvious to many of his contemporaries: Here was a man of great genius who had never reached maturity, an artist who had never achieved the Everlasting Yea and who, therefore, had little to offer a generation in search of assent.[20] Mill at the crisis in his development had turned to Byron for direction; but, he complained, "I got no good from this reading. . . . The poet's state of mind was too like my own. His was the lament of a man who had worn out all pleasures, and who seemed to think that life, to all who possess the good things of it, must necessarily be the vapid, uninteresting thing which I found it." [21] Macaulay, who warmed to Byronic description, was yet perplexed to understand the peculiar disease of mind that led the poet to forsake the hum of human cities for the high solitudes of self-communion.[22] And Browning could see no help for mankind in the misanthropist forever climbing mounts "to 'scape [his] fellow." [23] In 1838 Bulwer-Lytton had angrily declared: "When the multitude ceased to speak of Lord Byron, they ceased to speak about poetry itself." [24] But by 1850 the major Victorians had grown tired of Byron's subjectivity, suspicious of his rhetoric, and disgusted with his scorn of struggling humanity; and by 1850 even Bulwer-Lytton, arch-timeserver that he was, had replaced his own early Byronic attitudes by more popular literary gestures.

In the second *Hyperion* Keats was moving towards a conception of the artist's role in society far more relevant to Victorian needs than Byron's apparent self-absorption. Yet the second *Hyperion,* unfortunately, was not published until 1856 when the new generation had already achieved its own working aesthetic. Keats, accordingly, if read at all in the twenty years following his death, was known chiefly as the determined "escapist," the apostle of an unsocial art for art's sake, the unhappy youth who preferred sensation to thought.[25] Such was the poor aesthete Carlyle dismissed, "a miserable creature hungering after sweets" beyond his reach, a hopeless dreamer of "weak-eyed maudlin sensibility." Browning, though from the first less unsympathetic, turned resolutely from the values of Keats to seek his own strength in a psychological style utterly alien to the great romantic. Temperamentally, Tennyson came perhaps closest to the Keatsian ideal, as the Victorians imagined it. And we are not surprised to learn that Keats was Tennyson's favorite nineteenth-century poet, the one whose influence most strongly colored his early volumes. But there were from the beginning other forces operating upon the young Tennyson; and before long he was driven to disclaim charges that his lyrics echoed Keatsian music. Between

1832 and 1842, he strove consciously to reduce any possible likeness; he carefully toned down the sensuous elements in his verse to emphasize the prophetic. And ultimately he forsook his palace of art hung with its "Keatsian" brocades to face the Victorian conflict on the darkling plain that was so to perplex Matthew Arnold. Indeed, it is perhaps significant of early Victorian culture as a whole that Arnold, himself not unindebted to the odes, harshly arraigned Keats as unconcerned with the issues of modern life, as lacking high seriousness and the "matured power of moral interpretation." [26]

Less eager for aesthetic precision, Shelley from boyhood yearned to move unawakened earth with passionate prophecy. Yet his fierce spirit seemed to the Victorians too impatient of earth's essential disciplines. The vagaries of his private life troubled his early biographers, who found it more than difficult to reconcile an intense idealism with a quite imperfect sense of human relationships. And the violence of his revolutionary program shocked even the political liberals, who were committed to the orderly processes of parliamentary reform. If his concerns were undeniably moral, his morality at best seemed dubious, fashioned from his own unchristian visions, ill-adapted to the practical demands of an industrial society.[27] The young Thackeray felt that Shelley's "strong and perhaps good feelings" had been perverted by an "absurd creed," and his "high powers" misguided by conceit and false religion.[28] Others questioned the strength of his emotion and the range of his intellect. To Kingsley he was "a sentimentalist pure and simple; incapable of anything like inductive reasoning." [29] And to Sir Henry Taylor he was merely a man of feeling intent upon leading his followers to "regions where reason . . . is all but unknown, . . . to seats of anarchy and abstraction, where imagination exercises the shadow of an authority, over a people of phantoms, in a land of dreams." [30] A half-respect for such ethereal unreason led Mill, the "unpoetical nature," to think of Shelley as one of England's most enduring poets, the ideal type of the poetical mind;[31] and a half-scorn prompted Arnold's description of the "beautiful and ineffectual angel, beating in the void his luminous wings in vain." Tennyson, significantly, praised the poet who gave "the world another heart," but admitted, "He is often too much in the clouds for me." [32] And Carlyle, as usual, delivered the harshest judgment, the estimate which by its overstatement best crystallized the early Victorian objection: "Poor Shelley," he said, "always was, and is, a kind of ghastly object; colourless, pallid, tuneless, without health or warmth or vigour; the sound of him shrieky, frosty, as if a *ghost* were trying to 'sing' to us; the temperament of him, spasmodic, hysterical, instead of strong or robust; with fine affectations and aspirations, gone all such a road: — a man infinitely too *weak* for that solitary scaling of the Alps which he undertook in spite of all the world." [33]

Yet, whatever the heresies of Carlyle, at least one great Victorian remained fixed in his devotion to Shelley's memory. From his first discovery of *Queen Mab* the young Robert Browning was under the spell of a high "romantic" ecstasy. Shelley it was who almost converted him to radical politics and even, briefly, to vegetarianism. And Shelley it was who for a while inspired a religious disbelief, so ardent indeed that it very nearly shook the faith of Miss Sarah Flower, the youth's confidante — until the maturing poet might recover to defend Shelley's essential Christianity and Miss Flower could rally to indite "Nearer My God to Thee." But, in spite of his willingness to emulate, Browning achieved little of literary value under Shelley's direct influence. Largely an extended tribute to his master, his first volume, *Pauline* (1833), is hardly more than an eloquent failure; before long the "Sun-treader," so reverently saluted, is lost in the mist of cloudy meditation. Designed as a spiritual autobiography, *Pauline* betrays unusual vagueness of theme and direction; the poet lacks faith in his intuitions; his dreams lay bare no personal reality. Yet the poem occupies an important place in Browning's development; it marks his own dissatisfaction with the subjective method and the effusive confessional style. The introspection breeds only a deep despair; increasing disillusion overcasts an early hope, until at last the poet is driven to renounce his visions for a selfless view of the outside world:

No more of the past! I'll look within no more.
I have too trusted my own lawless wants,   6m
Too trusted my vain self, vague intuition —
Draining soul's wine alone in the still night.

Henceforth a rigid objectivity of manner and matter was to serve
as Browning's central aesthetic standard. However much he would
continue to value Shelley's Platonic ideal, his own best poetry was
to be rooted in a grasp of concrete dramatic detail. His personal
philosophy, stemming from "romantic" sources, might color his
whole work, but his private hopes and fears would be sealed from
an inquisitive public. And no matter how far from present actualities he might retreat into a past culture, he was, in this respect at
least, essentially in accord with the first principles of objective, unromantic art in early Victorian England.

On its lowest level the rejection of romantic writers may have
represented a fundamental distrust of literature itself, the basic uneasiness that the practical artisan, the builder of a material economy,
forever experiences in the presence of art. At any rate, the common
reader received from the first systematic encouragement towards
philistinism. In 1824, the year of Byron's death, the *Westminster
Review* was founded to propagate Benthamite doctrines of social
action and, quite incidentally, to pronounce aesthetic judgment insofar as things aesthetic could have any remote bearing on the sum
of human happiness.[34] While its editors felt a lingering respect for
Byron's radicalism, they found on the whole very little "utility" in
the literature of their time. One reviewer, evidently convinced that
poetry was but a dull opiate diverting the innocent from immediate
political issues, went so far as to warn his readers against all pur-
poseless composition: "Ledgers," he remarked with perfect reason,
"do not keep well in rhyme, nor are three deckers built by songs,
as towns were of yore. . . . Literature is a seducer; we had almost
said a harlot. She may do to trifle with; but woe be to the state
whose statesmen write verses, and whose lawyers read more in Tom
Moore than in Bracton." Not all the utilitarian critics bore so close

a resemblance to Gradgrind of Coketown, but many agreed on the dangers that attended the seductions of literature. If the creative writer selected detail to fit a predetermined design, his work could not reproduce an actuality, and it might, therefore, be both untrue and insidious. It might easily, argued one Peregrine Bingham, "tend to disqualify any man for the severer exercise of his reason." Even John Stuart Mill failed to escape entirely the Benthamite bias; the philosopher David Hume, he said, had been "completely enslaved by a taste for literature, . . . that literature which without regard for truth or utility seeks only to excite emotion." Absurd in theory, such criticism had perhaps some faint justification in actual practice. It was clearly fashioned to discredit the writings of the social conservatives who dominated the literature of the late 1820's. But, apart from its political aims, it cut directly into the heart of a sentimentalized "romanticism."

Exposed or not to the *Westminster Review,* readers of any critical acumen soon recognized that Byron had left no immediate successors worthy his mantle; and the rapid decline of poetry sales testified to a general impatience with pallid imitators. The early Victorian poets had to create a new audience responsive to new values, by which even Byron would suffer repudiation. That they were successful in doing so, we may gather from the good Colonel Newcome's consternation as he heard bright young bucks deliver new dicta with splendid assurance:

He heard opinions that amazed and bewildered him; he heard that Byron was no great poet, though a very clever man; he heard that there had been a wicked persecution against Mr. Pope's memory and fame, and that it was time to reinstate him, . . . and that a young gentleman at Cambridge, who had recently published two volumes of verse, might take rank with the greatest poets of all. . . . If the young men told the truth, where had been the truth in his own young days, and in what ignorance had our forefathers been brought up?

The Victorians did not return to Pope, but they soon found in the gentleman from Cambridge a highly satisfactory substitute; Tennyson became the most representative English poet since Pope's death, the one closest to literate readers, the one most fully aware of the conflicts, the purposes, and the ideals of his time.

In the first objections to "romantic" art, even in the narrow utilitarian reaction, were inherent the positive demands that were to shape the temper of early Victorian literature. Already by 1829 John Henry Newman, in decrying Byronic rhetoric, had asked of verse a more stringent technical and intellectual discipline.[35] For it was, he said, "the fault of the day to mistake eloquence for poetry; whereas, in direct opposition to the conciseness and simplicity of the poet, the talent of the orator consists in making much of a single idea." If the unruly passions of a Byron made for rhetoric, only mildness, restraint of emotion, calmness of judgment — in short, the Christian virtues — could produce true poetry; for "a right moral state of heart" seemed clearly to Newman "the formal and scientific condition of a poetical mind." The great artist was the one best able to make poetry "out of existing materials" and to endure measurement by the "principles of nature and good sense." Through careful labors the poet was to polish his verse, "not in order that his diction [might] attract, but that the language [might] be subjected to him" so as to serve as a vehicle for the expression of reality.

Five years later Sir Henry Taylor amplified Newman's prescriptions.[36] Gravity of theme, logical structure, intellectual balance — these, he insisted, were the prerequisites of meaningful verse. Byron and his contemporaries may admittedly have achieved force and beauty of language and easy versification, but they slighted the graver issues of poetry. The romantic poets were, he felt, deficient in theme, stronger in emotion than in thought: "A feeling came more easily to them than a reflection, and an image was always at hand when a thought was not forthcoming." They lived in an atmosphere of "poetical sentiment" remote from "the common earth." They divorced intellect and emotion; Byron, especially, did not "appear at any time to have betaken himself to such studies as would have tended to the cultivation and discipline of his reasoning powers or the enlargement of his mind." Poetry could no longer continue to exalt pure emotion at the expense of practical reason;

unpremeditated art, if indeed it ever existed, would henceforth seem a contradiction in terms.

Perhaps more insistently than any other critic, Matthew Arnold demanded for his time a subject matter sound in moral values and a style designed quietly to convey larger truths than private feeling could intuit. In a letter to Clough, he suggested that Keats and Shelley "were on a false track when they set themselves to reproduce the exuberance of expression" and the rich imagery of the Elizabethans; for a mature age of the world required greater "plainness of speech," if it were to achieve vital communication.[37] The romantics thus abided our question, and even Shakespeare was not free, for he was sometimes betrayed by his great gift of expression into fanciful play with language, and his "over-curiousness of speech" furnished a most unfortunate model for imitation.[38] To Arnold it was the romantic heresy that expression might weigh more than theme and that the accidental and the personal might replace the essential and the universal. But significant modern poetry, he said, could "only subsist by its *contents;* by becoming a complete magister vitae as the poetry of the ancients did; by including, as theirs did, religion with poetry." Since by such a standard his own *Empedocles on Etna* (1852) availed little towards life, Arnold felt compelled to suppress the poem. Like too many nineteenth-century works of the imagination, it seemed to him deficient in objective content; its hero, in whom "the dialogue of the mind with itself" had already begun, could find no vent for his suffering in positive action, no means of externalizing his private griefs in terms of inspiriting human drama.

Yet if Arnold in *Empedocles* and elsewhere failed for the most part to attain the objective narrative he admired, he nobly fulfilled at least a portion of his avowed didactic purpose; he taught in verse and prose the value of detached rational control and the danger of unleashed subjective emotion:

> Is the calm thine of stoic souls, who weigh
> Life well, and find it wanting, nor deplore:

> *But in disdainful silence turn away,*
> *Stand mute, self-centred, stern, and dream no more?* [39]

Arnold's stoic disillusion was, of course, in many ways untypical of an energetic age which understood few of his sharper cultural insights. But from the first years of Victoria's reign his desire for an increased objectivity had been shared by more sanguine artists emerging to produce a new literature — a literature concerned not with the classic generalities Arnold commended, but seeking its universals always in the particular, through an unromantic "realism."

If the Reform Bill of 1832 disappointed liberal spirits who had fought for a radical democracy, it still challenged the basis of a hierarchic social structure. It slowly swung open the parliamentary gates through which an insurgent middle class might pour to assert its dominance of an industrial economy. Already by the end of the thirties significant writing had lost much of its aristocratic tone, its primary appeal to an intelligentsia of wealth educated in the arts of the gentleman amateur. At Gore House Lady Blessington, herself somewhat *déclassée,* received the young leaders of a bourgeois society, men like Dickens, Thackeray, Disraeli, who were prepared to turn a withering satire upon all whose arrogance rested on mere accident of birth. To many of these spokesmen of the new culture, private passions came ultimately to count for less than public ills. For few could rest unconscious of the dire "condition of England," of widespread illiteracy, alcoholism, prostitution, hunger, and disease, of corrupt government and mob riots, of savage brawling in ill-lit streets and slave labor in squalid factories.

From the manifold unrest of the forties emerged a sociological fiction attempting, however crudely, to grapple with an immediate problem. Disraeli moved from the imagined romance of his *Young Duke* (1831) to "the two nations" of *Sybil* (1845), from the daydreams of a dandy to the living nightmare of coal-pits; and if his economics were naïve, his description was nonetheless vivid in its compelling detail. Mrs. Gaskell, whose best talents lay in the

quiet genre study, turned to the plight of the Manchester mill-
workers, in *Mary Barton* (1848), and before long to the turmoil
of Victorian England's own civil war, the clash of industrial and
agrarian interests, in *North and South* (1855). And Charles Kingsley welded Anglican ethics to social purpose in *Yeast* (1848) and
Alton Locke (1850), novels that were little more than dramatized
sermons animated by the intense earnestness of a vigorous personality. In *Yeast,* especially, lies a clue to the aesthetic doctrine that
guided not only Kingsley but all who sought from the painful
present their literary subject matter. Claude Mellot, the hero's artist
friend, who, admiring the "tinsel abstractions" of romantic verse,
has resolved "to live by art, for art, in art," is finally ready to respect only a specifically moral art, in which "the ideal is neither to
be invented nor abstracted, but found and left where God has put
it, and where alone it can be represented, in actual and living phenomena."

Dickens was less inclined than Kingsley to ponder the "ethics"
of fiction and far less able than Disraeli to present the machinations
of party intrigue. Indeed, he had no coherent theology to sanction
his art and no positive concept of government to reinforce his political satire. Yet he brought to the early Victorian novel a rich
imagination kindled by a deep though ill-defined moral consciousness and a broadly "liberal" view of social and economic conditions.[40]
If his swinging attack on decadent institutions implied no program
for reform, it clearly suggested a Radical distrust of historic precedent and an Evangelical sympathy with the victims of oppression
and injustice. For all his superb individual endowment, he was distinctly a child of his time, suspicious of ecstasy, contemptuous of
flight from the present into a remote Utopia or the glamour of a
"romantic" past. His emotion, lapsing at times tearfully into shameless sentimentalism, sprang from the moral heart of an English
middle class; it bore no kinship to the cultivated passions of a European romanticism. His heroes never rose from the ranks of the
aristocracy; if James Steerforth, exceptionally, aped the Byronic
dandy, Pickwick and Martin Chuzzlewit, Pip and David Copper-

field were distinctly bourgeois "gentlemen" struggling to make their way in a mercantile society. And his descriptive passages seldom resorted to the "view hunting" of which Carlyle had accused the romantic poets; for Dickens felt no response to tranquil or tempestuous nature; he focused his vision on the teeming city, the glooming alleys and draped interiors, the fog blurring ancient stone, the bright costumes silhouetted against brown walls — the whole crowded life of London in all its man-made detail.

Throughout his work the strength of his genius suffered surprisingly little from his more maudlin sensibilities. Dickens was somehow able to achieve, almost in spite of himself, the objectivity of pure laughter, the detachment from which an ever sharper indictment of his class and age might grow with the novelist's increasing knowledge of his craft and command of his materials. By his earliest books he had moved far from the manner of Scott and the long perspectives of historical romance; he had found his power in dramatizing the foibles and the vitality of little men with a sharp animation of gesture that often suggested the canvases of Brueghel and sometimes the more acid caricatures of Daumier. And by the later novels he had emerged as the satirist, the social analyst comparable to Balzac, ready to lash out against self-seeking materialism wherever he might find it. Though he could never have appreciated his role, he was among the first and greatest of the "anti-romantic" Victorians.

The attitudes that Dickens instinctively acquired by personal experience and sensitivity to public taste, Thackeray learned from a more rigorous and self-conscious apprenticeship. As the aspiring young journalist, he submitted cheerfully to the influence of William Maginn, the dynamic editor of *Fraser's,* whose burlesques in the late twenties had launched a vigorous campaign against "unsound moralizing" and "flamboyant romance." [41] Maginn it was who taught him to look upon style critically, to measure all writing including his own by the standards of reason and reality. Maginn it was who enlisted his talents in *Fraser's* war for the liberation of common sense. Together they continued a merciless assault on the

lesser disciples of Scott and Byron, on the pretentious Edward Bul-
wer and the "satanic" Robert Montgomery. They flayed alike the
rhetorical bombast of Mrs. Hemans and the lachrymose nostalgia
of Tom Moore. Castigating Harrison Ainsworth for a sentimentalization of crime, Thackeray insisted that actual Old Bailey records
and testimonials were far more convincing than sensational fiction:
"We back the reality against the romance," he said, "the lady in her
cups against the lady in her tears." And to illustrate the absurdity
of misapplied sympathy, he wrote his own crime novel, the ironical
Catherine (1839), inspired perhaps by Maginn's editorial encouragement.

Though his later development carried him far beyond the range
of periodical squibs and literary burlesques, he retained to the end
much of the Fraserians' distrust of sentimentalism. The practical
deviltry of Becky Sharp conveyed more of the novelist's genuine
force than the sententious scruples of Amelia Sedley. And the ludicrous antics of Miss Fotheringay rested on a surer foundation than
the loyalties of Laura Bell. The satirist's impatience with the gestures of romance remained long after the satirist himself had attained a mellower acceptance of all gesture. Indeed, the late ballad
retelling the tragic plight of hopeless Werther was within its limits
sufficiently characteristic of the Thackeray who pierced to the heart
of every false emotion; Charlotte the solid Hausfrau seemed the
only sensible actor in a foolish melodrama:

> *So he sighed and pined and ogled,*
> *And his passion boiled and bubbled,*
> *Till he blew his silly brains out,*
> *And no more was by it troubled.*
>
> *Charlotte, having seen his body*
> *Borne before her on a shutter,*
> *Like a well-conducted person,*
> *Went on cutting bread and butter.*

In the forties, especially, Thackeray made his witty contribution to
"the classic age of parody."[42] When he joined the staff of Mark

Lemon's young and "Radical" *Punch,* he identified himself with many wits who were discovering the potency of laughter in the shaping of a new culture; for the early Victorian humorists, even if they had like Thackeray little concern with political agitation, could not evade their broader social responsibility.

Visiting London in 1847, Emerson could see "a new trait of the nineteenth century" in the fact that "the wit and humour of England, as in *Punch,* so in the humorists, Jerrold, Dickens, Thackeray, Hood, [had] taken the direction of humanity and freedom." [43] Others closer to the scene could extend Emerson's observation. The new literature, humorous or not, seemed far different from the old, far more deliberately, even religiously, democratic in emphasis. "This," said Kingsley's Alton Locke, "is what I call democratic art — the revelation of the poetry which lies in common things. And surely all the age is tending in that direction: . . . and in all authors who have really seized the nation's mind, from Crabbe and Burns and Wordsworth to Hood and Dickens, the great tide sets ever onward, outward, towards that which is common to the many, not that which is exclusive to the few." Some years earlier Thomas Hood himself had reached a similar conclusion in considering the art of Dickens; *Oliver Twist,* he declared, was "wholesome reading" since it revealed an "honest independence of thinking" and its drift was "natural, *along with the great human currents, and not against them.*" [44]

Hood, in fact, had a rather unusual insight into the literary processes of his time, and it may be profitable to ponder for a moment his often neglected commentary. For Hood was one of the few poets of the romantic generation to linger on into the early Victorian period and to accept some of the first principles of the new Victorian aesthetic. His shorter lyrics of the 1820's had echoed somewhat reedily the verse of Byron, Shelley, and Keats, and his whole creative effort until the end drew much inspiration from his early models. Yet almost from the beginning he displayed a stronger social consciousness than any of the major romantics, except perhaps Shelley, who was always far more abstract and doctrinaire.

And as time went by, he came more and more to distrust "escape," to oppose excessive sensibility, precociousness, and nebulosity. Several autobiographical fragments sketched the course of his development in terms of a Cockney realism which foreshadowed the spirit of Dickens.[45] "For the sake," he wrote, "of our native sentimentalists who profess dying for love, as well as the foreign romanticists who affect a love for dying, it may not be amiss to give a slight sketch of the bearing of a traveller who had gone through half the journey. . . . I have had none of those experiences which render the lives of saintlings, not yet in their teens, worth their own weight in paper and print, and consequently my personal history, as a Tract, would read as flat as the Pilgrim's Progress without the Giants, the Lions, and the grand single combat with the Devil." Hood, we read, aspired to literature only in the face of a bitter economic struggle. His countinghouse career made inevitable a lower middle-class approach to poetry; for, as he said, "to commit poetry indeed is a crime ranking next to forgery in the countinghouse code." It was all

> *Now double entry — now a flowery trope —*
> *Mingling poetic honey with trade wax —*
> *Blogg, Brothers — Milton — Grote and Prescott — Pope —*
> *Bristles — and Hogg — Glyn Mills and Halifax —*
> *Rogers — and Towgood — Hemp — the Bard of Hope —*
> *Barilla — Byron — Tallow — Burns — and Flax!*

His apprenticeship thus riveted him to realities which became stronger forces in his career than any poetic influences to which he may have been attracted. He spoke from experience of a race to whom all art was luxury. And it was natural that a social purpose should underlie his most sober efforts in verse, "The Lady's Dream," "The Song of the Shirt," "The Bridge of Sighs."

Yet his greatest success lay in humor and burlesque, humor made grim by a macabre blend of pathos, and burlesque enriched with an inherent indignation at economic injustice. His most ambitious comic poem, "Miss Kilmansegg and Her Precious Leg" (1843), is essentially a satire on "romantic" extravagance, on traditional aristocratic values, and on the nineteenth-century bourgeois pedigree of wealth. Miss Kilmansegg, the fabulous heroine, had enjoyed fireworks at her nativity; yet had she been poor,

> *It's ten to one she had had to make shift*
> *With rickets instead of rockets.*

Even as a child her pleasures were expensive:

> *The yearly cost of her golden toys*
> *Would have given to half London's Charity Boys*
> *And Charity Girls the annual joys*
> *Of a holiday dinner at Highbury.*

As she grew older she would read only of "gentlefolks always possessed of fortunes so truly romantic." Then, when she lost her limb in a horse accident, she insisted upon a golden leg, surely a great advantage in the acquisition of male admirers. Not until she married a worthless count, however, did she receive her deserts; her bridegroom murdered her with the Golden Leg, and the coroner's jury brought in a verdict of suicide, "Because her own leg had killed her." The moral of the whole farce was implicitly serious. "Miss Kilmansegg" set out to deromanticize all illusions of grandeur, to expose the incalculable evils of economic inequality. And in so doing it introduced one of the key themes in Victorian literature, the role of money in the new society, a theme as central to the design of Thackeray's *Vanity Fair* as it was to Balzac's *Père Goriot*.

Hood, then, remains significant as a transitional figure who, looking before and after, acknowledged his debt to the eighteenth-century humorists, especially Smollett, and to the romantic poets, and yet shared with the early Victorians a deepened sense of moral responsibility and a broader sociological interest. Within the limits of his endowment, he worked amusingly and well. But whatever his awareness of shifting taste, he could in nowise divine the hidden forces inducing cultural change. With becoming good sense, he left analysis and prophecy to others; and the greatest of these, the senior "seer" of the new age, was Thomas Carlyle.

Carlyle was convinced that Martin Luther had fulfilled "the function of great men and teachers" as "a Prophet–Idol-breaker, a bringer-back of men to reality." And animated by his own brand of secular protestantism, he strove to emulate the iconoclast. Born the same year as Keats (1795), he lived through the English romantic period, resolutely hostile to its creative passion, though more deeply affected by its speculations than he would ever have admitted. His judgments of the great romantic poets were, as we have seen, almost uniformly splenetic — and indeed his literary opinions generally were marked by a characteristic overstatement which increased their verbal force as it diminished their critical power.[46] Lamb was a "Cockney to the marrow" with all the enthusiasms of shouting Cockneydom, and Hazlitt was a "thick-headed and discourteous boor of an Editor [with] almost nothing of the smallest moment to edit." Tennyson's *Princess* "had everything but common sense," and Newman's essays betrayed the "brain of a rabbit." It was natural, then, that Meredith, who felt Carlyle "the greatest of the Britons of his time," should find him great "after the British fashion . . . Titanic not Olympian; a heaver of rocks not a shaper." [47]

Yet it was as a shaper that Carlyle sought his influence. The Destroyer, having worked his will, strove to remain as the Preserver. And there was behind much of the destruction the sureness of intuitive insight that eventually gave the Idol-breaker his status as Prophet. From his negations arose more positive social and aesthetic doctrines than any he himself developed. However he might regard his warmest disciples or his severest opponents, the preachments of Kingsley and Ruskin, even perhaps of Engels and Marx, would have been rather different but for his example.

More than any of the English romantics, Carlyle steeped himself in German and French thought and literature.[48] From Kant and Fichte he borrowed the gospel of work and duty that inspired his recurrent hostility to the "greatest-happiness principle." From the Saint-Simonians he derived a theory of historical periodicity which colored his own less deterministic concept of cyclic change.

And from Goethe and Herder he drew the notion of palingenesis — of cultural death and rebirth — which gave to his iconoclasm the meaningful task of clearing the way for new growth. If he became impatient with the German metaphysicians as with all the other victims of enchantment, he subscribed fully to the revolt of Continental idealism from all mechanistic philosophies. More emphatically than Coleridge, he propounded an organic, a dynamic, view of society, an evolutionary explanation of the dread cataclysms shaping human history.

With consistent vehemence he rejected the Newtonian idea of an ordered world functioning with scientific precision within its predetermined and immutable laws. He repudiated all of British empiricism, with its continued reliance upon Locke's *Essay,* as a pernicious philosophy, "mechanical, in its aim and origin, in its method and results." Of all centuries, the eighteenth, the "Sceptical Century," seemed to him the bleakest, the farthest fallen from grace. And of all doctrines born of that dark age, he found utilitarianism the most distasteful — an avowed materialism recognizing only the ethic of self-interest, a confessed Atheism declaring hunger the only "ultimate fact of man's life." Yet even "this gross, steamengine Utilitarianism" helped provide "an approach towards new Faith"; for it meant, said Carlyle,

a laying-down of cant; a saying to oneself: "Well then, this world is a dead iron machine, the god of it Gravitation and selfish Hunger; let us see what, by checking and balancing, and good adjustment of tooth and pinion, can be made of it!" . . . It is the culminating point, and fearless ultimatum, of what lay in the half-and-half state, pervading man's whole existence in that Eighteenth Century.

But to the early Victorian with eyes to see, "the Unbelieving Century with its unblessed Products [was] already past: a new century [had] already come"; and "hollow Formulism, gross Benthamism, and other unheroic atheistic Insincerity [were] visibly and even rapidly declining." [49]

The belief that virtue was expediency and that the highest moral sanction was pragmatic, a belief which Carlyle ascribed to Hume and earlier eighteenth-century thinkers, seemed to him "the most melancholy theory, . . . the highest exhibition of scepticism — that total denial of everything not material, not demonstrable by logic." And it led directly, he thought, to the despair of a Rousseau and so to a sentimental unrest most vividly portrayed in *Werther* but thoroughly diffused throughout English verse of the Byronic period. Frequently it disguised itself as a sort of escapist "Dilettantism," a worship of the "beauties of art," a retreat to lonely nature, and a self-conscious nurturing of private emotion. Its inevitable outcome was suicide, physical or moral, for the life of man could not "subsist upon doubt and denial," and "if it had nothing to support itself upon but these poor sentimentalities, view-huntings, trivialities, this world was not really fit to live in." Among men of letters, Goethe seemed first to realize this vital truth, "greatly to his own profit, greatly to the world's profit." *Wilhelm Meister* represented to Carlyle Goethe's complete break with the cult of despair; it suggested to all men that the pursuit of "spiritual clearness and perfection" could be higher and nobler than happiness. It revealed "a man who has the soul to think, and be the moral guide of his nation and of the whole world," a man of "seeing eye" and "seeing heart," who turned his sorrows into useful work. By comparison Schiller seemed more and more monastic, "too aspiring, too restless, . . . he could not live in communion with earth." Only Goethe had learned to accept; Goethe alone had achieved complete assent, the full glory of the Everlasting Yea. And under such influence, the young Carlyle dreamed that his own generation, closing its Byron, opening its Goethe, might shake off "blind sensualism and egotism," might emerge at last from the "state of nightmare and paralysis." [50]

Though he may never have understood the disinterested artistry of *Tasso* or of *Faust*, Carlyle found in Goethe's breadth of vision and manful assertion a faith by which he himself might measure the values of English culture. With a far stronger passion for social justice than ever troubled the German poet, he probed the diseases of an industrialized, a mechanized, society. More forcefully than even Dickens or Thackeray, he dramatized the plight of the poor and the nonchalance of the Dandiacal Body. Leading Emerson through a London slum, he challenged an easier optimism; with deep intensity he demanded, "Do you believe in the devil now?" For to Carlyle the brand of evil was everywhere burned into fallen man. His "transcendentalism" allowed him no evasion of immediate wrong. *Sartor Resartus* (1834) with all its commerce in eternities and vague infinitudes tends to conceal its basic concern with tangible realities beneath a thick veneer of satire; if we fail to penetrate the burlesque of romantic philosophy, we miss the relevance of its allegory to the life of nineteenth-century England.

By insistence upon a "*natural* supernaturalism" as described in *Sartor,* Carlyle escaped the bloodless dance of the categories which had whirled too many of the European idealists beyond earth and reason. He sought the miracle of being, not in the remote realms of the ideal, but in the firm soil of actuality. If ultimate essences lay only in the creative mind shaping dead matter, the symbols, the clothes of the idea, were sensible to feeling as to sight. With the novelist's eye for significant detail, Carlyle seized upon particular appearances, specific incidents; the diamond necklace served as index to the intrigue of a whole decadent regime, and the battered shoes of Samuel Johnson became token of an uncompromising spiritual integrity. However eccentric may have been his prose style, however unique his insights, he was fundamentally at one with the major early Victorians in his preference for a sociological realism; he was by his own definition "a bringer-back of men to reality."

From his social philosophy Carlyle developed no aesthetic doctrine comparable to that of Ruskin or of Tolstoi, whose ethical premises were not markedly dissimilar. He remained always more or less suspicious of the artistic temperament, and he cared little for the artist's special problems or his technical accomplishments. The great poet was to him potentially the great priest or the great politician; he was by endowment and awareness the cultural hero whom circumstance had made the poet. Yet Carlyle recognized the place of poetry in a living society, and he explained in general terms its high significance. A poem, he said, is "a *musical* thought

. . . spoken by a mind that has penetrated into the heart of the thing; detected the inmost mystery of it, namely the *melody* that lies hidden in it; the inward harmony of coherence which is its soul, whereby it exists and has a right to be, here in this world." The poet's greatest gift, therefore, was an intuitive intellect which could apprehend and define the eternal essence embodied in the material shape; and the truth of his observation was of much higher importance than the strength of his rhetoric. That even a Byron could not permanently seduce a reading public "with all his wild siren-charming" seemed alone to vouch for "men's indestructible love of truth." [51]

The enduring writer, Carlyle insisted, must avoid straining after a "rosepink artificial bedizenment"; he must speak directly from a "healthy" mind, a mind at unity with itself. Since every work of art was "the outcome of a great soul," the expression of the artist's moral character, its social effect was essentially didactic. Though great literature was to teach by its picture of life rather than by rules and precepts, it had always to seek meaningful subject matter for dramatic presentation. Carlyle left Scott's romances no "wiser, better, holier, stronger," but in Dickens he heard "a real music of the genuine kind." [52] A true writer thus appeared to him "a Preacher preaching not to this parish or that, on this day or that, but to all men in all times and places"; and the preacher's gospel, if vital, seemed forever contemporary. Yet all who penned verse or prose of even the most transitory value must feel some responsibility to the culture they were shaping; for "the nation," he said, "is governed by all that has tongue in the nation: Democracy is virtually *there*." [53]

It was the tragedy of the later Carlyle who had deserted literature for history that he experienced the disillusion and despair he had once decried in others. Long before democracy had found its tongue, he turned from a free people's government to the controls of a state dominated by a rigorous hero-despot. By the time of *Frederick the Great* (1858–1865), many felt that the prophet, the truthseer, had come to prefer strength to truth, might to right. With some justice John Morley accused the greatest moral teacher of the age of thrusting from him "the only instruments by which we can make sure what right is, and that our social action is wise and effective."[54] Yet there was reason to believe that Carlyle himself was never fully satisfied with his estimate of the hero-king;[55] and there was an element of pathos in his portrait of the cynical Voltaire, child of that lost eighteenth century, who courageously undermined the pretensions of the autocrat. Readers of the *Heroes* (1841) had not forgotten that Napoleon had better have lost a regiment than murdered a helpless bookseller, for injustice paid itself "with frightful compound-interest." And the same ethical bias, the humanitarian impulse, remained inescapable even when prejudice and unreason strove to deny its cogency.

The best part of Carlyle's mission as Prophet–Idol-breaker was accomplished almost forty years before his death and posthumous fulminations. Younger Victorians who could ignore the metapolitics of *Frederick,* the ill-timed defenses of Bismarckian Germany, and the reactionary roar of *Shooting Niagara* (1867), might still recall the insights of *Sartor* and the perceptions of *Past and Present* (1843). Through the early lectures and essays they might catch a glimpse of the Carlyle sketched by Maclise, confident, ironic, ingenuous yet poised, lounging with tousled rectitude and earnest indolence at the threshold of a brave new world. And again and again they might hear the note of assent that had given direction to their whole long crowded age:

We have a faith in the imperishable dignity of man; in the high vocation to which, throughout this his earthly history, he has been appointed. . . . Doubtless this age also is advancing. Its very unrest, its ceaseless activity, its discontent contains matter of promise. Knowledge, education are opening the eyes of the humblest; are increasing the number of thinking minds without limit. This is as it should be; for not in turning back, not in resisting, but only in resolutely struggling forward, does our life consist.[56]

It mattered not that Carlyle's own hope faded or that the promise of the new society might never be quite fulfilled. It had meant much to the artists and artisans of the thirties and forties that their leader in breaking with a "romantic" past, their chief "bringer-back of men to reality," had instilled a positive faith which might guide their immediate labors. In the voice of Carlyle the early Victorians could have detected, if they would, the passionate intuition, the "natural supernaturalism" of a greater prophet who two centuries before had inspirited rebellious Englishmen:

We reckon more than five months yet to harvest; there need not be five weeks, had we but eyes to lift up, the fields are white already.

III

The Spasmodic School

Critics and poets both (save I who cling
To older canons) have discarded sense
And meaning's at a discount. Our young spirits,
Who call themselves the masters of the age,
Are either robed in philosophic mist,
And, with an air of grand profundity,
Talk metaphysics — which, sweet cousin, means
Nothing but aimless jargon — or they come
Before us in the broad bombastic vein,
With spasms, and throes, and transcendental flights
And heap hyperbole on metaphor.

— WILLIAM EDMONDSTOUNE AYTOUN

As Lord Byron swam the Hellespont to emulate Leander's athletic example, so some fifty years later Sydney Dobell mounted a seacoast near Naples to recapture the feelings Saint Paul must have experienced on his arrival in Italy. Both gestures were no doubt dramatic; but Byron's desire was propelled by a physical prowess which assured its fulfillment, whereas Dobell's saintlier ambition was frustrated by the hostility of earth itself — by the collapse of the ground beneath his feet and a sorry fall into a subterranean cavern.[1] If, in terms of symbol, the romantic's success might typify the attainment of a highly personal literary ideal, the Victorian's failure might no less betoken the high aspiration and descent to oblivion of the poetic group to which he belonged. Byron, after all, was Byron in art as in life; but the so-called "Spasmodic School," despite its Evangelical sympathies, was for the most part merely Byronic.

Though long since forgotten, the Spasmodic poets once assumed, even to more sober artists, considerable proportions; they once cast so long a shadow across the whole verse of their time that their frenetic volumes cannot even now be quite ignored in any estimate of early Victorian taste. While the major "anti-romantics" were following Carlyle's lead in shaping a new sociological aesthetic, a host of lesser writers, not unaware of social demands, were reluctant to break with their avowed "romantic" masters. Many could listen respectfully to the doctrine of *Sartor* and at the same time continue a sedulous imitation of the style and substance of *Manfred*. A few like Philip James Bailey learned to open their Goethe without closing their Byron. Some strove to reproduce the opulence of Keats. And nearly all were warm in their admiration of Shelley — so warm indeed that Charles Kingsley suspected that their "spasmodic, vague, extravagant, effeminate school of poetry" had been "unfairly fathered upon Byron." [2] But apart from its doubtful parentage, it seemed clear to Kingsley that the Spasmodic School had inherited from both Byron and Shelley a view of art which the principal Victorians were seeking to disown, the concept of the poet as a divinely inspired creature with an inalienable right to eccentricity, a right to despise the conventions that bound other men and to indulge a brooding genius in studied self-absorption.

Inflamed by borrowed passions and their own ranting emotion, the Spasmodics yielded to a titanic egotism, vigorous enough at times to shake a susceptible public into the conviction that these were the new Elizabethans, young men of gusto, of spontaneous feeling, of amazing verbal fluency. Godlike, they sought to create worlds in their own image; theirs was a thoroughly subjective art peopled by men of sensibility, heroes very like themselves. Each played his own "romantic" Hamlet, heedless of Kingsley's reminder that the gloomy prince was "Shakespeare's subtle reductio ad absurdum of that very diseased type of mind which has been for the last forty years identified with 'genius.'" [3] Yet each would have denied a will to evade the realities of his age. Many courted modernism with reckless assurance, quick to intuit its problems, but quite unable to achieve the rational detachment essential to analysis. More consistently than their greater contemporaries, they dreamed of a Victorian epic ample enough to embrace the manifold aspiration of the nineteenth century. Yet none possessed an architectonic sense at all commensurate to his high vision; and none would submit to the formal discipline requisite for the proportioning of an epic structure. Uncertain of their ultimate design, they neglected over-all theme and action to magnify isolated emotions, to embroider random sentiments often quite irrelevant to the given mood. Inevitably they were betrayed into the "occasional bursts of fine writing" which Arnold deplored as detrimental to a general texture.[4] Though they often produced striking figures of speech, compelling metaphors, suggestive similes, they were repeatedly carried away, like some of the Renaissance poets whom they revered, by their own embellished images, their own laborious conceits. Careless of larger wholes, most of them were nonetheless almost pedantically concerned with specific detail, with accurate reference and esoteric allusion. Time and again the appeal of quaint and curious lore proved irresistible; and many a young Spasmodic on the road to Parnassus lost his way in the British Museum, where Karl Marx was ordering his fervor somewhat more methodically. Had they been content with the smaller instruments of verse, they might have secured more durable effects; as it was, however, obsessed with their lofty ambitions, they remained minor poets failing in a major key.

The Spasmodics can be classed together as members of a "school" only insofar as, with all their deliberate eccentricities, they subscribed to a common body of poetic principles and, with an unexpected unanimity, rationalized their practice by a fairly coherent philosophy of incoherence. Yet it was not until the fifties that their articles of faith became fully apparent even to themselves; and only then, when the School had established its vogue, was it forced to face the challenge of a criticism which had evolved other literary standards. The Spasmodic School did not spring full-grown from the drooping head of a moribund romanticism. It developed its ideals gradually, over the course of some fifteen years and through the work of many writers often quite unconscious that they were contributing to the growth of any aesthetic theory. Perhaps the earliest and most significant of these was Philip James Bailey, who more than any other set a precedent for much poetizing which he himself could view only with jaundiced eye.

On first looking into Bailey's *Festus* (1839), Tennyson felt "like a wren beating about a hedgerow," cowering before a great eagle soaring to the sun.[5] For Bailey's epic-drama, expanded ultimately to a length of forty thousand lines, disarmed critical judgment. Its torrential cascades of emotion, its sententious religiosity, its highly wrought rhetoric, carried the reputation of a Victorian Goethe through edition after edition, into the literary consciousness of an awe-stricken England and a reverential New World. Within nine years of its first appearance, the flashes of metaphoric lightning that illumined its deserts of vast verbosity had been dutifully culled by an American admirer who issued the gilt-edged *Beauties of Festus Compiled with a Copious Index by a Festonian*. Whether or not such an anthology isolated any true touchstones of poetry, its very existence helped suggest the nature of Bailey's total performance, his almost calculated unevenness, his predilection for the purple patch.

Irregularity of form was indeed essential to the theory of inspiration baldly stated again and again throughout the long unedited text. It is Festus, the universal knower, who advises the helpless Student to follow the tides of passion in preparing his compendium of human experience:

> *Let that thou utterest be of nature's flow,*
> *Not art's; a fountain's not a pump's. But once*
> *Begun, work thou all things into thy work;*
> *And set thyself about it, as the sea*
> *About earth, lashing at it day and night.*
> *And leave the stamp of thine own soul in it.*

And it is Bailey himself who adds in an envoy an explanation of his own technique:

He spake inspired:
Night and day, thought came unhelped, undesired,
Like blood to his heart. . . .
God was with him.[6]

Divine inspiration apparently could rush Bailey into regions where Goethe feared to tread. His intuitions laid bare the "Heaven of Heavens"; and his mysticism fathomed the final "Judgment of the Earth." *Festus* was no mere *Faust*. With swelling metaphors and jangling metaphysics, it transcended space and time to lay its scenes in Hell, in the Sun, in "Everywhere"; it explored Eternity and the annihilation of the senses; it caught a vision of the larger hope by which even a politely Byronic Lucifer, having assumed the proper attitudes, might find reëntry into Paradise. Beside so fecund an imagination, the defect of formlessness seemed of little consequence.

Built on a more modest scale, most of Bailey's later works exploited the basic style and subject matter that had given *Festus* its incredible popularity. *The Angel World* (1850) and *The Mystic* (1855) continued his metaphysical speculations in a recondite vocabulary, his conjurings with exotic symbols and "awful rites, hinted in sacro-sanctities of the wise." But neither poem compelled the same attention as the first aspiring epic; and even *Festus,* as the years went by, lost its power to move an audience by sheer force of rhetoric and wild chatter of immensities. By 1858, after the younger Spasmodics had disbanded, Bailey was able, in a quiet dialogue, to indicate his aesthetic principles, which had also to a great extent been theirs. Enlivened by much good sense, *The Age* seems at first detached enough in its view to indict Bailey himself; the Critic in the satire attacks the writer who

conceits himself inspired; mistakes
Impressibility for power, and makes
A volume of his blunder for our sakes.

But before long it posits definite values clearly representative of the author's literary ideal. A good poem, we learn, reveals "an eye of all imaginative might" and "the vast completeness of one master mind";

it demands both capacious design and lofty moral; it deals in passion that raises no blush and causes no pain; and it presents heroes, larger than life, exhibiting the "true power of mind and genius." [7] So conceived, the good poem would be a production hardly less than *Samson Agonistes;* yet Bailey and his disciples uncovered talents somewhat smaller than Milton's.

Though among the first Victorian critics to laud Tennyson's craftsmanship, Richard Hengist Horne still found in *Festus* an "unrepressed vigour of imagination" which might well afford to shirk the narrower disciplines of form.[8] To the modern poet, he said, structure is undoubtedly important, but some souls may be wrongly confined by rigid patterns, for in some may have been kindled "a yearning towards some vaster region than the world which surrounds them, and an aspiration which would cleave its crystalline walls and soar away towards illimitable heavens, unknown ecstasies, and the eternal mysteries of Divinity." Such a poet, Horne felt, was Bailey, a writer of true passion, standing in direct contrast to one like the coldly correct Henry Taylor, who stunted "the growth of the imagination by never suffering it to rise beyond the calm level of reason and common sense." Taylor's philosophy might, he admitted, for the moment dominate verse; but there was coming, he felt sure, a struggle between the two opposed poetic ideals. Whatever the outcome of such a conflict, he himself preferred to *Philip van Artevelde* works cast in a Festonian mold such as the *Vivia Perpetua* of Sarah Flower Adams or the *Record of the Pyramids* by J. E. Reade. And he chose to stake his own poetic fame on a diffuse "Hellenic" epic called *Orion* (1843), an allegory of the "contest between the intellect and the senses," avowedly intended to counter a more restrained and rationalistic verse, as well as "the far-sweeping tide of broad-farce literature, caricature, and burlesque" which he saw overwhelming the "anti-romantic" forties.[9] Yet his efforts to resist the surge of reason and of laughter were ultimately as futile as Mrs. Partington's struggles with the sea.

But if Horne's preference for emotive verse brought him close to the Spasmodic bias, his dislike of contemporary themes alienated his sympathies from some of the School's most characteristic work. As he had repudiated realistic farce and burlesque, he attacked J. Westland Marston's notion that "reality and the present time constituted the best material and medium for modern poetry, especially dramatic poetry." [10] Yet Marston's *Gerald* (1842), even in its contemporaneity, derived far less from the new "realism" than from the "romantic" theory of the imagination to which Horne himself subscribed. Published a year before *Orion,* this modern "tragedy of genius" set out consciously to explore moments of high passion, to illuminate *"certain points* in Gerald's mental history — to show the *crises* of his developements, not their *progress."* [11] Its plot, accordingly, moves from climax to climax, spurning the logic of structure with nonchalant indifference. Gerald, the poet-hero, deserts his beloved Edith to seek literary fame in London, where he suffers the trials of authorship but steadfastly refuses to compromise with a bourgeois materialism. Repelled by a man-of-capital's insistence that art is pernicious and that poetry taught to his office clerks would "disturb — nay, ruin — my whole mercantile economy," Gerald is about to commit suicide when one Lord Roxmore, the benevolent aristocrat, takes him home to seek a natural death in the long-suffering Edith's arms. By the end, his purged faith is fixed on a spiritual immortality and his ambition flattered that his poems are at last making their mark in a hostile world. Throughout his sad pilgrimage, Gerald retains his conviction that "To Fancy's vision rapt, Nature reveals her mission," and his sublime confidence in poetic insight:

> *Ah, sure the sacred pathway to the skies*
> *Winds through the region of the sympathies;*
> *The Realm of Feeling to the Bard is given,*
> *A Human Empire, but it neighbours Heaven!*

And he dreams constantly that his heartfelt throbbing song — "Child of my Soul," "my vague, wild rapture" — may provide escape from earth's miseries, may

> *Visit the poor; sweeten their daily toil*
> *Who ply the loom, or cultivate the soil,*

And by a holier world's expectant bliss,
Lighten the load, and soothe the pains of this. . . .
In Mammon's empire still assert thy claim
To prompt the impulse warm, and lofty aim.

In view of Marston's accomplishment, Horne was obviously quite right in censuring *Gerald*. Yet he seemed to ignore the fact that its failure was the inevitable product of Bailey's emotionalism applied by a writer more sensitive than he to the plight of an industrial England. The poem, at any rate, remains historically important as an early example of the Spasmodic approach to social problems, an approach which misdirected the efforts of many less poetical reformers. And it is not without some interest as an experiment in a new technique, later to be imitated by Dobell and Smith and even by Tennyson. In a note to *Gerald,* Marston explained his distinction between the soliloquy and the reverie, the latter of which he reserved for "thoughts which one would scarcely express in language to oneself — far less to another — involuntary thoughts by which the mind is borne along without any conscious effort of its own." [12] Developed in such terms, the reverie remotely suggests the kind of poetic expressionism which Virginia Woolf achieved in *The Waves.* But more immediately it anticipated the method by which the lyric drama or monodrama would become a vehicle for the projection of psychological values, for the poeticizing of subjective experience or private intuition.

Many a Spasmodic of the forties found his poetic sensibilities thwarted by economic conditions as harsh as any that balked the unhappy Gerald; and none discovered a more satisfactory means of bringing his creative impulse to bear upon the tragic realities before him. Of all the forgotten lyrists, the most pathetic may well have been Ebenezer Jones, who, yearning for status as a "poetical thinker," produced his *Studies of Sensation and Event* (1843), frenzied verses of "wild desire" and "the glorious fire," which Rossetti thought "full of vivid disorderly power." [13] In his writing Jones sought release from the rigorous Calvinism of his childhood and the poverty and disease that overshadowed his maturity. But his defiant pursuit of passion led only to a deliberate and circumstantial sensuousness. From the beginning he was obsessed with a sense of his own failure. Some buried faculty of self-criticism kept warning him that his verse lacked form, unity, and direction, until eventually he came to wonder whether from his excitability, his impatience, his desire to be heard, could ever have come finished poetry. Yet he had at no time the leisure or the knowledge to discipline his exuberance. When he, working twelve hours a day, asked of his employer an occasional recess for reading and recreation, he was told that self-culture led to a "pride of intellect," which was "one of Satan's peculiar snares." Sometimes he answered trade's hypocrisy with a savage irony, as in his intense "Song of the Gold-Getters":

> Let us lie like statesmen, like fathers, and gold
> We shall heap and keep; — the world is war,
> And out of war's articles none will uphold
> The virtue of truth when a falsehood gains more.

And for a while he saw a solution in the socialism of Robert Owen, to whose *New Moral World* he made several contributions. But ultimately, disillusioned with both politics and poetry, he contented himself with residence in Chelsea where he might behold the author of *Sartor* stalking down Cheyne Row — behold and admire in silence, forever fearful lest the dread voice should ask, "Young man, what have you *done?*"

Had he fixed his hero worship elsewhere, Jones might have had less reason to fear the stern voice of duty; he might have found another prophet-critic more warmly sympathetic to the struggles of an impressionable young poet. For as early as 1840 Carlyle himself had written of "a poor meritorious Scotchman, a burgher minister in Dundee" named George Gilfillan, an ebullient reviewer who wrote in "a strange, oriental, Scriptural style; full of fervour, and crude, gloomy fire, — a kind of opium style." [14] Dogmatic in judgment, pontifical in tone, this Gilfillan rapidly established a wide reputation by his animated *Galleries of Literary Portraits* (1845–1854) and his articles in the *Quarterly,* the *Eclectic, Tait's Magazine,* and the unfortunately titled *Hogg's Instructor*. For nearly a decade he exerted an influence on early Victorian taste second only to that of Carlyle, who was both less conservative in his theological opinions and less liberal in his political sentiments.[15]

Though as ready as Jones to "press to his heart and bedew with his tears" a cherished copy of *Sartor Resartus,* Gilfillan kept the faith Carlyle had lost in the great romantics. He praised Shelley as a "lofty enthusiast" comparable to Israel's prophets, and he saw in Byron the noble fire and "the genius of convulsion."[16] He confessed to his own romantic restlessness and uncertainty of soul,[17] and he yearned Byronically "to retire to some Highland wild, and there muse and dream, and think and write." But in all his visions, tormented or beatific, he sensed always a strong religious light, the intuition of "a Divine procession of spiritual instincts passing like solar waves over the being."[18] Nearly all his personal or aesthetic judgments bore some trace of his theological conviction, of his unwearied search for God's chosen emissaries. On meeting Harriet Beecher Stowe, for instance, he thrilled to the presence of an elected one: "It seemed," he said, "a moment of the Millennium sent before its time."[19] It was natural that he should prefer "Festus" Bailey to Tennyson and indeed to all writers of his age, for Bailey most fully had experienced the ecstasy of sublime emotion, and no one had achieved "passages which heave and hurry along with a more genuine afflatus." And it was inevitable that he should foster Bailey's epic ambitions in the "cluster of new poets" who came to him for advice and encouragement.[20]

By intellectual bias and emotional endowment, then, Gilfillan — or Apollodorus, as he sometimes chose to sign himself — was the champion of Spasmodic art, the patron saint of Spasmodic genius. To many young writers he acted as guide and counselor; he praised their manuscripts often with outrageous generosity, suggested corrections and improvements, found willing publishers, and wrote highly eulogistic reviews intended to assure a fitting response from an impercipient public. He warmed to the effusions of Gerald Massey, in whom he discovered "separate sparkles of intense brilliance,

. . . like moonbeams gleaming on a midnight wave."[21] For he felt earnestly prepared to understand Massey's troubled revolt from the social system that had condemned him as a child of eight to the servitude of a silk factory; and he sympathized with his contention that "a poor man, fighting his battle of life, has little time for the rapture of repose which Poetry demands."[22] Yet Gilfillan rather regretted that the rebellious youth showed little of the capacity for epic synthesis which was to him the true mark of creative talent.

This he found fitfully present in the work of John Stanyan Bigg, whose *Night and the Soul* (1854) seemed to attain "a certain rich pervasive spirit of poetry" and "that noble rush of thought and language which is so characteristic of genuine inspiration."[23] Bigg indeed was fired by a transcendental passion, a kind of Christianized Byronism which could not but touch Gilfillan's heart. His heroes hung cloudy trophies in Nature's shrine, beseeching grace from a God "pavilioned in glooms . . . In brooding night for ages, perfecting / The glorious dream of past eternities." Festus-like, they thirsted for knowledge — "Great thoughts oppress me like an incubus. / They sit upon my soul like thunderbolts" — and Bailey-like, they speculated on their craft and the grandeur of their mission:

> *Words are earth's forgeries,*
> *And pass not current either in Hell or Heaven.*
> *It is as if, on mighty themes like this,*
> *Language with puny, frantic arms, strove hard*
> *To fold a mountain in its weak embrace.*
> *We seek to paint the darkness, and our brush*
> *Smears nothing but itself.*[24]

Gilfillan deeply respected their will to snare the infinite in the limited nets of language; but he could not quite condone the diffuseness of effort that must needs attend it. And since the poet-heroes were but pale shadows of Bigg himself, *Night and the Soul* seemed, even to its most zealous advocate, sadly defective in its glory.

But of Alexander Smith's talents, Gilfillan had no doubt. With poorly concealed excitement he wrote to Sydney Dobell in 1851 of his great discovery: "I half-fancy that while in you I found another Shelley, of a manlier and Christian type, in Smith I am to find another Keats." Two years later he sent Smith's *Life Drama* on its way with ringing eulogy and just a word of caution: Mr. Smith, he said, has given ample proof of "the power and truth of his genius"; let him now "burn his Tennyson and his Keats, . . . let him advance to nobler models," to Milton and Shakespeare's sterner tragedies, that he may "roll their raptures and catch their fire," and, "for the sake of poetry, let him proceed to veil the statue of the Venus, and to uncover those of the Apollo, the Mars and the Jupiter." [25] Though frankly disturbed by certain fleshly elements, which he could ascribe to his protégé's youth, Gilfillan exulted in the tremendous popular reception accorded the *Life Drama*. No poem since *Childe Harold* had won its author such widespread acclaim. George Meredith wrote a sonnet of appreciation for the *Critic*. Clough hailed "the latest disciple of the school of Keats." And Arnold grudgingly admitted to "an extraordinary faculty" in Smith, though a faculty perhaps of doubtful value. For the moment seriously adverse criticism was silenced. Smith like Browning's patriot had his hour of triumph,[26] thoroughly beguiled by his own success, quite unprepared to see his fame and the reputation of the whole Spasmodic School led within a year to the shambles' gate of literature.

It should, however, hardly have needed an agile satirist to expose the weakness of Spasmodic art. For the *Life Drama* itself exaggerates almost to the point of burlesque many of the qualities inherent in the verse of Bailey, Marston, and Jones. It presents a gloomy Walter, the typical Byronic artist, pacing to and fro in "an Antique Room," at war with himself, aspiring towards the discourse of "great thought-wealthy souls," erotically wooing the flighty Muse:

> *For Poesy my heart and pulses beat,*
> *For Poesy my blood runs red and fleet,*
> *As Aaron's serpent the Egyptians' swallowed,*
> *One passion eats the rest. My soul is followed*
> *By strong ambition to out-roll a lay*

Whose melody will haunt the world for aye,
Charming it onward on its golden way.

Walter takes his craft seriously. Poesy is to him "the grandest chariot
wherein king-thoughts ride," and the poet is one destined to "go
forward in his spirit's strength / And grapple with the questions of
all time." Yet like the true Spasmodic, he scorns disciplined emotion: "I'd rather be the glad bright-leaping foam," he insists, "than
the smooth sluggish sea." He indulges an aesthetic sentimentalism,
fain "to feed upon the beauty of the moon." And he strains after
fanciful images and lurid descriptions as when he salutes "the pas-
sion-panting sea" watching "the unveiled beauty of the stars, like a
great hungry soul." His impulsive courting of the lovely Violet is
marred by a fierce sensualism that repels the lady and shocks his
own finer sensibilities. But his fundamental innocence emerges in his
sweet song, "The Garden and the Child," which Gilfillan lauded as
"one gush of tender or terrible beauty. . . . The child is another
little Eva." And in the end Walter is worthy the love of Violet when
he can beg of her, "Teach me, for thou art nearer God than I!" He is
at last proud to wear "the armour of a pure intent," convinced that
"great duties are before me and great songs." [27]

Though the *Life Drama* bore some traces of a comic spirit[28]
which might have restored a sense of perspective to Walter's unbalanced rhapsody, Smith's purpose was essentially grave. And his apparent success as delineator of turbulent passions encouraged his
friend Sydney Dobell to issue *Balder* (1853), the most inchoate of
all Spasmodic tragedies. From the beginning Dobell had been in
many respects better qualified than Smith to attain the epic heights
towards which the whole School aspired. The son of a puritanical
publican, he had been taught from childhood to probe his soul by
introspection and self-catechism, to respect his own genius, and to
worship his high predestined calling. At the age of four he had already experienced moods of Wertherian self-pity; and by seven he
had learned to commit his deepest religious meditations to a commonplace book. As a young man he had endorsed the liberal revolu-

tions of 1848 and after their failure had penned *The Roman* (1850),
a long blank-verse tribute to the invincible cause of freedom.

Early in the fifties, George Gilfillan, discovering *The Roman,* had
described Dobell as "our most rising and sincere poet," the author of
what seemed "unquestionably a very striking, poetical, and impassioned production; . . . many of the individual passages burn with
the fire of genius." [29] Later lyrics in loose verse-paragraphs, formless,
digressive, shamelessly sentimental, merely confirmed the critic's
opinion that he had come upon "one of our greatest spiritual poten-
tates." And even his wife shared the tearful enthusiasm: "Mrs. Gilfillan," he wrote to Dobell, "thanks you for your forthcoming 'Snow-
drop.' She keeps no album, but she will put it in her heart." [30] Yet
Gilfillan could not rest content with the touching shorter pieces; he
urged Dobell to think at once in terms of a great epic. You may
write, he said, comparative trifles "like treatises of Reformation and
'Comuses,' till the time for the Epos come. Only, don't underrate the
'Paradise Lost.'" So directed, the poet turned towards the form in
which alone he might realize his Miltonic ambition, the Drama,
which was to him "merely an Epic produced under compulsory external conditions that interfered with the natural laws of epical production." [31]

If Gilfillan was the critic of the Spasmodic School, Dobell was
certainly its ablest aesthetician. Throughout his life he propounded
an art theory which helped both to determine and to explain his
poetic practice — and propounded it, in fact, so passionately that he
is said to have impaired his lungs by delivering a lecture on the
nature of poetry to the Philosophical Institution. From his notebooks
and essays, we may gauge what *Balder* ideally was intended to accomplish. Combining a post-Kantian idealism and a Hartleian psychology, Dobell insisted upon the importance of poetic intuition and
poetic association of ideas; for "the Truth on which the inward eye
is chiefly fixed becomes a solar centre and other truths are apprehended by rapid excursions from this central point — to which they
become, therefore, accessories; each accessory (in proportion to the
attention paid to it) itself the centre of still subordinate excursions."

The poet, he believed, was, by the very act of creation, transfigured, lifted to a higher level of perfection, manifested more clearly as an image of the Perfect Being, and his art accordingly gave a unique insight into the ultimate harmony of multiple relations. The great poem was, he said, a kind of microcosm, an organized aggregation of parts, in which the principal truth of the whole was its "sublimity or beauty," and the truth of the parts "their relationship, near or remote, to the central truth of the Greater Whole." But the microcosm of art could not have strictly rigid proportions, for then it would be "artificial not natural, architecture not Nature." The artist who sought to delete irrelevancies failed at dynamic composition; his work fell, in its theoretical completeness, "from Art to mechanics." But the true poet able to relate diverse ideas rejected all mechanical designs and all the unnatural patterns of logical thought. He scorned the painful processes of reasoning; he understood directly by immediate perception. And the truths he had apprehended he conveyed by metaphor, the peculiar language of poetry. Communication through verse demanded use of a fact which might "produce in the mind another fact," and poetic response in the reader was excited by the metaphorical images which the poet set afloat in the imagination. Metaphor, then, was to Dobell a sort of objective correlative, "not a work of conscious human intellect at all" but "the perfunctory work of a piece of Divine machinery which produces the *alter ego* of a fact involuntarily." [32]

As published late in 1853, *Balder* was to be understood as the first part of an ambitious trilogy charting "the Progress of a Human Being from Doubt to Faith, from Chaos to Order." If the enormous fragment in itself did not carry the reader far beyond Chaos, the larger whole, said Dobell, would establish the prerequisite relationship to a universal harmony. Yet few not endowed with Dobell's faculty of association could be other than confused by the excursions and "still subordinate excursions" from the central point, or rather, by the interminable and arbitrary digressions from a focus in nowise clearly defined. None would deny that Nature had triumphed over architecture or that metaphors grew like exotic flowers in the unpruned jungles of interlocked emotion. But all who lacked Spasmodic intuition failed to detect the functional significance of the resplendent images or the means by which any thematic pattern might be disentangled.

Gilfillan, however, was undisturbed by captious criticism; with all its faults, *Balder* still impressed him as "the richest volume of recent poetry next to 'Festus,' . . . a wilderness of thought — a sea of towering imagery and surging passion," the work of one who was "intensely and transcendentally a poet." [33] And by his own canons, Gilfillan was undoubtedly right. For *Balder* represented the culmination of Spasmodic art. Living high above ordinary mortals in an "old tower gloomy and ruinous," its hero was torn by the half-awakened social consciousness that invaded the metaphysical dreams of all Spasmodics:

> *In the form*
> *Of manhood I will get me down to man!*
> *As one goes down from Alpine tops with snows*
> *Upon his head, I, who have stood so long*
> *On other Alps, will go down to my race.*

Yet his ambition was repeatedly frustrated by the familiar Byronic morbidity, the awareness of dark desires. "I sit here," he lamented,

> *Within my passions; and that writhing round*
> *Of rooted serpents rises like a ring*
> *Of licking flames about me. Some are dead*
> *And others gnaw them. Of the living, some*
> *Lie lank as worms; some roar as dragons.*

Caught in the webs of self-analysis, Balder experienced most deeply the romantic *mal du siècle;* and his one gesture of assertion, the murder of his insane wife Amy, was less the humanitarian act he imagined it than a vain protest against the common paralysis of inaction. Throughout the course of his melancholy, he inflicted upon the vacant air reams of verse typical of many a protagonist since Festus; but once, in less literary mood, he achieved a unique expression of gasping despair, surely the most remarkable line of English blank verse, the most striking example of what we may call the "clinical" style:

> Ah! ah! ah!
> Ah! ah! ah! ah! ah! ah! ah! ah! ah! ah!
> By Satan! This is well. What! am I judged? [34]

Balder was indeed "judged," by a lesser court than he had deigned consider; and the sentence passed upon him indicted not only his creator but the whole Spasmodic School.

Before it entered a second edition, Dobell's "epic" fell into the hands of William Edmondstoune Aytoun, a versatile Scottish satirist already provoked by the extremes of Smith's *Life Drama* and angered by the critical judgments of Gilfillan.[35] In attacking the principles and practice of Spasmodic verse, Aytoun could draw upon an enviable apprenticeship as parodist. Ten years before, he had collaborated with Sir Theodore Martin on the amusing *Bon Gaultier Ballads* and had scored a popular triumph with his own version of Tennyson's "May Queen":

> You may lay me in my bed, Mother — my head is throbbing sore,
> And, Mother, prithee, let the sheets be duly aired before;
> And, if you'd do a kindness to your poor desponding child,
> Draw me a pot of beer, Mother — and, Mother, draw it mild.

But the assault on the Spasmodics was to be no simple burlesque. With the connivance of his publisher, Aytoun prepared an elaborate literary hoax. In *Blackwood's Magazine* for May 1854, there appeared an anonymous critical review of a forthcoming production entitled *Firmilian, a Spasmodic Tragedy* by T. Percy Jones. Though no recent poem, said the reviewer, had "so many symptoms of unmistakable lunacy," there was a method in the madness of *Firmilian* and "a rapidity of perception and originality of thought which contrast[ed] very favourably with the tedious drivelings of some other writers of the same school," and the author, alone among the Spasmodic poets, seemed to have the sense not "personally to evoke Lucifer or Mephistopheles." Yet Mr. Jones, the critic continued, was at one with his fellows in the use of apostrophe and figurative language, for they all were "simply writing nonsense-verses; but they contrive[d], by blazing away whole rounds of metaphor, to mask their absolute poverty of thought, and to convey the impression that there must be something stupendous under so heavy a canopy of smoke."

Having deftly antagonized the admirers of Spasmodic poetry by what seemed unfair attack upon an unpublished drama, Aytoun now allowed the imaginary T. Percy Jones to preface his work on its appearance the next month with a justification of his aesthetic theory. "The office of poetry," declared Jones, "is to exhibit the passions in that state of excitement which distinguishes one from the other. . . . I am perfectly aware that this poem is unequal, and that some passages of it are inferior in interest to others. Such was my object, for I am convinced that there can be no beauty without breaks and undulation." So familiar was his defense that many were prepared to accept it as perfectly sincere and altogether logical. And in view of serious Spasmodic verse, it is not quite incredible that some critics should have found the drama itself a wholly sober production. Even Aytoun privately expressed his alarm at the closeness of certain passages to good poetry, and his friend Martin was struck by the way in which the poem showed how anyone could write "pages of sonorous and sparkling verse, simply by ignoring the fetters of nature and common sense, and dashing headlong on Pegasus through the wilderness of fancy." [36]

Firmilian indeed remains a perplexing *tour de force,* lit by fitful gleams of a fiery rhetoric, often all too like the bombast it seeks to parody. Its poet-hero, the "Student of Badajoz," who is writing a tragedy on the subject of Cain, is hardly less restrained in his passions than Smith's Walter, and his basic motives are scarcely less pure; as his friend Haverillo explains to lorn Mariana of the Moated Grange,

> *His heart's in the right place. He's wayward, doubtless,*
> *And very often unintelligible.*
> *But that is held to be a virtue now.*

In both his egotism and his devotion to his craft, he is almost as steadfast as Marston's Gerald. And in his erudition, which enables him to discourse for twelve pages of blank verse upon the glacial theory, he rivals Bailey's Festus. Above all, he suggests Dobell's Balder, who likewise began in a library his search for the full experience and also found himself driven to murder as a means of savoring the pangs of remorse. Even his most absurd soliloquy, spoken as he is about to hurl Haverillo from a tower, might have been Balder's meditation when, craving action, he grappled ineffectually with his wife's physician on the ramparts:

> *Courage, Firmilian! for the hour has come*
> *When thou canst know atrocity indeed*
> *By smiting him who was thy dearest friend.*
> *And think not that he dies a vulgar death —*
> *'Tis poetry demands the sacrifice!*

Yet it is something of an innovation to Spasmodic drama that Haverillo's body should actually fall and, falling, crush the sentimental critic Apollodorus (who is, of course, none other than Gilfillan) just as he is praising the unpremeditated song of the fruit-peddler Sancho:

> *He labours not to sing, for his bright thoughts*
> *Resolve themselves at once into a strain*
> *Without the aid of balanced artifice.*[37]

And the final scene of retribution, in which Firmilian wandering through night-fog over a barren moor is hounded to his doom by a "chorus of Ignes Fatui," has many parallels but no exact duplicate among the intense Spasmodic originals.

Though Dobell and Smith were at first heartily amused by Aytoun's satire,[38] they had no intimation of the extent to which their fame would suffer from his indictment. But as the burlesque elements in *Firmilian* became clear to a wider public and as the Spasmodic label gained currency, it seemed more and more difficult to approach with proper gravity any future work of either poet. Their collaborated sonnets on the struggle in Crimea, though far more disciplined than *Balder* or the *Life Drama,* attracted little serious attention. Dobell's own volume, *England in Time of War* (1856), a collection of quietly sentimental ballads and topical lyrics, by no means retrieved the reputation he had won with *The Roman.* And Smith's best and most restrained verse, the *City Poems* of 1856, was arraigned on a groundless charge of plagiarism which called into question his whole artistic integrity and rendered suspect his every utterance. Gilfillan, meanwhile, repudiated Smith's later work and declared *Balder,* which he had once praised, to be merely "that hideous spasm of a true poet." [39] But few were longer interested in the opinions of Apollodorus. Gilfillan in vain denounced Aytoun as a "heartless dog" and helplessly complained to the already forgotten Bigg that he had endured more "systematic abuse and slander than anyone since Hazlitt and Shelley." Though he might ultimately feel within him "the buddings of a great truth . . . including all being in its sweep and forming a unity . . . out of 'ruin reconciled,'" [40] he could never recover his influence, and his principles were no more a power in the land.

After *Firmilian* some of the energies that had animated the Spasmodic School may have been diverted, through the sixties, into the sensational fiction which carried a similar rant and melodrama and a like interest in exploring insane passion, from the best seller *Lady Audley's Secret* to the subtler psychological thrillers of Wilkie Collins. At any rate, the Festonian drama and the Spasmodic tragedy disappeared from serious verse.[41] Rossetti and the Pre-Raphaelites discovered new methods of objectifying lyric emotion. And Swinburne with all his diffuseness rapidly achieved a technical virtuosity by which he could channel his exuberance. Lesser writers, revolting self-consciously from Spasmodic looseness, followed Frederick Locker-Lampson in cultivating the epigrammatic *vers de société* and Austin Dobson in turning to the rigid discipline of Old French forms.[42] Only a few like Robert Buchanan, who admired Smith and Dobell and dedicated his first book to Gilfillan, remained loyal to the Spasmodic ideal.[43] Yet Buchanan was promptly recognized and easily ridiculed as advocate of a lost cause. W. H. Mallock, for instance, explained with considerable verve "How to Make a Spasmodic Poem like Mr. Robert Buchanan" (1873):

Take ten verses-full of star-dew, twenty-five verses-full of the tides of night, fifteen of passion-pale proud women, . . . fifteen of aching solitude, and twenty of frost-silvered mountain peaks. . . . Into these put the moon, with stars *ad libitum;* and sprinkle the whole over with broken panes of a Grub-street garret window. . . . Then take an infinite yearning to be a poet, and a profound conviction that you never can be one, and try to stifle the latter. This you will not be able to do. The aim of the endeavor is to make the conviction restive. Then put the two together into yourself; and the conviction will immediately begin to splutter, and disturb you. This you will mistake for the struggles of genius, and you will shortly after be thrown into the most violent convulsions.[44]

In preparing his recipe, Mallock was able to draw upon literary opinion quite general since Aytoun's parody. But during its productive years from *Festus* to *Balder,* the defects of the Spasmodic School were seen in no such sharp perspective. Many serious writers were impressed by its driving rhetoric and quite in sympathy with its high purposes. Emily Brontë, whom Dobell was among the first to praise, may have gained not a little for her own passionate art from the post-romantic theory of the imagination held by Bailey and Marston and later by Dobell himself. And the work of Elizabeth Barrett Browning was most certainly affected by Spasmodic principle and practice.

In her close room on Wimpole Street, Elizabeth Barrett heard echoes from the outside world which encouraged her own feverish lyricism. Early in the forties she opened correspondence with R. H. Horne and made her contribution to his *New Spirit of the Age* (1844), which so warmly endorsed the genius of Bailey. Horne's *Orion* she considered the major epic of her time. Yet her own early pieces were often closer in tone to the verse of Ebenezer Jones; and her "Cry of the Children," a poem strangely intense in its vicarious intuitions, might stand as companion to Jones's "Song of the Gold-Getters," which was born of far harsher personal experience. Years later in Italy she retained the highly emotional attitude towards aesthetic and religious problems which characterized the work of many younger Spasmodics.

It was not remarkable, then, that she should greatly have admired *Balder* or that Dobell should have read her *Aurora Leigh* with peculiar interest and enthusiasm. For *Aurora Leigh* (1856), more than any of her other efforts, throbbed with a Spasmodic faith in the poet's mission and the sanctity of subjective impulse. She described the diffuse verse-novel as "the most mature of my works, and the one into which my highest convictions upon Life and Art have entered." And to a friend she confessed in terms that Dobell might have used in writing to Gilfillan: "I have put much of myself into it — I mean to say of my soul, my thoughts, emotions, opinions." [45] Like Balder or Walter or Gerald, the poetess Aurora expended much of her energy in lamenting the evil of the world, in worshiping the beauties of nature, and in theorizing for the author on the function of creative artists as interpreters of a multitudinous society:

> Their sole work is to represent the age,
> Their age, not Charlemagne's, — this live, throbbing age,
> That brawls, cheats, maddens, calculates, aspires,
> And spends more passion, more heroic heat,
> Betwixt the mirrors of its drawing-rooms,
> Than Roland with his knights, at Roncesvalles.

Yet there were, even in the insistence upon a passionate modernity, elements in *Aurora Leigh* quite alien to Spasmodic art. The will to approach social issues directly, the emphasis on immediate human values, the scorn of the aesthete's recourse to poetic imagery derived far less from the School of Gilfillan than from the "anti-romantic" preachments of Carlyle and Kingsley. Again and again we catch the sociological accent of early Victorian "realism":

> Humanity is great;
> And if I would not rather pore upon
> An ounce of common, ugly, human dust,
> An artisan's palm, or a peasant's brow,

> *Unsmooth, ignoble, save to me and God,*
> *Than track old Nilus to his silver roots,*
> *And wait on all the changes of the moon,*
> *. . . set it down*
> *As weakness, strength by no means.*

And though *Aurora Leigh* may seem quite as shapeless as the *Life Drama*, we find in it a demand for architectonic form, to which Smith had paid little heed, and an attack on the impulsive young poets who, tumultuous in their affections, "weak for art only," disregarded pattern. If Elizabeth Barrett Browning approached Spasmodic verse with some respect, she thus remained ambivalent towards its ultimate abandon. She preserved some ability to consider the obverse of every emotion and some final capacity for intellectual detachment.[46] And it was very likely this pervasive restraint that led Dobell to qualify his glowing eulogy of *Aurora Leigh;* the volume, he wrote, "contains some of the finest poetry written in the century; poetry such as Shakespeare's sister might have written if he had had a twin. . . . But it is no poem. No woman can write a poem." [47]

While in London before the publication of *Aurora Leigh,* Mrs. Browning held a literary soiree, at which her husband recited "Fra Lippo Lippi," the monologue that may well have embodied his own highest convictions upon life and art. But to most of those present the event of the evening was the Laureate's reading of *Maud,* an impassioned declamation which the young Rossetti, withdrawn to a quiet corner, recorded on his sketch pad in bold black shadows. Far more consciously than *Aurora Leigh, Maud* (1855) bore traces of Spasmodic emotion. Modestly designed as "a little *Hamlet,* the history of a morbid poetic soul, under the blighting influence of a recklessly speculative age," the monodrama in form, theme, and substance recalled the more ambitious efforts of Smith and Dobell.[48] Its cursing, distraught, Byronic hero, sentimental and violent, "the heir of madness, an egotist with the makings of a cynic," though clearly in direct descent from the narrator of "Locksley Hall," lived largely in the same world of delirious fancy that produced Walter and Balder.

His rant touched the same depths of insane despair, hovered over the same obsessing evils:

> *What! am I raging alone as my father raged in his mood?* . . .
>
> *At war with myself and a wretched race,*
> *Sick, sick to the heart of life am I.* . . .
>
> *Prophet, curse me the blabbing lip,*
> *And curse me the British vermin, the rat.* . . .
> *Arsenic, arsenic, sure, would do it,*
> *Except that now we poison our babes, poor souls!*
> *It is all used up for that.*

Yet his rhetoric at times reached such heights of eloquence as Byron himself seldom attained; and his ecstasy found images, "objective correlatives," infinitely beyond the starry metaphors of the Spasmodic School:

> *Here will I lie* . . .
> *Who am no more so all forlorn,*
> *As when it seemed far better to be born*
> *To labour and the mattock-harden'd hand,*
> *Than nursed at ease and brought to understand*
> *A sad astrology, the boundless plan*
> *That makes you tyrants in your iron skies*
> *Innumerable, pitiless, passionless eyes,*
> *Cold fires, yet with power to burn and brand*
> *His nothingness into man.*

If like his Spasmodic prototypes he repeatedly substituted rhapsodic intuition for logical analysis, he did so with the grandeur of diction, the lordship of language, that gave his creator preëminence among Victorian poets. Even in the midst of his rant he could recover moments of self-possession and with them a sense of his own absurdity:

> *Ah, but what shall I be at fifty*
> *Should Nature keep me alive,*
> *If I find the world so bitter*
> *When I am but twenty-five?*

For there was in the hero of *Maud* much of Tennyson himself, much of the "black-blooded" passion that threatened to consume, much of the awareness forever insistent that

> *It is time, O passionate heart and morbid eye,*
> *That old hysterical mock-disease should die.*

In its melodrama, *Maud* may have drawn freely upon Spasmodic materials; yet it subjected them to the discipline of a painfully acquired technique and the self-consciousness of a mind trained to distrust the egotist's escape. Whatever its possible debt to a passing literary convention, *Maud* derived its ultimate intensity from the author's understanding of his hero's divided emotion. Long after the Spasmodic School had been forgotten, the monodrama retained a personal significance; it stood as the last major expression of a conflict in Tennyson between "romantic" inclination and Victorian demand, a conflict which had animated his whole poetic development.

Tennyson—
The Two Voices

I seem'd to move in old memorial tilts,
And doing battle with forgotten ghosts,
To dream myself the shadow of a dream;
And ere I woke it was the point of noon,
The lists were ready. . . .

— THE PRINCESS

WHEN Tennyson as a small schoolboy at Louth climbed a wall to expound his political views, a stern usher, ordering him down, rebuked his aping of the parish beadle.[1] Yet the time came when few would so rudely question his capacity for public speech. By 1842 Tennyson had become to many the true Laureate of Victorian England, long before the Queen's minister was able to offer him that title. And for a full half-century he retained his place as oracle, as prophetic interpreter of the ideals, the fears, the tastes and prejudices of a troubled and tumultuous age. Then, on the poet's death, even Thomas Henry Huxley, the ablest of the prose controversialists, was moved to rhyme:

And lay him gently down among
The men of state, the men of song:
The men who would not suffer wrong:

The thought-worn chieftains of the mind,
Head servants of the human kind.[2]

Like many of his fellow Victorians, Huxley must have recognized the struggle in Tennyson between a personal art for art's sake and an art keyed to the interests of nineteenth-century society; for like most, he applauded the decision that had led the poet from the land of dreams to the hard realities of modern science.

Later critics, however, have usually been less disposed than Huxley to accept the oracular Tennyson, less ready to place him among the intellectual leaders of his time. Far from being the thought-worn chieftain, he has often seemed quite incapable of rational discourse, a lyrist who deserted his true inspiration whenever he mounted the wall or descended to the arena of Victorian controversy.[3] For his gifts, we are told, were primarily emotional, elegiac, the source of a melancholy meditation occasionally exquisite in its sensibility, but seldom conducive to a meaningful grasp of broader social problems. Harold Nicolson, accordingly, pictures him as a lonely frustrated singer of the foggy moors, a tortured soul most sincere in his heart-sick despair.[4] Hugh I'Anson Fausset feels him "essentially the poet of delicate, sometimes mystical sensuousness," rarely able to transmute his opinions into passionate convictions.[5] And W. H. Auden, granting him perhaps the finest ear in English poetry, finds him "undoubtedly the stupidest" of English poets, learned only in the arts of melancholia.[6]

To such readers, Tennyson's tragedy was an ill-considered surrender to an inhibiting convention. Yet, as Professor Bush reminds us, an objective survey of his life's work "does not suggest that he was notably warped, that he took or was pushed into the wrong road."[7] For the course of his development was apparent almost from the first; and his "failure," if such in any real sense it was, can never be dissociated from his triumph. Tennyson in truth had no better an ear than Pope, and no more obtuse an intellect. Like Pope, he had thoroughly assimilated the common knowledge of his England and willingly had subjected current themes and values to his controlled craftsmanship. He sang to the Victorians, as Pope to the Augustans, what oft was thought but ne'er so well expressed. His orientation towards his place as Laureate had, therefore, a wider than personal significance. His conflict, though highly individual, was also broadly typical of the conflict which all major Victorian artists had to face. In his early work we see both the Spasmodic impulse that culminated in *Maud* and the "anti-romantic" bias that produced a sociological aesthetic.

Tennyson's zealous apprenticeship to his craft began with his boyhood in Somersby.[8] Indeed, the melancholia which Mr. Auden considers so remarkable may well have been part of the meager legacy left him by his parson-father, a disinherited elder son whose gloom at times drove the child to solitary prayer in the dark churchyard. But from the first his despondency, whatever its personal inspiration, stemmed also in large part from literary sources. It was undoubtedly, to some extent, of a piece with the devotion to romantic verse that prompted the youth of fourteen to carve on the sandstone, "Byron is dead." For Tennyson lived from the beginning in the golden realms of poetry. His earliest ambition was to follow that poetic Gleam to which in fact he dedicated his long career. "Well, Arthur," he told his brother, tramping across the Lincolnshire fields, "I mean to be famous." And with fame as the spur, he produced his first Thomsonian blank verse and his early Popian couplets.

At the age of twelve he felt able to instruct his Aunt Marianne in Milton's prosody, which he deemed very fine, though its classical derivations, he supposed, might be unfamiliar to a less informed English reader. Two years later he discovered the Elizabethans in unbowdlerized texts and attempted to adapt their vigorous idiom to the exuberant fancy of his own inventive adolescence. *The Devil and the Lady,* his unfinished drama of the necromancer Magus, is the work of an extraordinary boy, saturated in a wide, if rather sophomoric, erudition, and endowed with a certain deeper sophistication, a premature insight, and a dash of Byronic worldly wisdom. Exploiting the theme of cuckoldry, the play develops through a broadly masculine diction and an uninhibited imagery the old story of January and May, expanded with the proper Mephistophelian additions.

With much of its rhetoric, the mature Tennyson was rightly dissatisfied. Still, its heroine Amoret, the lusty wench who fondly bids
farewell to her dotard husband, the "yellowest leaf on Autumn's
wither'd tree," the "fireless mixture of Earth's coldest clay," her "antidote to love," retains in all her unsubtle rant a vitality which his
purer ladies rarely equaled. But proud as the young poet may have
been of his creation, he must have seen almost immediately that its
literary derivations were too remote from approved models. At any
rate, he carefully excluded the play from *Poems by Two Brothers*
(1827) "as being too much out of the common for the public taste." [9]

By February 1828, when he matriculated at Cambridge, Tennyson
had grown thoroughly sensitive to "public taste" and had already
practiced his skill in imitating currently popular verse forms and
motifs. "In Deep and Solemn Dreams," an unpublished poem begun
at Somersby, represented a quite conventional "romantic" musing on
death and the passing of joy:

> Dear lips, loved eyes, ye fade, ye fly,
> Even in my fear ye die,
> And the hollow dark I dread
> Closes round my friendless head.

And "The Outcast" echoed a nostalgia not unlike the plaintive sentiment of Thomas Moore's "Oft in the Stilly Night":

> And oh! what memory might recall
> If once I paced that voiceless Hall. [10]

At Cambridge, Tennyson continued to follow literary modes with
the artisan's interest. The fashionable gift-books, the annuals, acquainted him with the verse-portrait designed to accompany graphic
illustration, a genre in which he could exercise his metrical talents
more or less objectively. Experimenting with varied stanza patterns,
he called upon his young man's fancy to produce a gorgeous gallery
of gallant inventions, dream figures, charming or tedious, remote
from reality, untroubled by intellect: Lisette, Isabel, and Amy; Eleä-
nore with her "swan-like stateliness," "sweet pale" Margaret, "airy,
fairy" Lilian, "shadowy, dreaming" Adeline, fickle Madeline, "wild-

eyed," disdainful Rosalind. Some of these ladies, the poet kept hidden in his notebooks; some, like Lilian who saw the light with laughing eyes, must have tried his patience:

> *Praying all I can,*
> *If prayers will not hush thee,*
> *Airy Lilian,*
> *Like a rose-leaf I will crush thee,*
> *Fairy Lilian.*

None of them bore close relation to his academic experience.

"Timbuctoo," which won the Chancellor's Medal for 1829, was no doubt a more serious experiment — the first prize poem to be written in Miltonic blank verse rather than the usual heroic couplets, a work in which the *Athenaeum* critics detected "a really first-rate poetical genius." [11] Yet Tennyson valued "Timbuctoo" scarcely more than his exotic "Anacaona," the ballad of a West Indian siren, which he withheld from print because of its faulty rhymes and dubious natural history. With a few exceptions, his earliest Cambridge verses carried little of the intense conviction which he himself demanded of true poetry. On occasion, however, he did approach the spiritual analysis that later would lend tragic depth to *In Memoriam*. In the "Supposed Confessions of a Second-rate Sensitive Mind," he explored the timorous unfaith of a dejected soul, a soul conscious of its falling away from the grace of childhood but hearing no timely utterance to reconcile it to maturity:

> *I am void,*
> *Dark, formless, utterly destroyed. . . .*

> *I am too forlorn,*
> *Too shaken: my own weakness fools*
> *My judgment, and my spirit whirls,*
> *Moved from beneath with doubt and fear. . . .*

> *O weary life! O weary death!*
> *O spirit and heart made desolate!*
> *O damnèd vacillating state!*

Here the "confessor" was and was not Tennyson, eager to find life's meaning before the busy fret of the sharp-headed worm could begin. And his confession revealed both the deliberate melancholy of a literary convention and something also of the miserable bewilderment that actually marked the first months of the poet's college career. For it seemed certain to Tennyson that "there was a want of love in Cambridge" and that its apathetic pedants, "feeding not the heart," could inspire little confidence or courage.[12]

Yet if his instructors were blind to "the Day-beam . . . New-risen o'er awaken'd Albion," many of his classmates had glimpsed the dawn of a regenerated culture, and some indeed had borne it in their own radiance. Before long, Tennyson had found a place among the Cambridge Apostles, a group of brilliant undergraduates from whom his person and his poetry commanded instant respect. Tall, handsome, muscular, he seemed to incarnate "the union of strength with refinement." FitzGerald remembered him as "a sort of Hyperion"; and Brookfield remonstrated, "It is not fair, Alfred, that you should be Hercules as well as Apollo." For his prowess as fencer and oarsman was surpassed only by the compelling charm with which he recited "Oriana" to enchanted tables or from manuscript read epic paragraphs, like his own Everard Hall, "mouthing out his hollow oes and aes, / Deep-chested music."

But with all due regard for his manly bearing, his friends perhaps saw, in his fastidious response to form and color and cadenced rhythm, not a little of the self-conscious aesthete; at all events, they may well have suspected that the interest with which he watched the coilings of a tame snake on his college carpet was not merely scientific. With no considerable indirection, the allegorical fragment "Sense and Conscience" betrayed Tennyson's own fear that the appeal of a sensuous art might prove stronger than the attractions of a dutiful life, that the force of reason might be led captive by

> *witching fantasies which won the heart,*
> *Lovely with bright black eyes and long black hair*
> *And lips which moved in silence, shaping words*
> *With meaning all too sweet for sound.*[13]

Yet his new admirers suggested to him poetic standards by which he might escape the fierce Maenads of sensuosity. That he rapidly succeeded in doing so, we may gauge from the fact that Cambridge men, soon after his withdrawal, were prepared to debate the question, "Tennyson or Milton, which the greater poet?"

Richard Monckton Milnes, who considered "Timbuctoo" "certainly equal to most parts of Milton," [14] was soon ready to defend Tennyson's general superiority. For Tennyson was clearly the strongest poetic voice of the same bright company in which Milnes made his debut as glittering "bird of paradox." [15] Whether or not their influence on the poet was wholly beneficial, the Apostles provided him the intellectual stimulus that alone could free him from a recurrent indolence and a self-absorbed aestheticism. Open alike to the broad theology of Frederick Denison Maurice and the eloquent skepticism of John Sterling, they reminded him that a faith could come of honest doubt and that a free intelligence need imply no lack of conviction. They forced upon him none of the dogmatism that later alienated Arnold from the Oxford Movement; but they demanded the earnest resolve requisite to the building of a new culture.[16] Though John Kemble announcing, "The world is one great thought, and I am thinking it," might view German metaphysics with becoming levity, Tennyson could commend his essential seriousness of purpose:

> *My hope and heart is with thee — thou wilt be*
> *A latter Luther and a soldier priest.*

When Kemble lapsed into Anglo-Saxon scholarship, his actress-sister Fanny complained that the fine sonnet had been "poetry but not prophecy." [17] Yet Kemble was among those who urged upon Tennyson the poet's prophetic mission. And Tennyson, accepting his responsibility, hymned the ideal lyrist who, seeing "thro' life and death, thro' good and ill," gave to Freedom "one poor poet's scroll" wherewith "she shook the world." Once, in mock rage he read before the Apostles his rejoinder to the irreverent Blakesley[18] who, as self-appointed practical iconoclast of the group, had dared attack his verse:

Vex not thou the poet's mind
  With thy shallow wit;
Vex not thou the poet's mind,
  For thou canst not fathom it. . . .

Dark-brow'd sophist, come not anear;
  All the place is holy ground;
Hollow smile and frozen sneer
  Come not here.

Still, the playful declaration of independence granted no poetic license to yield to the charms of an isolated dreamworld. Like the stern Apostle he was, R. C. Trench warned the poet, "Tennyson, we cannot live in art." [19] Tennyson pondered the admonition, himself aware that there could be no vital escape from human affairs, for

he that shuts Love out, in turn shall be
Shut out from Love, and on her threshold lie
Howling in outer darkness.

And to illustrate his own belief that "the Godlike life is with man and for man," he wrote "The Palace of Art," an allegory of the aesthetic soul that vainly shrinks from the encroachment of "uncertain shapes," the lengthening shadows of a dark reality. [20] Yet he was in truth still too preoccupied with the studied depiction of dreamful ease to vitalize the artist's conflict; the lush *décor* of the pleasure dome remained more vivid to him than the homely "cottage in the vale" where the converted soul was to learn the alchemy of love. James Spedding, though ready to quote the entire poem with high approval, recognized the poet's one lingering sin as "an overindulgence in the luxuries of the senses," a tendency towards excessive ornament and overwrought imagery. [21]

Tennyson himself, however, had been consciously struggling against his own taste for "escapist" art ever since he had drawn his early caricature of the Cambridge aesthete who "smooth'd his chin and sleek'd his hair,"

And said the earth was beautiful, . . .
And with a sweeping of the arm,

> *And a lack-lustre dead-blue eye,*
> *Devolved his rounded periods.*[22]

Now under "apostolic" guidance he was turning more and more to a consideration of broader cultural and intellectual problems. At one meeting he advanced the unorthodox theory that human development might be traced back to lower organisms. At another he opposed nature worship and resisted all attempts to deduce an intelligible First Cause from natural phenomena.[23] If his political views derived much from the Burkean conservatism propounded by Spedding, he expressed considerable sympathy with various "liberal" measures. He supported both the Anti-slavery Convention and the movement to abolish subscription to the Thirty-nine Articles.[24] For a while he was more sanguine than most of the Apostles about the probable effects of a widened franchise; and he eventually joined with abandon in the bell ringing that celebrated the passing of the first Reform Bill.

In many ways the moving spirit of the Cambridge Apostles, Arthur Hallam was assuredly Tennyson's liveliest inspiration. More than all others, Hallam could convince him that human values ultimately transcended the seductions of a rarefied art, that "poems are good things but flesh and blood is better." [25] It was Hallam's exuberance that kindled the revolutionary idealism that carried them both across the Pyrenees to a romantic rendezvous with the rebel Torrijos. And it was Hallam's irresistible vitality that made memorable a holiday excursion to the Rhineland, the ascent of the Drachenfels, and the eating of cherries beneath a castle wall. Hallam intimately understood Tennyson's delicate sensibility, his basic diffidence, his deep self-consciousness; yet he valiantly strove to encourage a firmer emphasis upon the moral interpretation which he deemed essential to high poetic achievement. "You say pathetically," he wrote, " 'Alas for me! I have more of the Beautiful than the Good!' Remember to your comfort that God has given you to see the difference. Many a poet has gone on blindly in his artist pride." [26] He agreed with Tennyson that the poet "ought to be lord of the five senses," but he insisted that the artist who lacked a higher intuitive sense had "left out the part of Hamlet in the play."

Hallam's faith in intuition was central to his whole philosophy; the work of the intellect seemed to him always posterior to feeling, for "the latter," he said, "lies at the foundation of the man; it is his proper self — the peculiar thing that characterizes him as an individual." [27] And the same intuitive faith in the reality of spirit eventually provided Tennyson his one avenue of assent when Hallam was gone and alone he had to find life and meaning in a world whose law was death and change:

> *If e'er when faith had fall'n asleep,*
> *I heard a voice, "Believe no more"*
> *And heard an ever-breaking shore*
> *That tumbled in the Godless deep;*
>
> *A warmth within the breast would melt*
> *The freezing reason's colder part,*
> *And like a man in wrath the heart*
> *Stood up and answer'd, "I have felt."*

In Hallam's untimely death, Tennyson experienced not only the shattering impact of a profoundly personal loss but also the sharpest reminder of an all-possessing mortality. Though deeply shadowed by the pathos of specific remembrance, his grief brought before him the general problem of evil, the tragic issue of man's struggle against a malignant destiny. Beside his present despair, his earlier moodiness seemed puerile or academic, born of adolescent fears or literary archetypes. Always before he had found release from despondency in the charms of verse. But now that the good had vanished, the beautiful gave little satisfaction; it remained the artist's futile protest against reality; for art, too, partook of death. In utter anguish he asked if life could hold any lasting worth.[28] And from his questioning, his "thoughts of suicide," arose "The Two Voices," his earliest attempt to resolve his misery. Like a medieval debate relentlessly focused upon the abstract verities, the dialogue, stripping away mere ornament, cut in pendulum rhythm across the "divided will" of a broken soul. Tinged with Satanic irony, the voice of negation, cynical and realistic, puncturing a desperate idealism, forced upon the reluctant ego an awareness of man's fundamental insignificance:

> *This truth within thy mind rehearse,*
> *That in a boundless universe*
> *Is boundless better, boundless worse. . . .*
>
> *Forerun thy peers, thy time, and let*
> *Thy feet, millenniums hence, be set*
> *In midst of knowledge, dream'd not yet.*
>
> *Thou hast not gain'd a real height,*
> *Nor art thou nearer to the light,*
> *Because the scale is infinite.*

Yet the self, rid of its illusions, could still call upon a dim intuition, unvanquished by the logic of reason, shielded by the inexplicable "inward evidence" that in life not death, in "more life and fuller," lay the one last hope. Recovery might yet begin if the soul could bless humanity — even though humanity might be seen in unfortunate guise as a grave father postured between "the prudent partner of his blood" and their demure child, a group frozen in their attitudes, as if drawn not from the fuller life at all but from the unrealities of gift-book illustration. And then at last the second voice might raise its little whisper, its tentative suggestion that all was well on the Sabbath morn. But compared to the promptings of the tempter, the murmur of good cheer strikes us as thin and ineffectual; "The Two Voices" remains intense as the colloquy of denial with doubt in the dark night of the soul.

"Ulysses," written to convey the poet's "feeling about the need of going forward," [29] quite convincingly objectified the vital assent which the voice of hope had timidly commended. In the heart of the aged wanderer, Tennyson placed the firm resolve which he himself had determined to feel, the defiant strength, the stoic assertion of life snatched from the eternal silence, the will — more Victorian than Greek — "to strive, to seek, to find, and not to yield." But "Ulysses" no more adequately represented his own true state of mind than

"The Lotos-Eaters," which before Hallam's death had dramatized an antithetical mood, the leisured absorption in sense perceptions, a thoroughly "unapostolic" retirement to an isolated art for art's sake. Indeed, now that an elaborate sensuousness had lost its seductive appeal, Tennyson subjected "The Lotos-Eaters" to extensive revision. The catalogue of exquisite impressions with which the poem had originally closed he now supplanted by a final chorus, inspired by Lucretius, but here designed to suggest the effects of lotus-eating, of selfish aestheticism, upon man's moral fiber; he sought now to emphasize not a harmless delight in exotic form and color, but the fatal willingness of the drugged soul to ascribe its indolence and defeat to the decrees of irresponsible destiny.

As he struggled both as man and artist towards an active acceptance of tragic experience, Tennyson paid increasing attention to the moral implications of self-indulgent despair. "The Vision of Sin," his most powerful dream-allegory, traces the degeneration of a weak-willed poet who forsakes his arduous mission, yielding to the allure of gross sensual pleasure. In the castle of sin, really a desecrated palace of art, the beguiled spirit joins a fearful *danse macabre* led off by intoxicated phantoms, "half-invisible to the view," reeling to the mad music, creatures "twisted hard in fierce embraces," the prototypes perhaps of the abandoned marionettes silhouetted against the window blind in "The Harlot's House" of Oscar Wilde. Then, as the melody dissolves before the corroding years, a gap-toothed specter crosses the dead heath, the gray shadow of the once sensitive soul, whose cynicism has sprung from decayed faith and a belated awareness of everlasting damnation:

> *Thou shalt not be saved by works,*
> *Thou hast been a sinner too;*
> *Ruin'd trunks on wither'd forks,*
> *Empty scarecrows, I and you. . . .*
>
> *We are men of ruin'd blood;*
> *Therefore comes it we are wise.*
> *Fish are we that love the mud,*
> *Rising to no fancy-flies. . . .*

> *Fill the can and fill the cup;*
> *All the windy ways of men*
> *Are but dust that rises up,*
> *And is gently laid again.*

With helpless fascination, the dreamer beholds the soul's destruction and hears the easy moralists pass judgment, hears a destitute voice cry, "Is there any hope?" —

> *To which an answer peal'd from that high land*
> *But in a tongue no man could understand;*
> *And on the glimmering limit far withdrawn*
> *God made Himself an awful rose of dawn.*

Yet if sin, the deliberate effort to gainsay inexorable law, merely hastened the process of decay, a self-conscious asceticism could scarcely, Tennyson felt, avail more towards life. As a complement to "The Vision of Sin," "St. Simeon Stylites" attacked the pride of calculated renunciation with a bitterness which could not but suggest the poet's own struggle against self-righteousness and self-deception. The martyr no less than the sinner had cut himself off from the demands of society and also, therefore, from the sources of energizing life. From solitary brooding no truth could come; introspection, if guided by the soured conscience, could lead only to a desolating self-pity. Despite his "Spasmodic" rant, even the narrator of "Locksley Hall" remained uncomfortably aware that a heaven-storming rhetoric could not long conceal a ridiculous egotism:[30]

> *I must mix myself with action, lest I wither by despair. . . .*

> *Hark, my merry comrades call me, sounding on the bugle-horn,*
> *They to whom my foolish passion were a target for their scorn.*

Though less melodramatically, Tennyson himself responded to the same call. More and more he inveighed against retreat from the vital world. And that the aesthete's isolation might seem more culpable, he added to "The Palace of Art" several stanzas of political allegory to indicate a deathful disdain of social values, values which the converted soul would have fully to recover. The personal assent of a

Ulysses was now meaningful to the poet only if it carried with it a social dedication. For the second of the two voices, growing clearer, had inevitably become the voice of society itself.

The decade of "silence" following Hallam's death was in reality among the most productive periods of Tennyson's life. Amid personal griefs and responsibilities, he was able to reshape his best Cambridge verse and to compose many more mature pieces, objective poems quickened in insight and deepened by what Hallam had once called "the ideas of time and sorrow." [31] From visits to many parts of Britain, he gained impressions which contributed much to his grasp of Victorian realities. And as he recovered from his desperate gloom, he learned to view his private doubts in broad perspective. "Will Waterproof's Lyrical Monologue, Made at the Cock" chronicled, with all the humor of the "anti-romantics," the triumph of redeeming common sense over bright illusion:

> For, something duller than at first
>   Nor wholly comfortable,
> I sit, my empty glass reversed,
>   And thrumming on the table;
> Half fearful that, with self at strife,
>   I take myself to task,
> Lest of the fulness of my life
>   I leave an empty flask;
> For I had hope, by something rare,
>   To prove myself a poet,
> But, while I plan and plan, my hair
>   Is gray before I know it. . . .
>
> I hold it good, good things should pass;
>   With time I will not quarrel;
> It is but yonder empty glass
>   That makes me maudlin-moral.

Though finally persuaded by Milnes to submit a lyric to *The Tribute*, he could now see the vapidity of all "aristocratic" gift-books: "To write for people with prefixes to their names," he protested, "is to milk he goats; there is neither honour nor profit." [32] His own energies were concentrated on matters more serious and less sententious. For many months he followed a self-imposed program of daily study, in the sciences, in history, in Greek, German, and Italian. So fortified, he turned purposefully to the early sections of *In Memoriam;* and the whole intellectual pattern of the intensely personal elegies took coloring from his disinterested concern with astronomical theory and Newtonian physics, his close examination of Lyell's *Geology,* and his general readings in natural science. Self-discipline, deliberately achieved, channeled and directed his most heartfelt emotion.

"Self-knowledge, self-reverence, self-control," these became the cornerstones of a philosophy grounded upon a cognizance of natural law; the individual will would henceforth find perfect freedom only in conformity to an impersonal moral order. In "Love and Duty" Tennyson disavowed the tragedy of thwarted passion and the consequent "brooding in the ruins of a life" and "the long mechanic pacings to and fro" dear to the Spasmodics; for Love, he argued, could find no real fulfillment if Duty, "this world's curse — beloved but hated," refused its complete sanction. To Browning, as "The Statue and the Bust" seems to suggest, the denial of passion might itself be the cardinal sin. But to Tennyson — as indeed to Kierkegaard — unleashed passion could lead only to moral collapse and social disintegration. In *Queen Mary* an unreasoning devotion to the lustful Philip would incite national calamity. And in the *Idylls* the surrender of a weakened duty to a coarsened love would bring disaster to Tristram and the whole realm of Arthur.

Self-control born of self-conquest was thus central to the mature Tennyson's thought and "message." And from 1840 onwards it was also the key to his poetic technique. By the time he had won his personal assent, he had proven himself the accomplished stylist in full command of the formal devices peculiar to his medium. "I suppose," he wrote many years later, "I was nearer thirty than twenty before I was anything of an artist." [33] Certainly the 1842 volume betrayed a surety of craftsmanship far beyond the ornate aestheticism of the Cambridge poems. Unlike the early Spasmodics who were already striving to emulate *Festus,* Tennyson aspired to clarity of form and precision of statement — especially in his shorter pieces, which he considered generally superior to his more ambitious efforts. "Every short poem," he told Aubrey de Vere, "should have a definite shape, like the curve, sometimes a single, sometimes a double one, assumed by a severed tress or the rind of an apple when flung on the floor." [34]

Intent upon distinct pattern, he rather regretted John Stuart Mill's favorable review of early work with which he himself had since grown dissatisfied.[35] Most of the poems carried over from the second volume suffered radical change before their reappearance after the long "silence." "The Lady of Shalott," for instance, was thoroughly rewritten; its diction was made more exact and less sentimental; its vaguer images were displaced by precise detail; and its rich ornamentation was as sharply reduced as the apostolic Spedding could ever have demanded. In nearly all the verse, revision meant deletion of countless lines which had once pleased the poet but now seemed inorganic to the requisite shape, the single or double lyric curve. If his own first models had been diffuse and spontaneous, Tennyson now sought concentration and finish, since "only the concise and perfect work" would, he felt, endure.[36]

But however apparent his craftsmanship might be to even the most casual reader, he in nowise felt that mere dexterity of form could compensate for want of subject matter. With self-assured modesty he saw the danger of his gift: "in expression," he said, "I am not perhaps below Sophocles, but there's nothing in me." [37] Yet he could hardly have gone on writing had he really considered his basic themes inconsequential. In collecting his 1842 poems, he had given at least as much attention to content as to technique; and his styles indeed had been evolved not for their own sake but for the ideas they were to carry. Now for the first time he was concerned with addressing a general public rather than a select audience predisposed to admire. His classical poems were accordingly adapted to the spiritual needs of the nineteenth century. And his allegories like "The Vision of Sin," his monologues like "St. Simeon," even his poems of personal conflict such as "The Two Voices," were sufficiently objectified to dramatize universal problems or to utter common moral truths. Lest the "Morte d'Arthur" seem too remote from immediate experience, it was placed in a colloquial frame designed as a conscious apology for the exploitation of old heroic materials. Though he would frequently return to the grand style, he experimented a good deal with verses in an easy conversational idiom, which seemed to him, for the moment at any rate, the language of vital communication.

Probably his most popular ventures into the middle style were the "English Idyls," sketches clearly emanating from the "cottage in the vale," though shadowed here and there by an awareness of grimmer realities. "Walking to the Mail," a conversation piece not far removed in accent from the dialogues of Robert Frost, suggested the evils of political violence through a gruesome anecdote of a child's sadism; while "Audley Court" merely described a holiday experience without serious implication, a picnic by the sea, revived in a sharp vignette of the savory meat pie, the cider jug, and the talkative companions. "Edwin Morris" lightly touched upon the subject of women's rights, as prologue to the tale of a country girl's *mariage de convenance* to a lame-brained aristocrat of "watery smile and educated whisker." And "Dora" more soberly developed a parable of feminine patience and self-sacrifice, with a conscious simplicity which Wordsworth thought more ideally Wordsworthian than his own "Michael." [38]

None of the idyls dealt in complex or rounded characters troubled by two inner voices. Each strove, not to motivate human action, but rather to set recognizable types against familiar backgrounds; each presented a genre study of materials which seemed curiously important to a generation more than ever concerned with discovering the homely beauty of native scenes and objects, the local color of a rural England. Essentially topical in interest, they thus made an appeal to early Victorian tastes which later readers could never wholly understand. "The Gardener's Daughter," for example, as the longest and most elaborately wrought of the first series, depicted a lovers' meeting in terms of gesture quite alien to the conventions of twentieth-century passion. Indeed, the idyllic maiden, poised by the porch, her long sunlit hair cascading to the flowers athwart her arm,

Yours faithfully,

I hate the dreadful hollow behind the little wood

Tennyson reading *Maud*
Sketch by Dante Gabriel Rossetti, 1855

may very well have suggested the attitudinizing girl of T. S. Eliot's "Figlia che Piange," who likewise compelled the imagination many autumn days. But whereas Mr. Eliot was bent upon burlesquing the situation with a cryptic self-consciousness and a dread of romantic emotion, Tennyson with perhaps as high an aesthetic intention chose to accept the ingenuousness of his subject as itself sufficiently worthy. Few of the 1842 poems were explicitly didactic; and one, "The Day-Dream," actually moralized upon its failure to furnish a moral:

> O, to what uses shall we put
> 　The wildweed-flower that simply blows?
> And is there any moral shut
> 　Within the bosom of the rose?

Yet in their quiet portraiture the idyls surely underlined the values of individual charity and ordered living towards which the poet's contemporaries were earnestly struggling.

In a composite review of *The Princess,* the *Works* of Shelley, and Milnes's *Life of Keats,* an *Edinburgh* critic contrasted Tennyson and the great romantics.[39] The writings of Keats and Shelley had the defect, he said, "of appearing poetry distilled from poetry rather than drawn from the living sources of life and truth," while Tennyson's verse seemed to have moved deliberately away from an "ideal" art of fanciful invention towards a "national" art centered upon immediate actualities. Whether or not he could accept any indictment of Keats, whom he consistently revered, Tennyson by the mid-forties had undoubtedly found his place among the "anti-romantic" Victorians. He showed a common interest in new books by new authors,[40] books as widely different in tone as the notorious *Vestiges of Creation* by Robert Chambers and the *Poems* of Miss Barrett or the first volume of a work on modern painters "by an Oxford undergraduate, I think." He was warmly received by Dickens and Thackeray, by Maclise and Macready, by Coventry Patmore and John Forster. And he became intimate with Carlyle, who on long nocturnal rambles harangued him about the condition of Peel's England. Though he attacked the philosophy of heroes, Tennyson apparently accepted the gospel of work.[41] At any rate, "The Golden Year," published in 1846, urging the claims of a broadened Christianity, of free trade and a free press, insisted with Carlylean certainty that the golden age of man's desiring lay neither in the past nor the future, for

> *unto him who works and feels he works,*
> *This same grand year is ever at the doors.*

While he felt no sympathy for the Grundyites, to whom poets were a "barely *respectable*" race,[42] he clearly identified his hope with the larger aspirations of an ascendant middle class.

Tennyson's eagerness to consider contemporary issues may have rushed him at times into premature debate. Thus *The Princess* of 1847, though carefully finished as verse, suffered from a basic confusion of argument; the poet throughout remained too ambivalent towards the ideal of liberated womanhood to achieve either a serious defense of feminism or a consistent mock-heroic satire. Yet the problem of women's rights was one that perplexed the whole age in its effort to reconcile individual freedom with the claims of a domestic culture; and Tennyson's failure to provide a meaningful solution was no real mark of incapacity as commentator on matters of public concern. His confusion, however it blurred the pattern of his "medley," sprang from too broad an awareness of diverse opinion rather than from too nice a regard for his own prejudices. For Tennyson, more than any other Victorian poet, more even than Matthew Arnold, was sensitive to the spiritual temper of his time; by power of will and imagination, he became the true interpreter of Victorian conflict.

If *In Memoriam* (1850) was his masterpiece, it was also the most representative and probably the greatest poem of the era. And its strength derived less from private grief nourished in bitter solitude than from the clash of intense emotion with solidly objective forces, with ideas crowding in upon the doubting soul from the dispassionate world of nineteenth-century science. Tennyson's crucial distinction between faith and knowledge meant no easy retreat from material realities. He was thoroughly disillusioned in his view of nature "red in tooth and claw." And he was no more able than Laplace to find God by scanning the starry heavens. He felt only contempt for the Brahmin who dismantled a microscope because it revealed an amoebic struggle for survival; the obscurantist, he said, was acting "as if we could destroy facts by refusing to see them." [43] Science, to be sure, might widen his whole perspective. It might lead him to speculate on the nebular hypothesis and the lapse of aeonian time, even on the identity of dynamic forces at the nucleus of the energized atom.[44] Science would certainly, he thought, do much to disperse the collective superstitions of mankind. Yet never could it stimulate individual assent; for never could it explain the strange miracle of selfhood. Deep within him Tennyson cherished an honest will to believe, the intimation of immortality, stronger and more persistent than any passing wish to rationalize his doubt. By faith alone, "believing where we cannot prove," could he discover purpose in the brute fact of existence. *In Memoriam* reaffirmed the possibility of keeping that faith — faith in a moral order, faith in the life of spirit — and of keeping it without denial or evasion of such knowledge as might seem to encourage a purely agnostic approach to the unknowable. No matter how personal Tennyson's hopes and fears may have been, the elegies developed them against an intellectual background familiar to all thinking Victorians; and the struggle of trust and despair thus became part of a common emotional experience. The final guarded but sure assertion of the Everlasting Yea had, therefore, significance not merely to the poet himself but to his whole troubled generation.

Less than six months after the appearance of *In Memoriam,* Tennyson was named Poet Laureate to succeed Wordsworth. With characteristic diffidence he accepted the honor, insisting that his decision had been prompted by the report that the Laureate, when dining out, always was offered the liver-wing of the chicken. From the beginning he was able to carry his dignity with becoming lightness and a wholly admirable sense of his own limitations. His thorough apprenticeship as craftsman had prepared him to speak with matchless clarity; and his awareness of Victorian objectives had made him, like the redeemed hero of *Maud,* one with his kind, broadly sympathetic to the basic ideals of the new culture. Usually on public occasions his thought ran parallel to the temper of his native land; and in a poem like his elegy to Wellington his voice could give definitive statement to a national sentiment. But if his private opinion collided with a public policy of which he could not approve, he felt no need to compromise his intellectual or artistic integrity. Throughout his long tenure as Laureate, he retained a wonderful candor of outlook, a remarkable independence of judgment. However frequently his verse was attuned to the spirit of the age, he could never be accused of acting as a political tool, a poetic timeserver.

By 1850 his orientation as a citizen of the Victorian world had been completed. But his growth as artist continued till the day of his death; and his development was by no means as anticlimactic as many critics have suggested. During his middle years he may have accepted too readily the conventions evolved by a dubious middle-class taste. But in his late poems he achieved a style and substance uninhibited by hollow standards, restrained merely by his own aesthetic discretion. Like his Ulysses, he lived to see himself become a name, esteemed as a knower of men and manners, climates, councils, governments. And he lived also to see his work recognized in quarters of which the earnest Cambridge Apostles could have had no inkling. Indeed, perhaps his warmest tribute came not from genteel eulogists but rather from the lips of a vagrant in Covent Garden who stopped the poet with humble entreaty: "Look, sir, here am I. I've been drunk for six days out of the seven, but if you will shake me by the hand, I'm damned if I ever get drunk again." [45] Such was the power of poetry; and Tennyson, who had himself known maudlin moments, was willing to answer with the voice of hope, though he realized from experience that the ethics of conversion were rather less simple than his friend had supposed.

The Pattern
of Conversion

Und so lang' du das nicht hast,
Dieses: Stirb und werde!
Bist du nur ein trüber Gast
Auf der dunklen Erde.

— GOETHE

I held it truth, with him who sings
To one clear harp in divers tones,
That men may rise on stepping-stones
Of their dead selves to higher things.

— TENNYSON

IN controlling his own "Spasmodic" impulse, Tennyson arrived with some reluctance but by deep necessity at the assent of the "anti-romantic" Victorians. Though loosely organized as an aesthetic whole, *In Memoriam* closely followed the general pattern of nineteenth-century conversion. Far from unpremeditated, its "wild and wandering cries" traced the soul's growth from unshadowed hope through the denial of life itself towards the final conquest of doubt and despair. By painful stages the poet learned to transcend an isolating self-consciousness, to achieve the saner perspective of dispassion, and ultimately to accept the tragic realities of an objective world:

> *I will not shut me from my kind,*
> *And lest I stiffen into stone,*
> *I will not eat my heart alone,*
> *Nor feed with sighs a passing wind.*

Through a determined social dedication, he rose above the paralysis of private grief, the stone-stiff inactivity which was death itself. Life, he concluded, could have meaning only if it were brought into harmony with the "eternal process moving on," with the purposes of all creation evolving slowly from form to form towards "one far-off divine event." For life to Tennyson meant vital motion, the motion as of a buffeted ship sailing into the baths of all the western stars. In "The Voyage" he developed a characteristic metaphor to describe the tireless struggle of his aspiring age: life was a sea journey over troubled waters, a pilgrimage which demanded fortitude of spirit and steadfast defiance of the laws that seemed to condition man's ineluctable free will:

> *And never sail of ours was furl'd,*
> *Nor anchor dropt at eve or morn;*
> *We loved the glories of the world,*
> *But laws of nature were our scorn.*
> *For blasts would rise and rave and cease,*
> *But whence were those that drove the sail*
> *Across the whirlwind's heart of peace,*
> *And to and thro' the counter gale?*

The aspiration towards spiritual fulfillment which Tennyson saw as the solution to a deeply personal problem was endemic to much verse quite independent of his direct influence. As a poetic motif, it undoubtedly owed much to the writings of Goethe, whose speculations on palingenesis, or the soul's rebirth to "higher things," animated the whole gospel of *Sartor Resartus* and lent authority to the opening section of *In Memoriam*. Throughout early Victorian literature the basic themes of *Faust* recurred with innumerable variations.[1] From *Festus* to *Firmilian,* the Faustian thirst for experience provided a thread of unity to the diffuse efforts of the Spasmodic School. The *Balder* trilogy, mercifully uncompleted, was intended to show at long last the gloomy egotist's acquisition of a nobler self through his un-wearied striving towards the infinite.[2] But few of the Spasmodics could follow their heroes beyond a first befuddling Walpurgisnacht. The major voice of aspiration was inevitably one that had mastered the logic of ebullient acceptance; it was Robert Browning who at-tained the immediate assent, far readier than Goethe's, far easier than Tennyson's. If "Ulysses" expressed an undaunted will to go forward, "Rabbi Ben Ezra," Browning's poetic testament, proclaimed an ecstatic joy of life in the living, the optimist's glory in the con-suming struggle:

> *Then, welcome each rebuff*
> *That turns earth's smoothness rough,*
> *Each sting that bids nor sit nor stand but go!*
> *Be our joys three-parts pain!*
> *Strive, and hold cheap the strain;*
> *Learn, nor account the pang; dare, never*
> *grudge the throe!*
>
> *For thence — a paradox*
> *Which comforts while it mocks —*
> *Shall life succeed in that it seems to fail:*
> *What I aspired to be,*
> *And was not, comforts me;*
> *A brute I might have been, but would not*
> *sink i' the scale.*

Aspiration so conceived was its own vital reward. To Browning the fulfillment of desire meant spiritual death, for it removed the high remote ideal that had given motive power to the soul. Man's imperfection was the certain mark of his humanity, a token of the infinite yearnings within him which would never leave the spirit content with even the highest form of a lower-scaled life, the finished and finite clod untroubled by a spark.[3] For it seemed, as John Stuart Mill argued to the defeat of his own "hedonism," far "better to be a human being dissatisfied than a pig satisfied." While Tennyson found evidence of immortality in half-mystic intuition, Browning saw sufficient proof in the righteous dissatisfaction of human beings, in their every triumphing failure. The faultless technique of Andrea del Sarto might be the measure of his moral inadequacy; for in many a less perfect painter there burned "a truer light of God." Heaven existed for him whose reach exceeded his grasp. And even Heaven might occasionally leave some provision for the heart not ready to forego the human aspiration; the lovers might still ride on

> *With life forever old yet new,*
> *Changed not in kind but in degree,*
> *The instant made eternity.*

Yet it was Heaven's deepest purpose to "perfect the earthen," to provide the completeness that imperfection augured:

> *The evil is null, is naught, is silence implying sound;*
> *What was good shall be good, with, for evil, so much good more;*
> *On the earth the broken arcs; in the heaven a perfect round.*

By his own brand of Christian Platonism, Browning thus postulated a solution to the problem of evil which was acceptable to many Victorians responsive to various idealistic philosophies. In *Festus,* though with greater turgidity, Bailey reached a similar conclusion; Lucifer, proclaiming himself "the imperfection of the whole," acknowledged good as "the sole positive principle in the world," the only ultimate that could inspire the ceaseless aspiration of relatively imperfect human beings.[4] Carlyle likewise discovered the source of man's blessed Unhappiness in the permanent desire for the Infinite which could never be quite submerged in the depths of the Finite. And Ruskin, applying the same principle to his art theory, insisted that "the demand for perfection," for "the perfect finish" rather than "the lovely form," was "always a sign of a misunderstanding of the ends of art"; for the great artist, he said, never stopped working till he had "reached his point of failure," and imperfection was "in some sort essential to all we know of life, . . . the sign of life in a mortal body, that is to say, of a state of progress and change."[5] But progress and change were, as Ruskin and most Victorians realized, not necessarily synonymous terms; for if man was now imperfect, he might as easily "sink i' the scale" as rise to a higher perfection. Alexander Smith saw in every human worthiness

> *a flaw*
> *That like a crack across a mirror's face*
> *Impairs its value.*

And man's weakness, he felt, was less a gauge of his immortal strength than a shield to hide him from his empty self, lest he "die of fright at utter nothingness." [6]

Even Browning, however, asked that human impulse be directed towards some nobler end than self-realization. *Paracelsus* (1835) illustrated the failure to "attain" through unbalanced pride of intellect; after long delirium the Faustian "knower" could awaken to the tragedy of misguided, loveless aspiration:

> *I learned my own deep error; love's undoing*
> *Taught me the worth of love in man's estate,*
> *And what proportion love should hold with power*
> *In his right constitution.*

For the spirit of man could transcend its fright at utter nothingness only by moving towards an active sympathy with the aggregate struggle of mankind. The soul's abiding hope lay in its conversion from the tyranny of self to the higher purposes of the "eternal process."

Only a few Victorians suffered the disillusion of a Faust or a Paracelsus defeated in the desire for self-perfection by reliance upon the unaided aspiring intellect. But many experienced milder frustration in their pursuit of "self-culture." The so-called age of individualism was remarkably conscious of the individual's limitations; and it preached the sober doctrine of self-denial quite as persuasively as the more facile gospel of self-help. However great the pressure of material values, the sensitive soul was not indefinitely to be diverted from its spiritual quest. Throughout Victorian literature ran the message of redemption. Poet, novelist, and sermon-writer joined to urge **the supreme necessity** of spiritual purgation, of the little death-in-life, the dying unto the corrupted self. Carlyle, significantly, selected Dante's *Purgatorio* as an "emblem" of all that was noblest in medieval "Christianism" with its stringent insistence upon "the Law of Human Duty, the Moral Law of Man." And Bailey, fired with his own Dantesque ambitions, allowed a Protestant archangel of *Festus* to explain the halfway house between denial and assent:

> *Between the two extremes*
> *Of earth and Heaven there lies a mediate state, —*
> *A pause between the lightning lapse of life*
> *And following thunders of eternity; —*
> *Between eternity and time a lapse,*
> *To soul unconscious, though agelasting, where*
> *Spirit is tempered to its final fate.*

If less "agelasting," the purgatory on earth, through which the soul seeking its redemption had inevitably to pass, was quite as real to the bewildered sinner as the lapse between time and eternity.[7]

In *The Sickness unto Death,* a work which would have spoken with peculiar cogency to Victorian Englishmen, Kierkegaard analyzed the "despair" of a soul whose torment lay in not being "able to die." Despair meant the refusal to realize the true self by devotion to the Eternal. And "the most dangerous form of despair," said Kierkegaard, was man's unawareness of his spiritual essence, his blind absorption in material values, the blank indifference which to Carlyle was Atheism itself.[8] For conversion, according to an able Anglican apologist,[9] came not to the careless profligate, but rather to the troubled soul beset with a liberating "despair," a genuine weariness of the ego, and "a passionate desire to find some new centre of life" which might "renovate the springs and purify the aims of the soiled and exhausted nature." And "the dark night of the soul" described by St. John of the Cross, or the "spiritual dryness" of medieval mysticism, could be experienced only by one who recognized the loss which his inability to "die" unto the old self had occasioned him, by one who, fallen into despair, could like the Psalmist cry aloud for succor "in a dry and thirsty land where no water is." If the Captains of Industry were complacently lost in their Mammonite dreams, there were other, more wakeful spirits, sleepless in the "dark night," seeking a faith in the "higher things" for which man was made.

Of all Victorian thinkers, John Stuart Mill was by training the most suspicious of mystic intuition and religious ecstasy. For he had been nourished from childhood on the hard Benthamism of an unimaginative father. Yet at the only real crisis in his "mental history" his utilitarian education seemed completely to fail him.[10] And then "in the dry heavy dejection of the melancholy winter" he sensed the dreadful despair that had overtaken less rationalistic souls. In his twenty-first year he "awakened . . . as from a dream" to the hopelessness of his will to reform the world by a philosophy which even he found void of inspiriting joy. He experienced — as the most moving passage of his *Autobiography* tells us — "one of those moods when what is pleasure at other times, becomes insipid or indifferent; the state . . . in which converts to Methodism usually are, when smitten with their first 'conviction of sin.'" His father, who had taught him that "all mental and moral feelings . . . were the results of association" with the ideas of pleasure and pain, could offer no help when the old objects of pleasure ceased to delight. The young man was thus, to use his own metaphor, "left stranded at the commencement of [his] voyage, with a well-equipped ship and a rudder, but no sail; without any real desire for the ends which [he] had been so carefully fitted out to work for." He thus felt the desolation of the forsaken soul: "The fountains of vanity and ambition," he said, "seemed to have dried up within me, as completely as those of benevolence."

Only when he could admit the claims of emotion, which the Benthamites had denied, could Mill find psychic release in tears and a consequent lightening of his oppressive burden. By slow degrees he reached "the anti-self-consciousness theory of Carlyle" which convinced him that all who fix their will on happiness as the end of life find only misery. And eventually he recovered his assent by seeking a new synthesis of mind and heart. From Wordsworth he learned the importance of inner culture, and from Goethe he gained respect for the "many-sidedness" of an integrated personality. If he continued to advance the "utilitarian" ethic, he was henceforth the utilitarian with a difference. Ever after his mental crisis, he held to a larger concept of social needs than an individual hedonism could postulate; for his recovery, to all intents and purposes, was a "conversion," a resurrection of the spirit after a dry and melancholy winter.

Though an avowed enemy of the "liberalism" to which Mill dedicated his renewed energies, John Henry Newman passed through a not dissimilar period of "spiritual dryness" in achieving his essential orientation.[11] Dissatisfied with the "do-nothing perplexity" of his church and haunted by visions of his own falling from grace, he endured a deep despondency when "all, save the spirit of man, [seemed] divine." Only after his crucial illness in Sicily, his bodily "sickness unto death," did he achieve a genuine conviction of duty, a resolve, specifically Christian in impulse but as broadly "Victorian" in accent as Mill's secular purpose: "I have a work to do in England." Then on the slow journey back to Marseilles he reflected on the source of his recovery, his surrender of the proud will that had once "loved to choose," and his full attainment of the humble desire for guidance through the dark night:

> Lead, Kindly Light, amid the encircling gloom,
> Lead Thou me on!

His longing for the physical reality of "home" was lost in the purged soul's yearning to seek atonement in self-denying work; and the becalmed Mediterranean naturally became to him a symbol of the despair from which the power of God alone might bring deliverance; for

> shouldst thou feel some fever's force,
> He takes thy hand, He bids thee rise.

> Or on a voyage, when calms prevail,
> And prison thee upon the sea,
> He walks the wave, He wings the sail,
> The shore is gain'd, and thou art free.

Newman's work in England demanded all the resources of his refined and refining intellect. Yet he consistently feared the pretensions of the independent reason; it became the great sin to value "intellectual excellence," which had once seemed the supreme good, more highly than moral submission. Throughout his strenuous activity during the Oxford Movement, he sought final authority from the faith that had led him over the dark waters. And his ultimate secession to Rome in 1845 was but an inevitable corollary to his earlier renunciation of the individual will, the "protestant" judgment. Indeed, to describe his emotion at that time, he again invoked, perhaps not altogether unconsciously, the metaphor of the ocean voyage; he felt, he said, that he had at last been brought safely "into port after a rough sea."

As the major Victorian autobiographers, Newman and Mill left the clearest record of actual conversion to self-sacrificing work guided by religious or philosophic principle. Yet neither, by the nature of his apology, could make his private history an object lesson in the ideal spiritual development; for each was limited to the specific facts and speculations of his own career. Each was thus denied the advantage of Carlyle, who was able to objectify in terms of allegory relevant details from his personal experience, and thereby to suggest what seemed to him the requisite pattern of all conversion. *Sartor Resartus* dramatized the general states of mind through which Mill, Newman, and Carlyle himself passed in achieving their assent, and it supplied useful categories to many other Victorians concerned with the common regenerative process. The "Everlasting No" fitly characterized the despair that regarded the material world as a dead mechanism and the spiritual as an impotent abstraction. The "Centre of Indifference" represented the soul's ability to cast aside an enervating egotism, in order to attain a broader perspective by which man's obsessing sorrows would seem of little cosmic import. And the "Everlasting Yea" explained the high significance for all men of "some purifying Temptation in the Wilderness" amid "the Droughts of practical and spiritual Unbelief," and emphasized the deep necessity of the little death, the "healing sleep" that accomplished the "Annihilation of Self (*Selbst-Tödtung*)" essential to the new life of work and service.

Denial, indifference, assent, such was the dialectic of Teufelsdröckh's "conversion," of an organic change which only the modern era could understand; for "the Old World," said Carlyle, "knew nothing of Conversion; instead of an *Ecce Homo,* they had only some *Choice of Hercules.* It was a new-attained progress in the Moral Development of man; hereby has the Highest come home to the bosoms of the most Limited; what to Plato was but a hallucination, and to Socrates a chimera, is now clear and certain to your Zinzendorfs, your Wesleys, and the poorest of their Pietists and Methodists."

But the modern conversion of Teufelsdröckh was far less comprehensible in purely rational terms than Hercules' reasoned choice between Duty and Pleasure. For it involved attitudes and values which escaped clear-cut definition and logical analysis. Yet language to Carlyle was in its highest function "symbolic";[12] and through its symbols, its metaphors drawn from the finite world of sense impressions, it could achieve "more or less distinctly and directly, some embodiment and revelation of the Infinite," some sharp suggestion of the truths that the soul of man might intuit. *Sartor Resartus* abounded in such verbal "symbols" employed as expressionistic devices to describe an elusive change of heart. Thus the materialism of "an atheistic century" which Teufelsdröckh had stoutly to resist was naturally evoked by the image of the wilderness, the wasteland familiar to the whole mind of Europe as token of sterility and despair.[13] And the crucial insight which delivered him from the Everlasting No was appropriately realized by richly connotative simile and metaphor: "There rushed like a stream of fire over my whole soul; and I shook base Fear away from me forever. . . . Ever from that time the temper of my misery was changed: not Fear or whining Sorrow was it, but Indignation and grim fire-eyed Defiance. . . . It is from this hour that I incline to date my Spiritual New-birth, or Baphometic Fire-baptism." With the purifying fire, Carlyle inevitably associated his favorite "symbol" of conversion, the symbol of the mythical Phoenix that sought its renewal through self-immolation in the consuming flames. To the spiritual life of a whole society as to the regeneration of a single soul, the fable of the Phoenix had for him the deepest relevance. The French Revolution itself seemed the necessary death-by-fire of a corrupt regime; it told once again, he said, "the story of the Phoenix which periodically, after a thousand years, becomes a funeral pyre of its own creation, and so out of its own ashes becomes a new Phoenix." Surely the life of the Phoenix, the life through death and change, was "the law of all things." [14]

The concept of the *Flammentod* had been central to several of Goethe's metaphysical lyrics. And it recurred from time to time in the considerable body of Victorian literature more or less directly concerned with the problem of conversion. In *Jane Eyre* (1847), for instance, an actual fire provided the visible means of purgation whereby the Byronic Mr. Rochester might attain the humility of a nobler self. And in *Bleak House* (1853), the much debated spontaneous combustion served to clear away the dead rubbish of "Chancellor" Krook's establishment and so to suggest, symbolically, the destruction of the more noxious Chancery, whose existence impeded the shaping of a sounder law. The Victorians in general, however, were usually less eager than Carlyle that death or baptism unto the new life should be accompanied by a "baphometic fire." And Goethe himself had been content, at least in his greatest work, with the cooler rites of watery baptism. Faust after the tragedy of Margaret passed through a little death, whence he arose, rainbowed on an Alpine hillside, new-souled, cleansed by the "Lethe-flood" of night dews — mysteriously sanctified by immersion in a healing element. Thus the damp mist became the water of life, the reality coalesced with the symbol, and the infinite intangible stood as "prophetically revealed" as Carlyle could have desired.

In tracing the varied courses of many a Spiritual New-birth, the Victorians were, as we have seen, quite familiar with the thematic motifs of *Faust*. Yet they scarcely needed Goethean example to discover the literary uses of baptismal symbolism. Everywhere throughout nineteenth-century England, the virtues of water as an agent of "purification" — in every sense of the word — were sung with strenuous insistence. Thoroughly Evangelical in a utilitarian crusade, Edwin Chadwick and his successive commissions demanded that the whole crowded island be quite literally scrubbed of its inherited grime, of the past's too freely consecrated dust. In an age at once religious and secular, physical purity became a spiritual obligation; the most obvious sort of cleanliness seemed clearly next to godliness, and an inevitable concomitant. But the water symbol had, of course, immediate meaning on planes of less material godliness, far beyond Chadwick's Benthamite concern. Its significance to organized religion was as antique as the ancient pagan rites of lustration and as contemporary to the Victorians as the orthodox christening ceremony of their common experience. Used interchangeably with the blood symbol, particularly among Dissenting groups, it appeared in countless hymns of conversion from Cowper's plaintive lyric cry, "There is a fountain filled with blood," to General Booth's rousing Army chant, "Are you washed in the blood of the Lamb?"

Symbolic baptism, symbolic cleansing of the soiled self, which had acquired new urgency since the work of "your Zinzendorfs, your Wesleys" — this was one constant theme in the diverse gospels of Victorian Christianity, fixed amid all the conflicting attitudes towards sacrament and ritual. It is perhaps instructive to compare a seventeenth-century paraphrase of the Twenty-third Psalm by Francis Rous with Sir Henry Williams Baker's version, "The King of Love My Shepherd is," written in 1868. While the earlier poem had adhered closely to the Old Testament original, the Victorian hymn rather deliberately introduced the Christian concept of redemption. In adapting "beside the still waters" to an iambic meter, Rous had made no shift in denotation:

> *he leadeth me*
> *The quiet waters by.*

Baker, however, sought a more heavily connotative image:

> *Where streams of living water flow*
> *My ransomed soul he leadeth,*

Sideboard by Fourdinois
Shown at the Great Exhibition, 1851

Centerpiece designed by Prince Albert

And where the verdant pastures grow
With food celestial feedeth.

In its context the "living water" clearly betokened not only spiritual refreshment but the baptismal regeneration of the thirsty soul.

As clergyman and moral propagandist, Charles Kingsley preached, with an energy that flagged not nor failed, the message of conversion. And it testified well to the diffusion of the water symbol that he made it the central motif of a widely popular fairy-tale allegory. From its first portrait of Tom, the soot-smeared chimney sweep, *The Water Babies* (1863) moves directly towards the problem of washing clean the lost worldling's body and soul. Escaping into the valley, the "brave little man" hears the deep river sing its song of purification as it surges past the befouled cities to a new life in the open sea:

Strong and free, strong and free,
The floodgates are open, away to the sea;
Free and strong, free and strong,
Cleansing my streams as I hurry along
To the golden sands, and the leaping bar,
And the taintless tide that awaits me afar,
As I lose myself in the infinite main,
Like a soul that has sinned and is pardoned again.
Undefiled, for the undefiled,
Play by me, bathe in me, mother and child.

Conscious of his own filth, Tom succumbs to a delirious obsession, "I must be clean, I must be clean." And so resolved, he enters the river where he sinks into a healing "death-by-water" which he has not learned to fear. But his salvation is not easily to be won. As a water-baby he must pass through pain and despair before his soul is sufficiently cleansed in "the taintless tide." He must journey alone "in black darkness, at the bottom of the sea, for seven days and seven nights" till he come to the Other-end-of-Nowhere.[15] He must suffer sore humiliation by doing "the thing he did not like," by killing his selfish desire, by sacrificing, as *Sartor* recommended, the pursuit of pleasure to the love of God. Then, having been tested and found true, he can emerge from his last ordeal, a clean soul, fit to take his place in the busy world as "a great man of science" — a player with railroads and maker of telegraphs! The great scientist, thus evolved, is ultimately above any "moral"; but the parable may still have meaning to less fortunate little men:

Meanwhile, do you learn your lessons, and thank God that you have plenty of cold water to wash in; and wash in it too, like a true English man. And then, if my story is not true, something better is; and if I am not quite right, still you will be, as long as you stick to hard work and cold water.

In fiction more serious than Kingsley's fairy tale, "cold water" appeared less explicitly as a medium of conversion. Yet a good many Victorian novelists made some dramatic use of water imagery, and a few even resorted to baptismal symbolism in describing the progress of the soul's rebirth. Dickens, for instance, though not given to subtle metaphor, was fully conscious of the evocative sea image and quite familiar with all the poetic overtones of actual "death-by-water." In *David Copperfield* (1850) the motif recurs with varying degrees of "symbolic" force: poor Barkis, resigned to his fate, simply drifts "out with the tide"; while troubled Martha passionately cries her identity with "the dreadful river" which, polluted like herself, seeks the purity of "a great sea"; and Steerforth, drowned in the Yarmouth tempest, retrieves in death his lost innocence so completely that David may once again see "him lying with his head upon his arm, as I had often seen him lie at school." [16] In *Hard Times* (1854) the purification theme is organic to the central plot; Stephen Blackpool, fallen into the rain-soaked pit, suffers in "th' fire-damp crueler than battle" a death to the "muddle" of a rotten industrialism, a death whereby he achieves a new vision of the turmoil he has escaped: "I ha' seen more clear and ha' made it my dying prayer that aw th' world may on'y come toogether more . . . than when I were in't my own weak seln." More than the other books, *Great Expectations* (1861) deals directly in the regeneration of a selfish hero and heroine — Estella humbled can at last confess, "I have been bent and broken, but — I hope — into a better shape." And fittingly, the climax of the novel comes with the death struggle on the dark river;

as the convict Magwitch is lifted prostrate from the Thames, Pip, himself drenched, his pride drowned, "melts" with a deep compassion: "I only saw in him a much better man than I had been to Joe." In *Great Expectations,* as elsewhere in Dickens, the watery "baptism" is clearly related to the events of a moving narrative; yet not a little of the emotional effect may spring from free association with the established images of spiritual renewal.

Meredith and George Eliot,[17] more deliberately than Dickens, integrated the water symbol into several intellectualized character studies. *The Ordeal of Richard Feverel* (1859) shows us the hero, who has fled from his fleshly sin, caught up in "the grandeurs and mysteries" of a Rhineland storm which purges him of all selfish desire: "Vivid as lightning the Spirit of Life illumined him" until he felt "a sense of purification so sweet he shuddered again and again." Similarly, *The Mill on the Floss* (1860) traces the passing of Maggie's weariness and self-despair as she is "driven out upon the flood — that awful visitation of God which her father used to talk of — which had made the nightmare of her childish dreams," but which now barely parallels "the strong resurgent love" rising within her, as she clings to her brother, reconciled in watery death, during one "supreme moment of realization." Here the symbolic and the real blend skillfully into a unified impression. But in *Romola* (1863) the symbol is too elaborately developed and too artificially linked to the central action of the spiritual epic. Disillusioned by the perfidy of Tito and the worldly ambitions of Savonarola, Romola feels "even the springs of her once active pity drying up and leaving her to barren egoistic complaining." Then at the crucial moment, she remembers Boccaccio's story of Gostanza, and, like that unhappy lady, she too resolves to seek escape on the deep-sea waters, "to commit herself, sleeping, to destiny which would either bring death or else new necessities that might rouse a new life in her!" Renouncing all self, she stretches out on the floor of her small boat, pulls a cowl over her head, and dreams of sleep in her own grave — or perhaps, as the psychologist might have it, of a return to the mother's womb. Then at length the dark night of the soul passes, the evil falls away, and the boat bears onward a reborn spirit: "Instead of bringing her to death, it had been the gently lulling cradle of a new life." So regenerated, Romola ascends from the sea to a plague-ridden village where, at one with her kind, she serves as a selfless sister of mercy. From her calculated "death-by-water" comes her earthly redemption, her self-dedication to the struggles of an Italian Renaissance community — which in manners and morals seems remarkably Victorian and English.

In verse, where all "symbols" appeared with greater inevitability than in fiction, the water image assumed various forms.[18] Arnold repeatedly invoked the metaphor to connote permanent values above and beyond the shifting conflict. In "Self-dependence," as in the last lines of "Sohrab and Rustum," the sea betokened the stoic calm of ultimate dispassion. In "The Buried Life" the river represented the surge of the soul in time, and the sea, once again, the peace of eternity. Similarly, in "Dover Beach" the ebb of the tide paralleled the recession from human shores of a vital faith; and in "Mycerinus," as Professor Lowry suggests, the Nile itself became "the image of a Necessity that rolls all things before it." [19] Few of Arnold's sea metaphors, it is true, related to the "conversion" of the wanderer between two worlds; yet all clearly intimated the values from which the unregenerate doubting soul was excluded.

Browning, on the whole, worked less deliberately with symbolism, but he drew from time to time more directly than Arnold on the "death-by-water" motif and the baptismal image. His Childe Roland, for example, forded a strange river of death as he approached the dark tower across a wasteland of perished hopes, and his Karshish wondered what great miracle might

> bathe the wearied soul and worried flesh
> And bring it clean and fair, by three days' sleep.

Tennyson and Swinburne developed the same figure in most explicit terms; again and again each associated the water image with the refreshment of the wearied soul and worried flesh. From the be-

ginning Tennyson's verse was pregnant with baptismal suggestion.
A precocious desire for renewal prompted a childhood lyric of despair:

> *The quick-wing'd gnat doth make a boat*
> *Of his old husk wherewith to float*
> *To a new life! all low things range*
> *To higher! but I cannot change.*

In his more mature poems, human change to higher things seemed
both necessary and possible. Life was the tempestuous voyage towards ever larger fulfillment; the Gleam called the "young Mariner,"
tossed in his "mortal ark," [20] from the broad rivers to the flood of the
eternal sea, and eventually at twilight across the bar,

> *When that which drew from out the boundless deep*
> *Turns again home.*

In the valley of Cauteretz the voice of the living water became the
voice of the dead Hallam calling from a timeless past, the same voice
that sent "a summons from the sea" [21] to the elegist of *In Memoriam*.
Unlike Lycidas or the Phoenician sailor, Hallam had met death far
from the dreaded ocean; but Tennyson not less than Milton or T. S.
Eliot could record the terror of a watery grave; for it seemed less
fearful to know the dead man safely buried in the dry land

> *Than if . . . the roaring wells*
> *Should gulf him fathom-deep in brine;*
> *And hands so often clasp'd in mine*
> *Should toss with tangle and with shells.*

Yet through the death of the old self could come a new and higher
life. Even Lancelot, tarnished though he was with earthly passion,
might glimpse the shining Grail, if, after his struggle of seven days
and seven nights "along the dreary deep," he still held steadfast to
his resolution:

> *I will embark and I will lose myself*
> *And in the great sea wash away my sin.*

And Galahad in his purity and strength could follow his vision over the burning bridges "on the great Sea," beyond death and death's token,

> *A great black swamp and of an evil smell,*
> *Part black, part whiten'd with the bones of men.*

To Tennyson water was thus the symbol both of life and the dying unto life, of the everlasting peace and the "eternal process" of regeneration.

To Swinburne it was all this — and perhaps something more, the expression of an overwhelming energy, the spirit itself of the highest freedom. In "the wild, various, fantastic, tameless unity of the sea," he found what Ruskin called "the best emblem of unwearied unconquerable power" and the ideal image of "majesty and deathfulness." [22] Until the last, the sea furnished many of his strongest themes and richest metaphors, for it exercised a remarkable compulsion upon his whole imagination. "A Channel Passage" (1904), for instance, revitalized the "rapture and radiance," the "supreme and supernal joy," the sense of oneness with eternity that he had experienced almost fifty years earlier as an ecstatic youth watching the fierce waves try the worth of a small ship, when

> *The joys of the lightnings, the songs of the thunders,*
> *the strong sea's labour and rage,*
> *Were tokens and signs of the war that is life and*
> *is joy for the soul to wage.*

And "The Lake of Gaube" recorded his lifelong delight in swimming, in plunging into the "passionate peace" of cool depths, and in seeking there, with "each nerve of the spirit at rest," to sound "the darkness . . . and strangeness of death" in "the ineffable and breathless purity of the clasping water";[23] for

> *Might life be as this is and death be as life*
> *that casts off time as a robe,*
> *The likeness of infinite heaven were a symbol*
> *revealed of the lake of Gaube.*

"Thalassius" (1880), his poetic apologia, made the sea symbol the key to an allegory of spiritual conversion. As surely as *Romola,* and far more spontaneously, it explored the full connotation of "living water." Born to the sun-god Apollo and the sea-nymph Cymothoë, the poet-soul learned from his ageless mother the sacred love of Liberty. But in the bitter world of man's experience he met Sorrow, whose name was Death, and felt the disillusion that left the heart "sear and numb." Vainly he sought to escape his desolating fear in the orgies of self-indulgence; but neither in the fleshly *femme fatale* or the Bacchanalian music was there real help or comfort. Only by a return to his great sea-mother's home did he find his lost peace. There, lying upon a rocky ledge, he awakened like Faust from a healing sleep, "pure as one purged of pain that passion bore," while

> *the sweet sea's breath*
> *Breathed and blew life in where was heartless death,*
> *Death spirit-stricken of soul-sick days, where strife*
> *Of thought and flesh made mock of death and life.*

Then at last revived, he could find in his heart what Apollo asked, the song of perfect freedom,

> *The song of all the winds that sing of me,*
> *And in thy soul the sense of all the sea.*

Thus the pattern of conversion was complete; Thalassius and so, therefore, Swinburne himself, the last poetic voice of his generation, had ultimately arrived at the solemn assent to the cause of man which many a Victorian, each in his own way, had painfully achieved.

By whatever "symbol" it might be represented, the process of Spiritual New-birth involved the crucial insight into a reality, human or divine, beyond the old self-absorbed life. Through an intense intuition the soul attained its "at-oneness" with the objective truth of earth and heaven. At the moment of crisis, it penetrated the mystery of a vital order until even the smallest natural object became token of the infinite; the threefold cup of the woodspurge, fixed forever in its indubitable form, blurred the memory of Rossetti's "perfect grief," and the flower in the crannied wall, fully apprehended, revealed essentially what God and man was. But the great revelation, the epiphany experience, which illuminated the purposes of all living, came as no arbitrary resolution to man's despair; it presupposed always the willingness of the dry soul to obey the call of a death-in-life, the irresistible summons from the sea. All conversion thus depended ultimately upon some faith in the immanence of spirit, whether the fullness of realization lay in "one far-off divine event" or in "the imperishable dignity of man." Such faith, born of awakened feeling, directed and controlled the active reason towards social or religious ends which the unaided intellect could neither perceive nor justify. Despite evidences everywhere of multiple conditioning, the Victorian of faith could cling to the dogma of free will essential to his moral action. By faith he could accept the tragedy of pain and death as prerequisite to a nobler spiritual evolution, the necessary discord in an all-embracing harmony.[24] And when his conviction was deepest, his art could edify in such a way that, as T. H. Green demanded, "the spirit, returning to it, [might] gain a fresh assurance of its *own* birthright, and purify itself, as in a river of Lethe." [25]

But when the faith wavered, when the providence of God seemed remote and the dignity of man merely hypothetical, the artist lost his capacity to trace the path of conversion and even his assurance that the higher self actually existed. Arnold lamented that his "Scholar-Gipsy" could in nowise "animate" or "ennoble" the despairing soul.[26] Yet the melancholy of the poem remained comprehensible to many light half-believers of their casual creeds, who were unable, in their self-conscious bewilderment, to reach Arnold's belief in "a power not ourselves that makes for righteousness." As the Sea of Faith ebbed, the intellect lay naked to all the winds of doubt. In an age of material advance and scientific discovery, the will to know frequently overpowered the will to believe; and the mind was left, without ethical sanction, to its own divided aims. Francis Newman, who set out for Baghdad as a semi-Christian evangelist, found the remnants of his faith shaken in Aleppo once by the reasoning of a Mohammedan carpenter.[27] And Bishop Colenso of Natal, who exposed himself to the skepticism of an intelligent Zulu, was forced eventually to repudiate the rites of baptism and so to surrender the essence of his orthodoxy.[28]

In the epilogue to *Dipsychus* (1862), Clough ascribed the confusion that gripped the doubter to an "overexcitation of the religious sense, resulting in this irrational, almost animal irritability of consciences." [29] Yet Clough himself suffered all his life from the conflict between an acute satiric intellect and an excessive moral sensibility. In the depths of his being he yearned for the "epiphany" that would deliver him from the hopeless fluctuation to which Arnold saw him continually subject.[30] For however far he might follow his questioning spirit, he consistently feared the bleakness of a thoroughgoing rationalism. His best work, therefore, was actuated by a strange ambivalence; his reason impeded his emotion, and his feeling denied his logic.

Of all Victorian poems, *Dipsychus* best illustrated the impossibility of completing a true pattern of conversion with all the familiar motifs, but without an underlying faith in the redemptive process. Though Faustian in inspiration, the dialogue reached no Goethean resolution; thesis collided inconclusively with equally weighted antithesis. Both tempter and tempted were clearly essential aspects of the one "twin-souled" personality; Dipsychus, the tender conscience, as sensitive and tremulous as any Spasmodic hero, had yet within him enough kinship with the worldly "anti-romantic" Spirit to discover the moral irony that permeated his cynicism and to accept without intellectual shock the common sense of his satire. The watery "baptism" consequently effected no real regeneration. Plunging into the sea, Dipsychus had confidently expected a renewal of youth:

> *Aha! come, come — great waters, roll!*
> *Accept me, take me, body and soul!*
> *That's done me good. It grieves though,*
> *I never came here long ago.*

But the Spirit soon destroyed his fond illusion with sub-acid comment which the idealist could not gainsay:

> *you with this one bathe, no doubt,*
> *Have solved all questions out and out.*

In his unflagging realism the Spirit, as the epilogue reminds us, "perhaps . . . wasn't a devil after all." For his honesty of vision, which was Clough's own, would permit no compromise with unalterable fact; and his sharpness of insight could detect the real motive of the individual beneath every assumed orthodoxy:

> *"There is no God, or if there is,"*
> *The tradesman thinks, " 'twere funny*
> *If He should take it ill in me*
> *To make a little money."*

His ultimate function was less to prevent man's salvation than to expose for his moral enlightenment the hypocrisies of a mercantile materialism. For all his awareness of the world's evil, the Spirit remained as conscious as Dipsychus of a larger aspiration, a standard of values which might refute his own cynicism. And Clough, who was both the Spirit and his victim, retained to the last his own reverence for the Truth whose eternality could fortify the doubting soul. If a skeptical intellect kept him from the full faith of the sincerely devout, he nonetheless recognized the strength of their creeds, and he viewed with genuine sympathy the courses of conversion which he himself could not pursue.

VI

God and Mammon

Behold yon servitor of God and Mammon,
Who, binding up his Bible with his ledger,
Blends Gospel texts with trading gammon,
A black-leg saint, a spiritual hedger,
Who backs his rigid Sabbath, so to speak,
Against the wicked remnant of the week,
A saving bet against his sinful bias —
"Rogue that I am," he whispers to himself,
"I lie — I cheat — do anything for pelf,
But who on earth can say I am not pious?"

— THOMAS HOOD

ON his honeymoon Walter Bagehot, the most urbane of Victorian economists, is said to have regaled his bride with a sermon by Frederick Denison Maurice, the most erudite of Anglican rationalists.[1] And the lady's edification was no doubt quite as authentic as her husband's unquestionable sincerity. For the early and mid-Victorians were wonderfully concerned with religious controversy and ethical debate; and the reading of sermons was perhaps the most popular of their literary pastimes.[2] But whatever their theological interests, their age was nonetheless in various ways devoted to the business of a material world which repeatedly denied the relevancy of their spiritual quest. For it was, as Jakob Burckhardt told his students at Basel, not at all remarkable that a generation given to metaphysical dispute and moral dogmatizing should also indulge in "the most platitudinous round of life and money-making." [3]

Though the poet or novelist aware of an engulfing materialism might urge the necessity of spiritual conversion, the absolute values towards which he aspired remained largely inaccessible to all who were bound by the relative standards of an industrial economy. The "practical" man, devoted to his own vision of success, had deliberately to resist a transcendental ethic. While he found good sense in Carlyle's doctrine of hard work, he considered the doctrine of "self-annihilation" highly irrelevant to the fierce struggle which engaged his energies. Had he confessed more freely to his real motives, he might at least have been spared the charges of hypocrisy which have been turned with undue readiness against his whole generation. But he was often sufficiently touched by the selfless moralities of his prophet-teachers to feel the need of rationalizing his own daily conduct. All too frequently he sought some spiritual sanction for his roughshod material advance.

As early as 1837 Hood recognized the uneasy compromise that was threatening to make of trade a sententious religion and of the warehouse an ugly shrine. [4] And before long Clough could prepare his stinging revision of the Decalogue to embody the articles of the new faith:

> *Thou shalt not kill; but need'st not strive*
> *Officiously to keep alive. . . .*
> *Thou shalt not steal; an empty feat*
> *When it's so lucrative to cheat. . . .*
> *Thou shalt not covet, but tradition*
> *Approves all forms of competition.*

Ruskin, who harangued the merchants of Bradford on their worship of "Britannia of the Market," the "Goddess of Getting-on," told "the workmen and labourers of Great Britain" that their employers subscribed to a new commandment writ large in the gospel according to Adam Smith: "Thou shalt take the name of the Lord in vain to mock the poor, for the Lord will hold him guiltless who rebukes and gives not." [5] And the miserable clerk of Tennyson's "Sea Dreams," betrayed like Tennyson himself by an unscrupulous speculator, denounced the piety of the rogue,

> *Who never naming God except for gain,*
> *So never took that useful name in vain;*
> *Made Him his catspaw and the Cross his tool,*
> *And Christ the bait to trap his dupe and fool.*

In prose and verse the writer of high principle and true spiritual conviction inveighed against the pharisaical race that had flagrantly appropriated his terminology. At the end of a lifelong moral crusade, Kingsley felt compelled to warn his congregation that their faith was being surely undermined from within; for it was certain, he said, "that the very classes among us who are most utterly given up to money-making, are the very classes which, in all denominations, make the loudest religious profession; that our churches and chapels are crowded on Sundays by people whose souls are set, the whole week through, upon gain and nothing but gain." [6] Yet the tradesman, unabashed, continued to find "practical" uses for the Christian and Mosaic law and to draw liberal profit from enlisting the interests of God in the service of Mammon.

In the preface to *Men of Capital,* a long forgotten novel of the forties, Mrs. Gore insisted that, "however vehement the disputes between High Church and Low," the Molten Calf remained the predominant idol of her country; for "the very sound of a sum in millions," she wrote, "tickles the ear of an Englishman! — He loves it so much, indeed, that it all but reconciles him to the National Debt." [7] But the national debt, as Mrs. Gore and every sharp-witted observer knew, was not to be measured entirely in terms of pounds sterling. Excluded from the records of the Exchequer were the incalculable losses in human life and talent which the ruthless acquisition of capital necessarily involved. As well-nourished animals, the Victorians, said Kingsley in 1848, were tolerably comfortable, unless they happened to be "Dorsetshire laborers — or Spitalfields weavers — or colliery children — or marching soldiers — or, I am afraid, one-half of English souls this day." [8]

The evils of the industrial system, as it affected the worker's body and mind, had, of course, been apparent enough long before "the hungry forties." And there had been considerable improvement in general factory conditions since the dark days following Waterloo when a Lancashire mill-owner could offer to relieve a London parish of one idiot child for every twenty sound urchins delivered to his looms.[9] But the social unrest and the ill-organized agitation that marked the first decade of Victoria's reign testified to countless abuses still crying for correction. And Lord Shaftesbury's reports on mine and mill, on slum and sweatshop, child labor and adult illiteracy, provided concrete evidence of Mammon's progress through England's green and pleasant land.

Between 1851 and 1873, the period of greatest economic prosperity, Britain became the "workshop of the world," a thriving industrial community willing to abandon its ancient agrarian heritage.[10] Yet the rising prices and increased employment of the "golden" years emphasized rather than diminished the problems of labor. As never before, the workers — the Populace as Arnold called them — recognized their role in the national economy and prepared through their growing unions to assert the essential rights of man. Meanwhile, throughout the fifties and sixties, the literary war against capitalism continued to draw the support of zealous intellectuals sympathetic to the cause of reform.

Typical of these in spirit was William Gilbert, a retired naval surgeon, now remembered, if at all, only as the father of the irrepressible librettist. Far more trenchant than his son's bouncing satire, Gilbert's social criticism claims our attention for its thorough analysis of London's lower depths. Published anonymously in 1858 as "the adventures of a medical man in a low neighbourhood," *Dives and Lazarus* provided an appalling commentary on the triumph of *laissez faire*. The notebook, replete with statistical documentation, presented actual case histories of those who had fallen in the feverish struggle for material advancement. It traced many an Alger story in reverse — the descent from riches to rags, from the heedless fraud of legal competition to the anxious necessity of overt theft. By specific charges

Gilbert indicted the money-mad society that would knowingly tolerate vast disease-ridden slum areas, whole districts of ruined hovels where beneath a single roof from forty to seventy human beings might be huddled together like whipped beasts. Much of the grotesque detail with which he buttressed his attack on the provisions of Dives would have seemed, if translated to fiction, merely the morbid imaginings of an embittered caricaturist; his portrait, for instance, of the half-crazed widower, reluctant to bury the twelve-day-old corpse of his wife in a pauper's grave, achieved the unreal horror of sensational melodrama. Actually, however, the contrived situations of *De Profundis* (1864), Gilbert's "tale of the social deposits," were less intensely grim than the true episodes taken over from his earlier book. For the novel was leavened by a comedy and sentiment which were largely alien to the sordid reality. After a fierce conflict conducted at a subhuman level of utter destitution, it reached a conventional "literary" dénouement; the good characters were preserved for an invented happiness, since, in fiction at least, "virtue, industry and honesty were sooner or later, sure to meet their reward." [11] Yet the only solution the novelist could imagine involved a complete escape from the oppressive environment; the hero and his friends were transplanted to a new life in Australia where, presumably, the old poverty could not exist. Like most reformers of his time, Gilbert saw the physical milieu itself as the single source of all misery and want. He failed to consider that the plight of Lazarus might demand more than the benevolence of Dives, that it might require a revision of the whole economic system.

The Captains of Industry, upon whose exertions depended the very real though unbalanced prosperity of Victorian England, subscribed wholeheartedly to an economic and political doctrine which sanctioned their aggressive individualism. From John Locke and his eighteenth-century successors they adapted to their own purposes the concept of the state as a community in which each man's claim was his personal property. Since the earliest British reaction to the tumult of the French Revolution, the dogma of individual ownership had been upheld with renewed vigor as the first essential of an orderly civilization; and the government had been expected, above all, to protect the right of private possession from the unreasoning violence of the masses, from the "brainless mobs and lawless Powers," "the red-fool fury of the Seine." The Benthamites, the most "practical" of philosophers, worked earnestly for "the greatest happiness of the greatest number." Yet they continued rather than countermanded the teachings of the classical economists who had seen individual enterprise as the necessary free functioning of a "natural" law, the law of supply and demand. And when John Stuart Mill eventually asked the social controls which Adam Smith had resisted, he was already in effect repudiating the principle of utility based on "enlightened" self-interest.

In the meantime, however, Herbert Spencer was reaffirming the classical defense of *laissez faire* on what seemed to him a broadly scientific basis. Published in 1851, his *Social Statics* was actually so outmoded in argument that a "Radical" reviewer could dismiss the first edition with caustic epigram: "We have heard of the Curiosities of Literature and some day this book will be numbered among them." [12] But to men of capital, who were considerably less disinterested than Spencer in denying the right of state interference with their private concerns, his apology for competitive industrialism still seemed sufficiently cogent. And his subsequent social theorizing, supported by fantastic analogies drawn from biological evolution, proved attractive to many "rugged" individualists who felt themselves living witnesses to "the survival of the fittest." [13]

In March of 1831 Macaulay described the proposed Reform Bill as a measure which, he trusted, would "admit the middle class to a large and direct share in the representation, without any violent shock to the institutions of our country." [14] By 1859, the year of Macaulay's death, his hope was amply realized. For the middle classes, assuming dominance of the national economy, had found their strength in reinforcing the established political order. As tradesmen, they espoused the cause of *laissez faire* with a zeal which arose from something more than economic conviction. Their religion itself seemed to sanction an individualism fearful of social encroachment upon the rights of private property and acquisitive capital. Since the Reformation there had been a working agreement between Protestantism and the bourgeois mercantile system.[15] A century and a half before the first Reform Bill enfranchised a considerable section of the middle classes, Dissenting preachers might advise their sectarians against prolonged morning devotions which would interfere with the business pursuits of the day.[16] Now in an early Victorian middle-class society, which was grimly destroying churches built by Christopher Wren to make way for new warehouses, the Evangelical faith could be invited to rationalize the practices of trade. For this influential creed clearly tended to inculcate a respect for the worth of disciplined conduct and strenuous labor and for the sanctity of individual judgment — in short, for ideals readily amenable to secularization.

Whether or not the Evangelicals were the major force in preserving England from social revolution, they generally tried to make the poor man content with his lot and occasionally even commended poverty as a useful training ground for the soul and a needed challenge to the mind relying upon self-help and godly living to lift the body to better things.[17] Small wonder, then, that Karl Marx saw religion being used as "the opiate of the people" while the capitalist proceeded to exploit his drugged victims.

Yet it is not always remembered that vital Christianity on various levels would expose the darkest sin committed in its name. Anticipating Marx's charge in his very phrasing, Charles Kingsley told the Chartist rebels that his fellow clergymen had seriously misrepresented their office. "We have used the Bible," he said, "as if it were a mere special constable's handbook — an opium-dose for keeping beasts of burden patient while they are being loaded — a mere book to keep the poor in order. . . . We have told you that the Bible preached the rights of property and the duties of labour, when (God knows!) for once that it does that, it preaches ten times over the *duties of property* and the *rights of labour*." [18] Let the worker, he continued, but read the Psalms to see "whether the book which contains such noble utterances of struggling freemen could have been

the invention of tyrants and hypocrites"; and then, however much
his superiors may misuse the scripture, he will rightly hold it as "an
everlasting testimony against them!" Amid all the deliberate gar-
blings of Christian doctrine, true religious spirit thus remained sufficiently alive and articulate to rebuke the hypocrisies and compromises of an expedient faith.

All concerned like Kingsley with the difference between a declared
ethic and the actual code of daily commerce could appreciate the
bitter immediacy of Clough's fourth commandment:

> *At church on Sunday to attend*
> *Will serve to keep the world thy friend.*

Yet the Sabbatarian rule had long before Clough's time established
an authority which its opponents, including Victoria herself, might
not easily defy.[19] For it was but one expression of the cult of "respectability"[20] that more than any other force had helped discipline the
physical strength of the middle classes at a time when the Whig
aristocrats were rapidly dissipating their material resources. The bourgeois reverence for an overt Sunday-school morality and the intol-
erance which accompanied it may often have concealed a basic ethical
uncertainty; but it seemed demonstrably clear to the successful
tradesman that only deliberate sobriety, self-imposed inhibition, consciously restrained living could conserve the energies demanded by
an industrious mercantile economy.

The literature of the pre-Victorian middle class was, accordingly,
expected to deal in civilized and respectable sentiments and to ex-
clude the description of those appetites, the excitement of which
might prove subversive to the disciplined social order. By the 1820's
a chastened public taste was no longer willing to endure the uninhibited prose of a lusty and sometimes lustful past. Scott told how
deeply shocked was his grandaunt by a re-reading in old age of
Aphra Behn's novels, which had been the delight of her youth when
they were "read aloud for the amusement of large circles, consisting
of the first and most creditable society in London."[21] And Francis
Place, a few years later, reporting to the House of Commons on the

improvement in public morals, produced evidence that books regarded as pornographic and illicit in the thirties had been freely advertised, displayed, and sold a generation earlier.[22]

When passed on to the Victorians, this literary reticence concerning matters of sex placed some real limitation upon the content of the novel. Thackeray deplored the fact that Fielding had been the last writer of fiction "permitted to depict to his utmost power a MAN," and rather archly warned the readers of *Pendennis* (1850) that, since they could not tolerate the Natural in Art, they would find little in his book of what moved in the real world of men, little of the actual life and talk of their own sons.[23] And other novelists felt it quite as difficult to portray a realistic Woman; for they were again and again forced to yield to the convention of the pure heroine, the selfless center of a tightly closed domestic universe. To the new "puritans," who constituted the core of a widened reading public, sexual license and unwed passion meant a permanent threat to the stability of the home, and the home itself seemed the essential fixed unit in an ordered community.[24]

Though the Evangelical code of behavior persisted into the Victorian period, it was subject from the beginning to serious qualification which gradually weakened its influence and power. By the end of the era, books to which the Evangelical censors once took exception enjoyed considerable popularity; readers might, if they wished, now peruse the novels of the infamous Aphra Behn; and writers could openly applaud the vigorous realism of Fielding and his uninhibited contemporaries. Even the mid-Victorians, however, were a good deal less constrained in their human relationships than we have often been led to believe. Their family life, as their most representative fiction and their most reliable memoirs indicate, was neither acquiescent nor dull, neither unduly sanctimonious nor alarmingly repressed. More and more the austere Victorian father, dominating an abject household with an impervious piety, appears to have been largely a figment of the post-Victorian literary imagination.[25] For the average English child of the fifties and sixties was actually accorded a deeper sympathetic understanding than childhood had known at any earlier time in the history of modern civilization; he experienced little of the parental despotism which, in after years, a Samuel Butler or an Edmund Gosse delighted to expose.

Throughout the age, a respect for emotional and intellectual independence challenged every effort to impose an absolute conformity to a "respectable" norm. Mr. Punch, for instance, though he had no kind word for Disraeli's politics, vigorously assailed the Grundyism that maliciously pried into Disraeli's private religious beliefs.[26] In more philosophical terms, Mill attacked the organized tyranny of public opinion which sought to encroach upon the liberty of the original thinker. Morley decried the same puritanical spirit, with all its fondness for oversimplified ethical judgments, as the source of "much injustice, disorder, darkness and immobility in English intelligence."[27] And Arnold denounced the moral dogmatism, the "coarseness and lack of spiritual delicacy," and the uncritical herd-instinct of the Philistines, all of which denied the sweet reasonableness of a true culture. However complete had been the dominance of a narrow pietism, its authority could in nowise resist the intellectual forces dedicated to the liberation of the nineteenth-century mind.

Many Victorians saw the limitations of the Evangelical discipline, but few were ready to deny its more positive social effects. Even Morley, who felt the theology "narrow, unhistoric, and rancorous," thought it only right to give "this dull and cramped Evangelicalism its due," for the churches and chapels, he admitted, had done a real service "in impressing a kind of moral organization on the mass of barbarism which surged chaotically into the factory towns."[28] If the Sunday schools instilled a moral code which the pharisees of trade could warp to their own unchristian purposes, they also worked tirelessly to extend the heavenly kingdom. It was to the high credit of the Evangelicals that they relied as firmly as they did upon the power of education to raise the ethical standards of the industrial community, even though the educated man might eventually repudiate their whole concept of respectable behavior. Long before the state was willing to accept the responsibilities of public instruction, the parochial schools, operating under manifold handicaps, had embarked on an earnest crusade against national illiteracy. And the lower middle classes, to whom the printed page was opening new perspectives, soon learned the rewards of reading and study. Gradually the roistering taverns yielded precedence to the sober coffeehouses or teashops, where the newly literate could forgather for group discussion or continued self-culture. By the 1840's there were nearly two thousand such establishments in London alone, all well stocked with the organs of "useful knowledge." One of the most successful shops, for instance, subscribed to forty-three London daily papers, seven country papers, six foreign papers, twenty-four monthly magazines, four quarterlies, and eleven weeklies; apparently, here at any rate, the appetite for information was quite as sharp as the thirst for tea.[29]

The moral zeal with which the conscientious Evangelical discharged his duties as educator animated the great humanitarians who carried the faith into social action, men like Sadler, Oastler, Shaftesbury, each essentially conservative in political temper but nonetheless sincere in his desire to mitigate the evils of the factory system. And a similar spiritual ardor gave impetus to the Victorian intellectuals who sought other ideals but yet retained a lingering respect for the serious convictions of their fathers. Leslie Stephen and Frederic Harrison brought a "puritan" conscience to their ethical humanism;[30] and Morley himself attacked the world's wrong with an intensity more "Evangelical" than he realized.

Following the Reform Bill of 1832 began the critical examination of things spiritual which continued throughout the greater part of the Victorian period. While the Evangelicals had concentrated their energies upon individual salvation, the men of the Oxford Movement seriously reconsidered the role of the Church in the process of conversion. Analytic and academic in training, they fought secularism and "national apostasy" with the resources of a thorough historical scholarship, rather than the "enthusiasm" of a private conviction. Concerned with dogma as few had been since the days of the seventeenth-century Anglican divines, they recalled the Establishment to its first principles, and, more subtly than any other theological group, they questioned what Morley called "the House of Commons' view of human life." [31] Kingsley, who rebuked their sacramentalism as "radically unEnglish," felt that they had "at least awakened hundreds, perhaps thousands, of cultivated men and women to ask themselves whether God sent them into the world merely to eat, drink, and be merry." [32]

But the Newmanites were not alone in demanding a quickened conscience and a deeper conception of the Church as a social organism. The Ecclesiastical Commission of 1835,[33] whose work they doggedly resisted, was moving in more immediately practical directions towards the removal of abuses within the Anglican settlement, anachronisms of finance and administration which had long kept the Church from a really active share in the life of the nation. Far from weakening the Anglican cause, religious reform actually aroused the whole episcopacy from a lethargic acceptance of privilege to a firmer definition of its purpose and a broadened sense of its spiritual responsibility.

In the fifties and sixties increased toleration furthered the sincerity of theological debate. The relaxing of the Test Acts, which had excluded Dissenters from Oxford, delivered the student from the need of a conformity based upon convenience rather than conviction. But it afforded him no excuse to lapse into religious indifference. For his educators, still broadly humanistic, saw in the moral truths of religion, whatever its dogmas, the only standards by which they could interpret and integrate all new knowledge. The intellectual's concern with science was both deepened and made meaningful by his awareness that every advance into the heart of nature might force him to revise his whole concept of man's spiritual function in the emperies of space and time. And his troubled interest in the "higher criticism" — in such controversial books as Strauss's *Leben Jesu* (translated by George Eliot in 1846) and Renan's *Vie de Jésus* (1863), or the English *Essays and Reviews* of 1860 and Seeley's anonymous *Ecce Homo* (1865) — arose largely from his half-conscious fear that he was being driven either to the defense of an old orthodoxy or the painful search for a widened creed. His literature, in general, was impregnated with religious emotion, even when it shrank most deliberately from the sanctions of organized belief. And his poetry, in particular, was devoted to ethical and metaphysical speculation, to the effort to discover the eternal principle in the transitory human experience. If his more prosperous contemporaries had turned too often to the worship of matter, the earnest intellectual, whether he declared himself theist or skeptic, struggled steadfastly to maintain his all-essential faith in the vitality of spirit.

Much of the religious controversy and all of the "higher criticism" proceeded on planes far above the industrial conflict which engaged the forces of Mammon. The Tractarian and the Christologist as such dealt for the most part in problems of dogma and historicity which bore slight relation to the tradesman's practical code. From the late forties, however, one religious leader sought to bring a militant Anglicanism to bear upon the dark struggle of the worker's under-world. Though opposed alike by Evangelical and High Churchman, Frederick Denison Maurice asserted the social immediacy of the faith with a wholeness of intent which his bitterest enemy could not impugn. He saw the competitive system as a clear violation of God's order, of the central law of love; and he believed a knowledge of that order the only possible criterion for a social morality which might comprehend the rights and duties of universal brotherhood. Accordingly, aided by his zealous followers, Charles Kingsley and J. M. Ludlow, he set out to "Christianise Socialism," to fortify the will for social justice with the requisite religious principle.[34]

None of the Christian Socialists aspired to prominence in a revolutionary movement; for all were in fact loyal admirers of the British constitution, and each was thoroughly convinced that no political action, however violent, could accomplish a true social reform unless it first touched the moral fiber of the people. Their mission, conducted through lectures, pamphlets, sermons, letters, novels, was thus ethical rather than economic in impulse; it suggested an approach to the ills of society rather than a method of solution. Yet it exposed to many reluctant eyes the tragedy of sweated labor and the failure of human charity; and it demonstrated to the laborer himself, in terms which he could understand, that his plight was unequivocally the concern of a vital religion.

Maurice's special efforts to encourage workers' unions and co-operatives were largely abortive. But his general influence as moralist and teacher spread in widening circles throughout mid-Victorian England. His scholarly discourses, despite a gnarled prose style, reached — and often shocked — a considerable reading public drawn from various levels of society, while his sermons, delivered with a persuasive logic, moved many a congregation to sympathy with his Christian purposes. In 1854, as founder of the Working Men's College, he began a remarkable experiment in adult education, intended in its modest way to help elevate the moral and intellectual standards of the forgotten masses who might one day control a social democracy. The success of the project, to be sure, depended in great measure upon the brilliant lecturers whom Maurice was able to attract, upon men like Huxley, Ruskin, Rossetti, Madox Brown, Fitzjames Stephen, Frederic Harrison — men who brought diverse creeds and varied talents to the school in Red Lion Square. Few of these felt compelled to adopt Maurice's faith; some indeed, rejecting his Christianity, accepted his "Socialism." [35] Yet to all he remained the guiding spirit of the college; his alone was the sustaining vision, the religious fervor, that inspired even the most secular of his associates.

Kingsley revered the teaching and example of Maurice without mental or theological reservation. But he entered upon the work of the Christian Socialist with a "spasmodic" zeal somewhat distasteful to his master.[36] Impatient with all the subtle introspections, he bluntly attacked Oxford ritualism as mere "belief-in-believing, . . . the parent of the most blind, dishonest, and pitiless bigotry." [37] Though he understood the dilemma of agnostic youth driven from orthodoxy, he urged a turning outwards to the spheres of overt action, where a vigorous religion might prove its value in charitable works and a numbing doubt could not subsist. From the beginning he was less at home in the scholar's study than in the world of manly men and virile exercise; and it is not surprising that the soldiers of

Aldershot were much impressed by what, to his chagrin, they called his "muscular Christianity." [38] For he was, by his own admission, "Esau's parson, not Jacob's"; and his valiant war against the filth of diseaseful slums was actuated, in part at least, by his horror that human beings could be permanently shut off from the fresh air of the open field.

In *The Water Babies* Kingsley retold the myth of Prometheus and Epimetheus, to the infinite advantage of the latter. For the fire-bringer seemed to him the archetype of the visionary, the impractical man of idle prophecies, and ultimately the father of all "the fanatics, and the theorists, and the bigots, and the bores, and the noisy windy people." But the earth-bound Epimetheus, untroubled by airy dreams, represented one who had learned "to till and drain the ground, and to make looms, and ships, and railroads, and steam-ploughs, and electric telegraphs, and all the things which you see in the Great Exhibition," and his children had become the men of science who got "good lasting work done in the world." Though naïvely conceived and whimsically presented, the fable embodied a serious will to relate a firm religious faith to the needs of an energetic population.

Kingsley as clearly as any social critic saw the tangible evils of the industrial system and the terrible consequences to body and soul of a determined Mammon-worship; yet he saw also that there could be no retreat from an age of railroads and steam-ploughs and electric telegraphs. He, therefore, chose to fight materialism by accepting matter itself and by arming its human agents with moral and spiritual purpose. If his victory was never won, he yet succeeded more than any other popular apologist in reminding the mid-Victorians that the objects of religion might animate their common activity no less than their lonely meditations.

VII

Victorian Taste

Then came that great event, the Exhibition,
When England dared the world to competition. . . .
But still, I hold, we were triumphant seen
In iron, coal, and many a huge machine. . . .
Peace-men had then their beatific vision;
And Art-schools were to render earth Elysian.

— PHILIP JAMES BAILEY

THOUGH hardly a Christian Socialist, Prince Albert was almost as eager as Kingsley himself to quicken the moral conscience of an industrial England. While he could have no recourse to direct attack upon the abuses of capital, he could at least rebuke the insularity of British manufacturers who remained suspicious of his alien tastes. Accordingly, guided by the vision of a universal brotherhood to be grounded upon civilized technology and peaceful commerce, he informed all plans for the Great Exhibition of 1851 with his own "religious" impulse; and ultimately on the memorable opening day he presided over this first world's fair with true Christian humility amid all the pageantry of pomp and circumstance. If few of the exhibitors he attracted to London shared the purity of his motives, none entirely escaped the sense of interdependence which Albert sought earnestly to engender. Even the official catalogue bore some impress of his moral purpose; its very title page announced — in Latin and in English — a divine sanction for the miracles of the nineteenth century's inventive genius:

> *Say not the discoveries we make are our own —*
> *The germs of every art are implanted within us,*
> *And God our instructor, out of that which is concealed,*
> *Develops the faculties of invention.*

Not all, to be sure, among the thousands who converged on Hyde Park were moved to religious awe by the visible triumph of the machine; for the actual "works of industry of all nations," for which the Crystal Palace had been designed, were in truth largely void of spiritual intent. But many felt dwarfed by the huge glass house and at the same time strangely exalted by the vague awareness that a destiny too large for their comprehension was shrinking the limits of the world community. On Sundays countless pilgrims to the shrine of industry crowded the metropolitan churches to offer thanks to the favoring Providence that had vouchsafed the incredible progress of man; and even St. Paul's and Westminster, closed to worshipers for many generations, were temporarily opened for public services. William Whewell, D.D., the Master of Trinity College, Cambridge, was quite overpowered by the spectacle of "millions upon millions, streaming to [the fair], gazing their fill, day after day, at this wonderful vision, . . . comparing, judging, scrutinizing the treasures produced by the all-bounteous earth, and the indomitable efforts of man, from pole to pole." And as he himself measured the science of the West against all the products of the gorgeous East, the Reverend Dr. Whewell felt that "surely that mighty thought of a Progress in the life of nations is not an empty dream; and surely our progress has carried us beyond them"; for "there," he said, "Art labours for the rich alone; here she works for the poor no less; . . . here the man who is powerful in the weapons of peace, capital and machinery, uses them to give comfort and enjoyment to the public whose servant he is, and thus becomes rich while he enriches others with his goods." [1] In the presence of such reassuring optimism, the congregation assembled in St. Margaret's four days after the grand opening of the Exhibition was naturally rather puzzled to make sense of Kingsley's bitter warning that no scientific advance could long conceal the fundamental atheism of modern culture.[2]

As newly appointed Laureate, Tennyson felt it only proper to commend Victoria's share in having

> brought a vast design to pass,
> When Europe and the scattered ends
> Of our fierce world were mixt as friends
> And brethren, in her halls of glass.[3]

But for his own part, he thought the halls themselves more remarkable than all the ingenious exhibits they sheltered. And however frequent his lapses as a judge of things aesthetic, his enthusiasm for the Crystal Palace was not misplaced. Long after Ruskin had dismissed the great greenhouse as "neither a palace nor of crystal," as merely a glass envelope built "to exhibit the paltry arts of our fashionable luxury," [4] Joseph Paxton's original plans were to find a vital place in the story of a new architecture.[5] For the Crystal Palace was on many counts the most revolutionary building of the Victorian era, the one most daring in its use of "functional" materials. The masters of an older style had thought that the outer wall must serve always as a weighty and weight-bearing mass designed with due proportion to enclose finite space. But the Crystal Palace, breaking all orthodox precedent, raised its airy shell, supported by a vertebrate structure of light blue iron girders, as a thin transparent cover assembled from light but strong portable units and shaped not to shut off an interior volume but rather to suggest all the unlimited outer world by the space within. Had the space within been filled with objects fashioned as organically as the great frame, the Exhibition might have effected a reformation of public taste which artisans far more pretentious than Paxton could not achieve with all their laborious contrivance. Unfortunately, however, the quality of its contents — at least viewed from a vantage point in time — merely helped explain Ruskin's disgust with the building itself.

But, despite the misgivings of the critical few, most visitors to the Crystal Palace stood long enraptured before the marvels of mechanical craftsmanship. Everywhere in the exhibits, said the sanguine Dr. Whewell, lay incontestable evidence that the inventive machinist might prove himself again and again the true Poet or Maker, since "man's power of making," he insisted, "may show itself not only in the beautiful *texture* of language, the grand *machinery* of the epic, the sublime display of poetical *imagery;* but in these material works." [6] Many of the "makers" themselves must have felt the praise well merited; for their wares alone were ample proof that they deemed their talents in the highest sense "creative." Not content with illustrating the range of applied science, they strove to make of their looms and reapers, their grates and boilers, obvious works of art. Impatient with the simpler devices of clean line and natural curve, they repeatedly sought to conceal the function of their machines with the intricacies of machine-made ornament. Like the exhibitors at every world's fair, they sacrificed the beautiful to the ingenious; and their search for the novel led inevitably to fantastic creation. One manufacturer, for instance, proudly displayed a walnut-wood couch, serviceable as a bed but stuffed with his own patent cork fiber to make it buoyant when placed in water — for the couch, "in case of danger at sea," was instantly convertible into a life raft with a floating surface of fifty square feet; and to this versatile piece were attached two cabinets of fine walnut, one hiding "a self-acting washing stand" and the other "as a Davenport, forming a patent portable water-closet." [7]

Less ambitious craftsmen, who had perhaps not learned the merits of cork fiber, devoted themselves to painful experiment with *papier-mâché,* the malleable pulp glued and shellacked, out of which they could shape vases and footstools and even pianofortes, all lacquered, tinted, and grained, bespangled with gilt or inlaid with mother-of-pearl.[8] Eventually the multiple-purpose furniture like the couch-bed-lifepreserver-watercloset would suggest the more immediately practical appointments of the Pullman car,[9] just as the manufacture of *papier-mâché* might foreshadow the elaborate processes by which a less synthetic plywood could be molded. But the artisans of 1851 felt little of the pioneer's humility; far from tentative, their works were designed as end products and so accorded final embellishment.

Whether working with strange or familiar materials, nearly all the exhibitors who brought their produce to the Crystal Palace struggled to achieve something of "the sublime display of poetical imagery" that betokened the "maker." With the intensity of the Spasmodic poets, whose impulses were indeed rather similar, they strained after fanciful "conceits" in plastic form, ornaments wrought in lush detail, existing for their own sake, often quite unrelated to the "prose meaning" of the chair or table or chimney piece they adorned. To beds and bookcases, to whatnots and newel posts, to twenty-foot mirrors and many-drawered chests, they applied their "metaphors" of wood and iron and plaster, Gothic peaks and finials, arches, arcatures, and arabesques, symbolic griffins and naturalistic camels, acorns and fish and twisted vines, ruddy cherubim and reclining elephants. Inevitably, the desire for copious "illustration" fought down all respect for unified design, until the various motifs that bedecked a single article of furniture might be not only irrelevant to the piece as a whole but also ill-proportioned to each other. Since the new machines of Birmingham could turn forth the florid as inexpensively as the simple, the manufacturer yielded readily to the demand of an uncritical public for size and quantity of ornament rather than balance and harmony of construction.

Though many of the official judges were happy to think that the factory had thus brought culture to the multitude by cheaply reproducing "the noblest works of art," several charged the British industrialist with some lack of restraint in his enthusiasm for the ornate. It might be, they mused, that English taste, generally, was inferior to French. For certainly no native artisan had created an original work so noble as "the grand buffet of M. Fourdinois," which was awarded the Council Medal as a piece "of rare excellence and merit in design, and of skilful and artistic execution as to carving." [10] But if the sideboard seemed a most effective antidote to excessive *décor,* it was nonetheless itself sufficiently complex to require descriptive commentary and interpretation. At its base, six dogs, "emblematical of the chace," rested on a parquet floor, supporting a slab fronted by a finely carved molding and inlaid "in geometric forms." Above the slab, standing on four pedestals were "female figures, gracefully designed as emblems of the four quarters of the world each bearing the most useful production of their climate as contributions to the feast" — European wine, Asiatic tea, African coffee, and American sugar cane. And in the center the products of the chase were "poured out on the very board," above which the space was "filled with a framed picture of rare fruits, giving an opportunity to enliven the work by the addition of colour, without militating against good taste." The figure of Plenty crowned the piece, and the bracketed cornice beside her carried boys "with the implements of the vineyard and of agriculture," while the ends bore figures with "the implements of fishing on the one side and of the chace on the other." All in all, the buffet — at least in the opinion of Richard Redgrave, R.A., the eminent authority on design — was "consistent and free from puerilities," and though "thoroughly fitted for its purpose as a sideboard, . . . at the same time of a highly ornamental character, without any of its decoration being overdone or thrown away."

By limiting his *décor* to motifs more or less closely associated with the festal rites, M. Fourdinois attained the coherence of "intellectual" pattern that had eluded most British craftsmen. But it hardly occurred to the judges that his motifs might be intrinsically ludicrous in their naturalism or that the over-all effect of his neo-baroque style might not represent the highest achievement in pure design. For his "simplicity" stuck fiery off indeed beside far more ornate examples of "spasmodic" artistry. In evaluating the exhibits, even Redgrave became at times "tired altogether of ornament" and eager for an absolute utility "where use is so paramount that ornament is repudiated." [11] His fellow critic, Owen Jones, saw the source of a confusion worse confounded in the failure of the artisans to agree on an aesthetic standard. "We have," Jones wrote, "no principles, no unity; the architect, the upholsterer, the paper-stainer, the weaver, the calico-printer, and the potter run each their independent course; each struggles fruitlessly, each produces in art novelty without beauty, or beauty without intelligence." [12] Though more inclined to applaud British invention, the *Spectator* admitted that the displays at the Crystal Palace betrayed "the chaotic condition of the civilized mind in respect to canons of taste." [13] And Bailey, whose *Festus* had not been distinguished for economy of selection, lamented a common deficiency of his countrymen:

> *What England as a nation wants, is taste;*
> *The judgment that's in due proportion placed;*
> *We overdo, we underdo, we waste.*[14]

Years later, on looking back from a new era, Frederic Harrison pointed to his revulsion, as a youth of nineteen, from the "appalling vulgarity" of the Exhibition, as proof that he had never been in spirit an "Early Victorian." [15] He felt it clearly necessary to acquit himself of that label; for the attack of the Edwardians on all the values of their grandfathers, and even on the standards of Harrison's generation, was stimulated in large part by the legacy of tangible unloveliness which the middle decades of the nineteenth century had left behind. Yet many of the Victorians themselves could recognize in their own time a complete failure of the plastic arts; and many could accept Kingsley's charge that "the mass of the British people . . . sits contented under the imputation of 'bad taste.' " [16] It was not for lack of criticism that the "bad taste" so long persisted. It was merely that the sanctions of the ornate and the ugly were too widely diffused and defended to be easily destroyed.

"If people only knew as much about painting as I do," said Edwin Landseer, "they would never buy my pictures." [17] But few among the middle-class public that most cherished his work could be expected to bring to any canvas any more than a sharp eye for lifelike detail. The same "puritan" disciplines that had abetted their rise in a mercantile world had from the first inculcated in them a distrust of all that was purely "aesthetic." Not before they had won financial security and political independence could they afford even to consider the claim of art as a means to a more abundant living. And then, unfamiliar with the proven standards that had long guided the judgment of the aristocrat, they were driven to their own trial-and-error attempts at culture. In control of industrial empires vaster than all the estates of the landed gentry, the upper middle classes sought to establish their own tradition of opulent elegance, an outward sign of their economic triumph. And the aspiring many below them, the smaller tradesmen and foremen, the shopkeepers and clerks, for the most part quite innocent of any trained tastes, set out to garner unto themselves such objects of intricate design and impressive bulk as it was within their means to procure — inexpensive replicas of the "finer things," produced in quantity to demonstrate that their purchasers were not exclusively devoted to the gross and the useful.

All levels of bourgeois society exercised their acquisitive powers at leisure moments in amassing great stores of bric-a-brac, wax flowers, ormolu candelabra, porcelain vases, plaster busts of literary idols, and iron or lead statuettes of pagan deities. For the sheer joy of possession, they accumulated innumerable oddments, especially novelties in glass — glass ducks and dogs and roosters, glass hats and slippers and sea shells, glass bowls in the "daisy-and-button" pattern, glass cups large and small, warted and welted with the "thousand-eye" design or branched and veined like the "tree of life." [18] They lined their shelves and spread their walls with tiny miniatures and huge prints in heavy frames as numerous as the characters in their three-volume novels. If they knew little of painting, they were nonetheless enthusiastic collectors of cheap engravings which preserved a wealth of gesture and sentiment for their constant perusal. And on occasion they could measure their own graphic treasures against enormous originals; when W. P. Frith first exhibited his "Derby Day" (1858), they came in such droves to the Royal Academy that the canvas had to be railed off to keep the picture-readers from "smelling" out its detail "like bloodhounds." [19] Ill-informed yet eager, many argued about styles in furniture and building with the determined assurance which a cultivated few brought to the elucidation of Browning's verse. Though the machine age was robbing their labors of diversity, their tastes in art and ornament reflected no willingness to accept the monotones of order.

Despite his sensitive responses to literature, Newman complained, in prefacing his own poems, of his ignorance of any fixed aesthetic values. Unable to find a standard "by which to discriminate aright between one poetical attempt and another," [20] he feared that all criticism of verse must remain personal and so more or less arbitrary and unscientific. In religion he could invoke the authority of dogma to confute the anarchy of dissent; but in art he felt forced to accept the canon of a nonconformist individualism. Much of the confusion that attended judgments of taste throughout the Victorian era arose from the failure of the artisan and his public to discover a common body of principles or to question the validity of their personal reactions. In the building trades, *laissez-faire* economics encouraged *laissez-faire* aesthetics; as long as the state refused to place controls on private construction or to assume responsibility for town planning, the jerry-builder was left as free as the conscientious architect to follow his own "designs." If individual enterprise determined the progress of industry, individual performance seemed largely to guide the course of music and the drama. From the forties on, the average concert audience was much less interested in abstract harmonies of sound than in the particular charms of the artiste occupying the center of the stage. The wide popularity of the Italian opera stemmed mainly from the occasions for emotional display which it afforded highly paid and highly eccentric prima donnas. And a native composer could enjoy great acclaim only if his work, like *The Bohemian Girl* (1843) of Michael William Balfe, showed sufficient technical virtuosity to strain the operatic talents of its principal singers. The theater, likewise, from Macready to Irving, was completely dominated by the star system; the play as a rule was written for the leading actor, adapted to his peculiar mannerisms, and directed to his best advantage. Since producer and spectator were alike more concerned with the versatile protagonist than with coherent theme or firm structure, most significant attempts at dramatic art were doomed from the first to failure. Tennyson, who could secure tragic effect in isolated scenes, knew no practicing playwright able to teach him the first essentials of serious stagecraft. And George Meredith, who might, in the opinion of Harley Granville-Barker,[21] have proven himself the great comic dramatist of the period, was quite unable to find the public that the comic muse demanded.

Unfamiliar with the formal conventions that governed the various aesthetic media, the middle-class critic would frequently resort to the sanction of verisimilitude. In judging ornament he would attach less value to the pleasing line than to a "truth to nature" quite literally conceived. He could, therefore, approve of such preposterous objects as the centerpiece designed by Prince Albert,[22] which arrayed upon ornate pedestals the Queen's favorite dogs, modeled from life, together with a dead hare, a caged rat, and the remains of a dead one, the actual tokens of happy hunting. Prince Albert had clearly "gone to nature"; yet he had made no attempt to deceive: the dogs on the pedestals were obviously not real dogs, since the metal of which they were molded could not be "mistaken for that which it professe[d] to imitate." In any other material, too, direct an imitation of nature might have been misleading,[23] for, as a popular aesthetician explained, "the perfect reproduction of the form would lead to demands for reality" — and the dogs themselves had no place on the tablecloth.

All successful ornament was thus expected not only to attain the appearance of actuality, but also to suggest that the illusion was merely illusion. Even the picture most admirable for its realistic detail was to remain a picture; heavily matted, it was to be hung in an embellished frame "to keep it totally distinct from its surroundings," lest it be mistaken for a window opening unto an illusory world.[24] For the Victorian of taste was loath to be betrayed by a wayward fancy; and he allowed the "lamp of literalism" to guide his judgment in queer directions. Redgrave at the Crystal Palace, for instance, objected to a table supported by swans, not so much because the piece was graceless and cumbersome, as because he himself was perplexed to know "why swans should make their nests under a table at the risk of having their necks broken by everyone seated at it." [25] Actuated by a like regard for truth, a later consultant on decoration saw fit to praise a bowl enlivened by cherubs clustering about its stem; for the bowl was supported by the stem *"resting upon a solid basis"* and not by the frail infants who could scarcely have sustained such weight.[26] Craftsmanship so faithful to the realities of experience, he thought, deserved special commendation at a time when most designers seemed content to violate all laws of "Common Sense" in their search for lifelike detail. "It might be too much to say," he wrote, "that one may knock for admittance with the head of a goat, wipe one's 'feet' upon a Newfoundland dog, approach the hostess over a carpet strewn with bouquets, converse with one foot upon a Bengal tiger, and contemplate birds of paradise upon the walls; that one may be called upon to interpose the Bay of Naples between an elderly lady and the fireplace, to slice a pine-apple upon a humming-bird, and place one's finger-glass upon the countenance of a Tyrolese peasant. Yet this as fairly describes the popular taste as when we say that the English people have a decided predilection for the imbibition of beer." What disturbed the critic, however, was not that the multiple imagery was bewildering in its total effect and quite incompatible with any harmonious interior design. It was just that the individual motifs were badly misplaced; for one should certainly not be expected to preserve a courteous poise in the presence of a life-size tiger or to converse with ease beneath walls from which great birds might momentarily descend. It was obvious to the decorator that "nothing within doors should suggest that one is out of doors." Such was the first dictate of "Common Sense"; and "Common Sense" was of prime importance, "for not only [was] taste unable to proceed without it, but owing to its non-cultivation, material prosperity [was] impeded."

In *Hard Times* Dickens caricatured the literalist, the man of Common Sense, who deplored Sissy Jupe's lack of taste: "You are not to have, in any object of use or ornament, what would be a contradiction in fact. You don't walk upon flowers in fact; you can not be allowed to walk upon flowers in carpets. . . . This is the new discovery. This is fact. This is taste." Yet Dickens himself throughout his novels strove to achieve the factual accuracy of an anti-romantic "realism"; he was quite as intent upon following with scrupulous care the exact procedures of Chancery[27] as he was eager to chronicle in minute particulars a child's first view of Mr. Peggotty's grounded ark. For a concern with circumstantial detail obsessed the "maker" of literature no less than the designer of household ornament; and the reader of novels and poems and plays expected to find in his favorite author the proper respect for fact. Charles Kean, was, therefore, disturbed by the anachronisms and logical inconsistencies of Shakespeare's *Winter's Tale* — so much disturbed, indeed, that, when producing the play in 1856, he not only clarified the plot but transferred the scene from a vague "Bohemia" to a definite Bithynia in Asia Minor, while his associate George Scharf designed settings which reproduced "the vegetation peculiar to Bithynia . . . adapted from his private drawings, taken on the spot." [28]

Writing in an age of analytic science, the Victorian poet felt less free than Shakespeare to depart from the literal truths of inanimate nature. Sydney Dobell, for all his "Spasmodic" rhapsodies, took pains to make his observations incontestably precise.[29] Once on a night journey, for instance, he noted for future poetic use the five main shifts in light and coloring before dawn, "the following symptoms of the dissolution of Night in the following order. . . ." And Browning, though not primarily a nature poet, delighted his admirers with ample evidence of his keen perceptions, his awareness of the tiny leaves round the elm-tree bole, and the short sharp broken hills, and the bell of the wild tulip "like a thin clear bubble of blood." But it was Tennyson who above all jealously guarded his reputation as a master of physical detail, as an unequaled recorder of sense impressions drawn from the natural world. Since, when in the Pyrenees, he had verbally sketched the cataract before him "Slow dropping veils of thinnest lawn," he was greatly irritated by a reviewer who objected to the image, claiming that the poet should not have gone "to the boards of a theatre but to Nature herself for his suggestions." [30] Again, while reading *Maud,* he is reported to have paused long enough to ask an authoress in his audience what sort of birds in a high hall garden would call, "Maud, Maud, Maud, Maud." When the embarrassed lady faltered that they might be nightingales, he impatiently rebuked her ignorance: "What a cockney you are! Nightingales don't say Maud. Rooks do, or something like it. Caw, caw, caw, caw, caw" — and then the reading continued.[31]

Though such self-conscious regard for exact detail helped discipline Tennyson's imagination, it frequently betrayed him — as it betrayed other Victorian writers — into the "ornate," the baroque style so distasteful to Walter Bagehot. The element of the ornate was, to be sure, utterly absent from many of Tennyson's most characteristic poems, especially from his personal epistles, which unfolded with a Horatian grace and purity of idiom. But it was disastrously present in a work like *Enoch Arden* (1864), where a desire for full literal presentation brought so much detail into sharp focus that the hero himself was barely distinguishable against the elaborated background. The "ornate" might thus be born of the will to document all the individual "realities" of a "romantic" setting; for in verse, as in the plastic arts, a reverence for the particular fact could often destroy the aesthetic unity of the whole.

George Eliot, whose *Romola* was sufficiently replete with factual data, insisted that the painter's imagination no less than the writer's should be rooted in the literal and the concrete. Even a picture of the Last Judgment should, she felt, be composed of details drawn "from real observation"; it should deal in "the veriest minutiae of experience" heightened by "ideal association." [32] To the representative Victorian painter such demands seemed only reasonable, since the canvas that lacked "truth to nature" could betoken only the artist's spiritual inadequacy or his technical incompetence. Frith, for example, attained his conspicuous popular success largely through his prolonged studies of setting, costume, and gesture and his careful selection of models who were eager to contribute their individual charms to his animated tableaux. His "Claude Duval," which illustrated an incident from Macaulay concerning a seventeenth-century highwayman, portrayed, against the "blasted heath" of a real Devonshire, an actual antique stagecoach which had been preserved at the estate of Lord Darnley; so grounded in fact, the painting derived little from a "creative" imagination. And his "Derby Day," which transcribed in paint the average man's response to an excited holiday crowd, was likewise characteristically objective. It was intended to reproduce a familiar scene not as it might strike an artist's unique vision, but rather as it might appear to the alert eyes of any spectator; and when the Prince Consort questioned the placement of certain shadows, Frith was naturally glad, in the interests of complete accuracy, to make all desirable changes.[33]

Though the Pre-Raphaelites had in general a far ampler concept of artistic truth than the "literalists," they were hardly less concerned with precise realistic detail. Millais used a magnifying glass when sketching veined leaves and tendrils; Rossetti burned wine and chloride to obtain the proper color for the flames about the feet of the Archangel Gabriel; and Holman Hunt journeyed to the Holy Land partly to pose his "scapegoat" against an authentic Dead Sea background. Most of the Pre-Raphaelites worked patiently with a medium over which they had little technical control; they painted, repainted, and overpainted layer upon layer of pigment; and in so doing they frequently altered their whole design after a long-pondered picture had been well begun. By blending a slow-drying varnish into their oils, they were able to match colors over protracted periods during which they could proceed deliberately with their innumerable revisions. They paid little heed to the fact that, with the darkening of the resin mixed into the very colors, their pictures so produced would eventually deteriorate beyond reclaim; for they were enabled by slow painting to attain, for a time at least, the illusion of a carefully transcribed reality.[34]

Insofar as they wished to achieve "a pretty mocking of the life," all Victorian painters, including the Pre-Raphaelites, were fighting a losing battle against mechanical means of reproducing the actual with consummate "realism." During the fifties the daguerreotype became so fashionable that Lady Morley scarcely expected the sun to shine elsewhere when it was "fully occupied every day in taking likenesses in Regent Street." [35] And by 1870 the camera had completely outdistanced the pencil and the brush as a recorder of factual detail. Charles Landseer spoke a sadder truth than he knew when he told Frith that science had at last produced "a *foe-to-graphic* art." [36]

But, however devoted he might be to a pictorial "naturalism," the successful painter could not content himself with a mere transcript of observable experience. In order to reach a public insensitive to the simple effects of line and shade, he often adapted each carefully depicted fact to a "literary" pattern — to the purposes of storytelling or moral instruction. Draftsmen like Landseer, Egg, Harvey, and Phillip, who derived their greatest popularity from the "subject-picture," diligently sought out topics for illustration, scenes from literature, history, and contemporary life, richly informed with narrative content. Calderon established his reputation with "Broken Vows" (1857), a piece of documented sentimentalism which portrayed the shock of a pure maiden as she glimpsed her perfidious lover (in the act of flirtation) through a chink in the kitchen-garden wall. And Frith, who considered subject always of prime importance, moved from triumph to triumph, financially at any rate, with such canvases as "Ramsgate Sands" and "The Railway Station," sprawling panoramas packed with dramatic incident, and "The Road to Ruin" and "The Race for Wealth," mildly Hogarthian sequences, animated tales of fallen virtue.

From the forties onwards, most avowed "lovers of art" were skilled picture-readers with a keen appetite for character and episode and a will to find story values, even in the works of masters quite unconcerned with anecdote and parable. Kingsley, for instance, drew many "a sharp sermon" from Bellini's portrait of a Venetian doge; for in the doge he saw the sort of man who would most surely fight the inhumanities of Victorian capitalism as he had once resisted "those tyrannous and covetous old merchant-princes who had elected him — who were keeping their own power at the expense of everyone's liberty, by spies and nameless accusers, and secret councils, tortures and prisons, whose horrors no one ever returned to describe." [37] Even the major Pre-Raphaelites, whose appreciation of fine art was rather more sophisticated than Kingsley's, refused to regard a picture as essentially a problem in graphic design. If they scorned the "anec-dotage" of Frith and the obvious appeals of "lettered" painting, Rossetti and Burne-Jones, nonetheless, surrounded their dream fig-ures with literary — or at least "poetic" — symbols chosen to lend a spiritual significance to each ornate detail.

Like the painter, the ornament maker found realistic reproduction not sufficient in itself. For men of "refined taste" self-consciously demanded of *décor* some "dash of allegory . . . imperceptible only to the uncultivated multitude." [38] The multitude, to be sure, had little difficulty in divining the "symbolic" import of the hens that nested on their egg warmers, or the cows that adorned their butter pots, or any other of the motifs, like animal paws or cherubs, promis-cuously carved to suggest the abundant vitality of nature. But the cultivated few, to whom the allegorical was no secret, sought subtler associations of thought and feeling in plastic forms. They placed urns on their gateposts as tokens of affluence, and they pointed the rail-heads of their fences like spears and arrows, to represent the pride of possession and the will to defend the rights of property. They read "animation" into the serpentining curves of baroque furniture. They believed that a green wall might be the proper setting for pic-tures since green was nature's background. And they carefully calcu-lated the "Rembrandt effects" of tasteful chiaroscuro to be attained by placing windows and lamps on one side of a room only. In gen-eral, though they allowed no common principle to dominate their individual prejudices, they showed a deep interest in the types and symbols of older and more coherent styles. Instead of creating their own "allegories," they drew eclectically on motifs to which time had attached complex connotations.

Interior *décor* could be readily adapted to suit changing fashions in ornament, and its excesses, indeed, may often be ascribed to the decorator's awareness that it was profitable to encourage successive vogues for old patterns newly minted. But architectural design was of its essence more durable. And it was, therefore, the architect rather than the ornament maker who left the most permanent reminders of the confusions and conflicts that vitiated Victorian taste. In *The*

Water Babies Kingsley described the home of Sir John Hartover; it was a most eclectic manor house, "built at ninety different times, and in nineteen different styles," including the Anglo-Saxon, the Norman, the Cinquecento, the Doric, and the Boeotian, and bearing traces of the Parthenon, the Pavilion at Brighton, and the Taj Mahal at Agra. Though admittedly bewildering in its aspect, the house nonetheless "looked like a real live house" that had had a history and accumulated many forms as it aged. And this was more than Kingsley could say of most Victorian buildings, finished as they were to look old at birth, that they might trail the clouds of vanished glories into a world of machine-made façades. Reluctant to break with established structural traditions, the academic architects, unlike Joseph Paxton, refused to shape their plans in accordance with the new materials which industry was making available to them. They preferred to compound their styles of many influences, and they gave themselves wholeheartedly to the various "revivals" — to the Renaissance of Barry and the neo-Greek of Cockerell, but, above all, to the Gothic.

At the Great Exhibition, Owen Jones deplored the omnipresence of Gothic motifs: "I mourn over the loss," he said, "which this age has suffered, and continues to suffer, by so many fine minds devoting all their talents to the reproduction of a galvanized corpse." [39] But by the fifties the revival of Gothic had already advanced so far on so many levels that protest was in vain. Thanks to the efforts of the Pugins and of Gilbert Scott, it was becoming "an intricate science of styles," [40] of Saxon, Norman, and Lancet, Perpendicular and Tudor, each of which found its earnest supporters. After an initial Protestant revulsion to a "Catholic" architecture, many a Victorian professed to see in Gothic the embodiment of a philosophy of life and work which his generation might do well to regain. In the offices of George Edmund Street, one of the most successful "Gothicists," young apprentices called to each other in Gregorian chants. [41] And from their drawing boards came many of the hybrid designs that were to be inflicted en masse upon the whole English-speaking world throughout the sixties and seventies. Yet it is unlikely that the borrowed spires and gargoyles, the scrolls and trefoils and traceries, the symbols once, perhaps, of the bountiful earth and the hopes and terrors of the aspiring soul, awakened in the factory worker, the industrialist, or the city clerk much of the emotion that may have stirred the heart of medieval man. Certainly most of the sham-Gothic mansions and colleges and stables, like the pseudo-Gothic furniture of Charles Eastlake,[42] conveyed little more than a nostalgia for the past and a feeling for the picturesque, alien to the best design of the Middle Ages and quite unworthy the demonstrable vitality of the Victorian era.

Convinced that the nineteenth century could not approach a true architecture until it had clarified its moral and social objectives, Ruskin strove to reawaken the ideal which he felt must have guided the original Gothic craftsmen. In so doing, much of his energy was misspent on a vain repudiation of the machine — which, for better or for worse, had long since established itself as an inescapable force in Victorian society. Yet he at least made it clear that a vital style in building was inseparably related to the environment that produced it. Aware that the best in Gothic had arisen from a trained regard for "function," he recalled his contemporaries to a serious consideration of the uses of art; and, almost in spite of himself, he thus prepared the way for the "functionalist," whose designs were to reveal rather than to hide the purpose of his structures.

As his ablest disciple, William Morris was likewise handicapped by an inability to see that the new building — and indeed the applied arts generally — must accept all the conditions and resources of an industrial system. But he succeeded, all the same, by precept and example, in attacking the most flagrant examples of bad taste and in suggesting the essentials of sound design. His Red House of 1859, built in collaboration with Philip Webb, represented not only the first modern attempt to shape a commodious home entirely from native building materials, but also the first effort to plan both exterior and interior as a single unit.[43] His furniture, though unduly cumbersome in its massive lines, dispensed with much unnecessary embellishment. And his flat patterns, based on a careful reworking of stylized motifs, supplied an effective antidote to the misapplied naturalism of household *décor*. If his emphasis on the handicrafts led certain ingenious manufacturers to mass-produce articles artificially roughened to look handmade,[44] it yet went far to broaden public concern for thorough workmanship. More than any other decorator, Morris helped clear the Victorian home of the ugly, the ornate, and the inorganic; for more clearly than all, he provided a standard of intelligent selection and a will to carry into practice the first principles of his creed: "Have nothing in your houses which you do not know to be useful or believe to be beautiful."

By 1880, when Morris turned his attention from art to socialism, Victorian taste had noticeably improved. The architect had grown impatient with imitative revivalism. The designer had learned to sacrifice florid ornament. The painter had come to prefer pattern of composition to the portrayal of incident in photographic detail. And the prose writer had mastered an urbane middle style freed from sentimental diction and turgid rhetoric. Yet Victorian taste had never been a static entity. From the beginning it had reflected the restless activity that was driving the whole era towards new horizons. But its "progress" had depended upon the curbing of an exuberance reluctant to undergo a civilizing discipline; and even as it gained in discretion and self-conscious tact, it lost something in spontaneity. Though the late Victorian could deride the absurdities of Prince Albert's Exhibition, he was uncomfortably aware that the splendor of the Queen's Jubilees might seem as contemptible to a new century. Whatever the extravagances of early Victorian culture, it had committed its sins with a religious intensity which a more disillusioned age could not recover; and it had called forth to denounce its follies earnest souls endowed with a range of enthusiasm and a capacity for synthesis which the narrow specialists of a later generation could not but envy.

VIII

The Moral Aesthetic

And I want you to think a little of the deep significance of this word "taste"; for no statement of mine has been more earnestly or oftener controverted than that good taste is essentially a moral quality. "No," say many of my antagonists, "taste is one thing, morality is another. Tell us what is pretty: we shall be glad to know that; but we need no sermons — even were you able to preach them, which may be doubted."

— RUSKIN

To the Crystal Palace exhibits the art critics brought memories of an aesthetic standard which the ingenious craftsmen were content complacently to ignore. Well aware of the principles that had guided the tastes of a less anarchic era, Wyatt and Redgrave and Owen Jones were all moved by a longing for the order of a neoclassicism vanished beyond recall. Whatever their desire to believe in the "progress" of culture, they saw a lack of common purpose as the source of much misdirected energy; and they shook their heads at "art's decline." Like their eighteenth-century predecessors, most early Victorian aestheticians strove to relate the beautiful to some fixed pattern in the harmony of nature, to an unchanging truth beyond the immediate object of contemplation. If art was to mirror a larger totality, its function, they thought, must be at least implicitly "moral"; the picture or the poem, the play or the statue was to edify as well as to delight by its reflection of an immutable design. Sydney Dobell, as we have seen, felt that art by recording a special perfection would help the soul to "rise towards Perfection Universal." [1] And Charles Kingsley, with all his respect for the particulars of experience, was confident that the actual, when fully realized, could by some miracle of suggestion evoke the timeless ideal and so turn the mind of man to thoughts of heaven.[2] Though few could explain the exact processes by which art was to accomplish its religious mission, none questioned its ultimate relevance to the ethical needs of an aspiring people.

In the year of the Great Exhibition, David Ramsay Hay founded the Aesthetic Society at Edinburgh to probe the metaphysics of design and to discover, if possible, the objective principles which governed the creation of beauty. Since the days of Lord Kames and Archibald Alison, speculative Scots had pondered the problem of art, its origin and effect, with a sustained patience and a reasoned logic not to be matched in English academic criticism of the same period. Now in the 1850's the aesthetic discussion continued with renewed vigor, though grounded as before in empirical philosophy tempered by Christian doctrine and a concept of innate intuition.

Convinced that "the sensibility of beauty was implanted in the human breast" for moral improvement, the Scottish theorists considered the material forms which might awaken the purifying response. John G. Macvicar argued that "the principles of aesthetic beauty" must be based upon what natural philosophers could tell us of the laws of nature, since these laws were, he said, a universally beautiful embodiment of God's "divine intelligence and feeling." [3] Hay, who agreed that a sound "aesthetic science" must be rooted in "the great harmonic law of nature which pervades and governs the universe," recommended to the artist the Pythagorean system of numbers or musical ratios as the fundamental rule for all design intended to image forth the all-beautiful cosmic harmony.[4]

Whether or not the rule proved helpful to craftsmen actually engaged in creative work, it seemed most acceptable to the elder John Addington Symonds, an English physician educated in Edinburgh, whose concern for aesthetic inquiry foreshadowed his son's critical interests. Citing Hay's formulation of "a precise scientific basis for the Beauty of Form," Symonds developed the theory in mathematical terms to demonstrate the existence of an intrinsic beauty, a beauty inherent in the art object and independent of the emotion it might arouse in the spectator. For the object produced by a mind fully cognizant of natural law would, he believed, have a life of its own higher than that of nature itself, since great art was "inclusive of nature, . . . nature exalted, refined, and glorified, . . . nature impregnated with humanity," shaped by "the highest nature of all, — the human hand and the human brain, those greatest of God's creations." [5]

In seeking to establish an "objective" science of beauty, the Aesthetic Society for the most part tended to discount the subjective, or psychological, attitudes necessarily involved in artistic production and appreciation. One member of the group, however, rapidly grew dissatisfied with every vain attempt to define the beautiful. It was Eneas Sweetland Dallas who turned from the search for art's essence to an analysis of its aims and to the means by which the artist could achieve communication. Eager for a "correct psychology" of criticism, Dallas early in the fifties began a study of aesthetics[6] which culminated in *The Gay Science,* a wide-ranging treatise published in 1866. With both courage and wit, he challenged Coleridge's notion of an "esemplastic power" as no more adequate than all the involuted theorizing of the German idealists who obscured discussion by "the fearful clatter of metaphysical phrases." [7] Disturbed by the manifest uncertainty of Victorian taste, he struggled to assert a critical principle purged of the vague generalities that beset much speculation on art. For he was throughout his work aware that aesthetics, as propounded by earnest coteries, was fast becoming "the dismal science" with its own odious jargon, while economics, properly humanized, was taking its place as one of the lively arts.

From an initial assumption that the first and last end of all creative design was pleasure, Dallas set out to describe the nature of aesthetic delight. But pleasure, he insisted, defied conscious analysis, since man ceased to be happy as soon as he became conscious of happiness. Pleasure belonged only to the buried life; it arose in the imagination, or the Hidden Soul,[8] "a secret flow of thought which is not less energetic than the conscious flow, an absent mind which haunts us like a ghost or a dream and is an essential part of our lives." This Hidden Soul was "nothing of itself"; it was function rather than substance, "the entire mind in its secret working." Within the dark subconscious, said Dallas, there must roll "a vast tide of life, which is, perhaps, even more important to us than the little isle of our thoughts which lies within our ken." Here, at any rate, the memory uncontrolled by reason or will acted as a kind of kleptomaniac which seized all impressions and held them to the death. The spectator, therefore, brought to the art object a total experience far deeper than he could consciously fathom, far wider than he could comprehend. For it was his Hidden Soul rather than his active intellect that discerned the intent of art and partook of its pleasures. Unlike the reason, the imagination alone never abstracted or dissected;[9] it worked through metaphor, comparing wholes with wholes, seeking from art parallels to its own latent intuitions, and achieving, when satisfied, "a subtle sympathy" [10] which transformed the whole mind into the image of what it looked upon: "I am that, or like that; that is I, or like me." Art thus succeeded by suggesting a wholeness, a harmony, a consistency; and the artist communicated by his careful selection of such details from nature as were "in magnetic relation with the hidden life of the mind."

Dallas felt that "the modern disease" [11] stemmed directly from "excessive civilization and overstrained consciousness," which were destroying all immediate assent to the full experience. As every poetic hero since Manfred had indulged in "incessant introspection," so the sensitive mind everywhere seemed to be yielding more and more to troubled self-examination and reasoned doubt. Yet the true aesthetic pleasure would, Dallas insisted, be permanently denied to all who assumed with Matthew Arnold that the essence of life lay "in thinking, and being conscious of one's soul." For great art grew in the free "play of thought" and revealed itself only to the untrammeled imagination; it shrank beneath the pressures of logical analysis. The supreme poet like Milton displayed, to be sure, an "immense intellect," but he achieved, without conscious intellectual effort, a grasp of totality which made him "the most complete man to be found in his day"; and like Milton he was prepared always to recognize the quickened sensibilities of his whole being as readily as any power of his controlled reason. The morality of his art rang true, since it was implicit in his very perceptions and so in his aesthetic designs. But an art more conscious than his of a moral purpose, of a will to teach, ultimately failed. The Hidden Soul could respond fully to a fundamental innocence of spirit, but not at all to a calculated virtue making its practical appeal to convention or expediency. The moral element essential to all art was, therefore, to be natural rather than artificial; it was to set up "love instead of law for its guide"; and then, however the prude might object to its naked truths, it would "have its foundations in the moral sense of a people" who would grasp its inherent purity.[12]

In the belief that art must speak to the nation from whose moral heart it had arisen, Dallas attacked the artist who invoked private symbols to convey his esoteric meanings. The French critics, he said, had betrayed French democracy by establishing "the theory of art as caviare to the general." For self-culture, careless of social values, could lead only to aesthetic decadence; and "solitary thinking" would thus prove as detrimental to the public health as "solitary drinking." Convinced that the creative inspiration of an age like the Elizabethan had been "not individual but general, . . . common to the country and to the time, . . . a national possession," Dallas dismissed all aesthetic activity that lacked popular appeal. "The true judges of art," he wrote, "are the much despised many — the crowd — and no critic is worth his salt who does not feel with the many. There are, no doubt, questions of criticism which only few can answer; but the enjoyment of art is for all. . . . Great poetry was ever meant, and to the end of time must be adapted, not to the curious student, but for the multitude who read while they run — for the crowd in the street, for the boards of huge theatres, and for the choirs of vast cathedrals, for an army marching tumultuous to the battle, and for an assembled nation silent over the tomb of its mightiest." [13]

Had this criterion — the preference of the crowd — been sound, Dallas would have had to accept "The Charge of the Light Brigade" as a greater poem than "The Two Voices," "The Lost Chord" as a finer composition than "The Blessed Damozel," *The Heir of Redclyffe* as a better novel than *The Ordeal of Richard Feverel,* and the Albert Memorial as an unparalleled triumph of sculptural design. Yet his own judicious taste, apparent throughout *The Gay Science,* is sufficient proof that he would have been unwilling to do so. Like many another aesthetician, he was in truth the victim of his own theory. And this theory was in many respects both valid and stimulating. More directly than all other minor critics of his time, Dallas approached the psychology of communication; and more skillfully than most, he distinguished between an overt and an intrinsic morality. He was essentially right in affirming the social function of the artist and in resisting a sterile aestheticism which would seek to divorce art from life. But he erred grievously when he suggested that popular response must be the infallible judge of aesthetic value. If his notion of the Hidden Soul helped him explain the effect of art upon the spectator, it furnished no canon of discrimination, no clear basis for a qualitative estimate of a given art object. Unlike Ruskin, from whom he derived many of his first principles, he failed to consider that a people must be worthy of its art and that it must expect of its creative spirits a not always welcome appraisal of its common attitudes and prejudices, an "imitation of life" often unflattering and so quite unpopular.

Ruskin showed little of Dallas's interest in the workings of the subconscious mind and none of Hay's concern for the Pythagorean ratios or any single fixed rule of beauty. Though he drew in his own fashion more than he ever acknowledged from the eighteenth-century aestheticians, he was far less familiar than his Scottish contemporaries with the general history of aesthetics. He expressed an impetuous contempt for the measured logic and the abstract theorizing of all formal philosophy, and he lauded the "adamantine commonsense" of Dr. Johnson which had secured him "for ever from being caught in the cobwebs of German metaphysics, or sloughed in the English drainage of them." [14] If he accorded a higher place to reason than the concept of the Hidden Soul could admit, his judgments were frequently informed with a quite irrational emotion and delivered again and again in a tumultuous prose, the surging cadence of which might only too often encourage the illogicalities of overstatement.

From the outset he had been, as a writer, the disciple of Carlyle — moved by the same awareness of social forces, driven by a like will to assert the claims of the spirit in an "atheistic" world. But his cultural sympathies were broader than Carlyle's, and his moral insights deeper. And he saw more clearly the dangers of his own eloquence; from the first volume of *Modern Painters* (1843) to the *Fors Clavigera* (1871–1884), his "Letters to the Workmen and Labourers of Great Britain," he struggled earnestly to adjust his richly evocative style to the shifting demands of his message and his audience. For he was, among all Victorian prophets, the most eager that his gospel be heard and understood. At times his abnormally acute social conscience, his sensitivity to the moral problems of his age, led him to introduce into his complex studies of aesthetic form issues extraneous to his subject, digressions which obscured and befuddled his analyses. But despite the strange confusions of his method, he achieved an essential unity of tone, a deep if chaotic coherence. And whatever his unresolved conflicts, personal and intellectual, he succeeded somehow in articulating a doctrine of art adapted as no other to the basic impulses of his generation.

As aesthetician, Ruskin was so driven by both prejudice and principle that it is frequently difficult to dissociate the one from the other. Sometimes parochial, often dogmatic or deliberately contentious, his judgments mingled in varying proportions a quite impersonal standard of value and a highly subjective impressionism conditioned by the anomalies of his peculiar psychological development.[15] When he felt a temperamental affinity to a painter or a poet, his private intuitions might go far towards comprehending the power of a picture or a poem; his sympathetic studies of Milton and Carpaccio, for instance, gave him unusual insights into the emotional meanings of "Lycidas" and "St. Ursula's Dream." [16] When, however, he allowed the bias born of a narrowed "puritanism" to dominate his critical sense, he was forced into such unjust verdicts as his estimate of Balzac's fiction as "full of blasphemies, subtle, tremendous, hideous in shamelessness." [17] Yet he was also capable of an amazing disinterest, often prepared to withhold opinion until he had examined the intrinsic merits of an artist and his work. Though himself infected with certain middle-class pruderies, he could assail "the piously sentimental public" who shrank "with anathema not unembittered by alarm" from the genius of Byron.[18] And despite his distrust of erotic emotion, he could defend the verse of Swinburne against all who found its passions dangerously seductive.

He was willing to admit his own mistakes and even (as when his remarks on Gothic seemed most inspiring to the neo-Venetian revivalists[19]) to deplore his own influence. A child might have seen the inconsistency of his personal impressions; indeed, Dora in *The Ethics of the Dust* (1866), a precocious little girl, did venture to indicate an apparent contradiction: "Well it may be all very fine and philosophical, but shouldn't I just like to read you the end of the second volume of *Modern Painters*." But Ruskin was ready with an answer, "My dear, do you think any teacher could be worth your listening to, or anybody else's listening to, who had learned nothing from seven and twenty to seven and forty?" [20] He was in truth never much alarmed by his inaccuracies of detail. Yet he vigorously persisted in clinging to judgments which he knew to involve the essentials of his theory. And his refusal to retract the fateful "libel" against Whistler rested on his firm conviction that he had brought his whole art doctrine to his criticism of the "Nocturnes" in the Grosvenor Gallery. For, however ingeniously his biographers may account for his reaction in terms of "automatic panic" [21] or personal prejudice, he himself saw clearly that he could never embrace Whistlerian aestheticism without denying his own first principles.

Throughout Ruskin's criticism recurs his desire for synthesis, his will to discover the universal harmony towards which his age aspired.

At no time could he find value in an art which bore no perceptible relation to the realities of human experience. He was himself a skilled draftsman and colorist[22] with much the same feeling for nature as we detect in the classical Chinese masters and a command of technique probably unequaled by painters like Holman Hunt to whose work he did not dream of comparing his own. Yet he was oppressed by a sense of irresponsibility whenever it occurred to him that his sketches might be useless to mankind;[23] his moral faculties rebelled against the pursuit of beauty for its own sake. Perhaps his deepest impulse was his urge to integrate all the varied knowledge he was able to amass during his crowded career. He was always a tireless collector, eager to sort, to catalogue, to classify the innumerable objects he had gathered; for material things became to him tokens of the richly diversified design that held the created world in unity.

His range of enthusiasms was prodigious, his capacity for interest almost unlimited. In 1855 he told Carlyle of the main topics which engaged his attention over a period of six months, during which time he had written and revised some six hundred pages of *Modern Painters* and other expository prose. "I have had to make various remarks," he wrote, "on German Metaphysics, on Poetry, Political Economy, Cookery, Music, Geology, Dress, Agriculture, Horticulture, and Navigation, all of which subjects I have had to 'read up' accordingly." [24] Twenty years later he listed the projects upon which he had already begun his researches:

A history of fifteenth-century Florentine art in six octavo volumes; an analysis of Attic art of the fifth century B.C., in three volumes; an exhaustive history of northern thirteenth-century art, in ten volumes; a life of Sir Walter Scott with an analysis of modern epic art, in seven volumes; a life of Xenophon, with analysis of the general principles of education, in ten volumes; a commentary on Hesiod, with a final analysis of the principles of Political Economy, in nine volumes; and a general description of the geology and botany of the Alps, in twenty-four volumes.[25]

And these sixty-nine volumes were, as Frederic Harrison pointed out, "to be written by a man shattered in body and mind at the end of a laborious life."

Though his restless energy often made him impatient with the details of the large "analyses" he wished to achieve, it continually broadened his awareness of human motives. As art teacher, Ruskin proved endlessly stimulating to many Oxford students who listened enthralled, while his pencil traced clear patterns, to his inexhaustible talk "about Plato and the Book of Job and the wickedness of modern politicians and industrialists." [26] For it was, he believed, the business of art to interpret and to edify; and no work designed as pure ornament was worthy serious consideration. However much a Whistler might seek to rid his pictures of social content, the great artist would remain the one who could grasp "great ideas," the one able to embody in his creation the wholeness of experience, to hold a cultural infinity in the palm of his hand.

While the aesthetes who succeeded him proclaimed the autonomy of art, Ruskin, even more emphatically than Dallas, stressed its social sources. Art, he insisted, was born of a distinct social milieu, and it served directly and indirectly the society that produced it. The best literature mirrored a complete world with a splendid objectivity and so suggested to the reader the depth of the full life, the richness of the human drama. And the vital architecture (as Frank Lloyd Wright would later agree) both expressed and influenced the national character; for a beautiful building, perfectly adapted to its social function, challenged all who looked upon it to achieve the purity of order. Historically, a great age could best be judged by its capacities for thought and feeling as reflected in its creative work. And if its art, indissolubly linked to its cultural traditions, had attained the requisite wholeness or "integrity," the age itself must have respected to some extent the ideals of discipline, balance, and harmony; it must, in short, have been a "moral" age.[27]

To Ruskin, then, great art was in some measure the expression of a great society. Yet it was also the product of a great individual, the medium by which the gifted artist passed on his vision to a public prepared to receive his meanings. Into its narrow compass was concentrated the essence of a complete, and so a "moral," personality. For however irregular were his habits, however unconventional his attitudes, the artist as "maker" had to be in full possession of his faculties, in absolute control of his materials. At the moment of creation he had to be an integrated person, a whole man, balanced in his emotions, right in his perceptions. Though to less intense souls he might seem alarmingly familiar with the depths of depravity, he would be at heart unsullied by his insights; and his work would show good "developed to its highest by its contention with evil." In his obedience to the laws of being, the true artist achieved "exquisite balance and symmetry of vital powers," restraint, perspective, superb command of form and content. Pope was the "most accomplished" writer Ruskin knew in English, since Pope had best learned to manipulate the strictest language within the briefest limits. And Veronese ranked high among painters by virtue of his "muscular precision . . . and intellectual strain," his physical mastery of line no less than his mental grasp of theme. Though an artist's "morality" could never be gauged in terms of his private life, it yet revealed itself unmistakably in the seriousness and breadth of his work, in a subject matter which betokened no warped or partial view of experience, and in a disciplined technique which could countenance no dissipation of vital energies.[28]

But before the spectator could appreciate the artist's "morality," he required a mind sufficiently noble to grasp the moral "ideas" which art might communicate. As soon as any aesthetic object evoked an impression, it became his duty to evaluate its worth, to distinguish the higher from the lower sensation. A well-trained moral sense would recognize immediately and instinctively the healthful stimulus. Operating by a kind of immanent vitalism, it would claim kinship with the "purity" of the art object, since "purity" was the energizing force of life itself. All great art impressed the mind by its correspondence with an integrated whole, a living truth. The vital reality beneath appearances, upon which the artist's "penetrative imagination" had seized, spoke to the basic vitality of human nature, which was "in its fulness . . . necessarily Moral." [29] To art the spectator brought his total personality; his entire past faced the adventure of the moment. And to the worthy art object he surrendered his whole consciousness, until by the principle of "love" he had achieved an empathic identification and so a moral self-effacement. The finer his capacity for such "love," the more complete would be his experience. Perfect taste in art was "the faculty for receiving the greatest possible pleasure from those material sources which are attractive to our moral nature in its purity and perfection." [30] And the greatest art was accordingly the art which most appealed to that receptive power, the art which conveyed "to the mind of the spectator, by any means, whatsoever, the greatest number of the greatest ideas." [31]

In his emphasis upon communication, Ruskin had no desire to minimize the importance of technique. As draftsman he knew that the artist must always feel a genuine concern for his medium, and as critic he found it necessary to examine in considerable detail the devices by which thought could be given aesthetic expression. Moreover, he was himself a conscious prose stylist, thoroughly sensitive to verbal color and cadence, to the shape of the sentence and the tempo of the paragraph. Yet he resented all who lingered over his harmonious phrases. "My vanity," he said, "is never more wounded than in being called a fine writer — meaning — that nobody need mind what I say." [32] For he wished to be known as a thinker with a meaningful message rather than as a "word-painter" with a well-stocked palette. And in all the arts he deemed the "language" of the artist "invaluable as the vehicle of thought, but by itself nothing." [33] There were few, he felt, who enjoyed "the mere artifices of composition or the dexterities of handling" more than he. But he valued that art most highly which forced him to forget its form and to turn his attention to its content. Fearing that excessive refinement of technique must be paid for by some loss of substance, he insisted that in painting as in literature "no weight, nor mass nor beauty of execution, [could] outweigh one grain or fragment of thought." [34] For if prose and poetry were to do more than lull the reader with beguiling rhythms, graphic art also was to appeal to the judgment as well as to the senses; it was to utilize line and curve and color not for their own sakes, but for the abstract "ideas" they might convey.[35]

Of painting and sculpture, which dealt in plastic surfaces, Ruskin could hardly ask the exposition of logical argument. Yet he could look to the material qualities of every art object for some embodiment of moral and intellectual values or "types." The infinite gradation of light and shade, for instance, suggested to him the idea of "infinity" and its associated emotions, admiration and awe. The appearance in material things of a "self-restrained liberty" evoked the idea of "moderation," the golden mean. And the skillful placing of masses represented "repose," on which depended strength, poise, and dignity. Similarly, balance, the opposition of equals, constituted "symmetry," which corresponded to the moral concept of justice. "Unity" was the principle by which many parts were related to one organic whole, to an essential pattern which could reflect in the microcosm of art the ordered design of a teleological universe. And "purity" was a material quality of light, the concentrated energy which made the matter of art a living matter, the power which, as we have seen, aroused love of vitality in the sympathetic observer. These, then, were the six main "ideas" of "Typical Beauty," from each of which Ruskin drew complex connotations. But besides the Typical, he discovered in art as in nature what he called a "Vital Beauty," arising from "the felicitous fulfilment of function in living things";[36] and to this, also, he assigned emotional meanings which he felt it needful to explain in replete detail. Many of his moral readings, to be sure, were fanciful or arbitrary, serving to confuse rather than clarify his aesthetic doctrine, forcing him into self-contradiction and tenuous rationalizing. Nevertheless, despite the difficulties he encountered in describing the "ideas" behind material forms, he remained firmly convinced that art had much of intellectual significance to say, and that it would always speak in its own fashion to the whole mind of moral man.

The artist intent upon real communication was to ground his work securely in the facts of physical life. He was to be guided consistently by a reverence for the actualities of human experience and a certain knowledge that all art cut off from the affairs of men, existing in its own patterns for its own sake, must be forever sterile and dead. Concerned from the outset with material shapes and forms, Ruskin advocated a thoroughly inductive approach to reality; he asked that every generalization about universals be fast rooted in a scientific study of particulars.[37] He was, in short, a "realist," decrying outmoded conventions and stereotyped formulas, urging the poet or painter to "go to nature" as the only source of adequate subject matter. Yet he saw his exhortation freely misunderstood, as more and more Victorians came to consider the faithful imitation of nature the final goal of art. He, therefore, found it necessary before long to shift his whole emphasis; for it was, he felt sure, the artist's highest function to interpret and not merely to copy natural phenomena.

"The picture," he declared, "which is looked to for an interpretation of nature is invaluable, but the picture which is taken as a substitute for nature had better be burned. . . . All that is highest in art, all that is creative and imaginative, is formed and created by every great master for himself, and cannot be repeated or imitated by others." The literal transcription, whether in paint or in words, was clearly not enough. M. Tissot's pictures, "despite their conscientiousness," were "mere coloured photographs"; George Eliot's "realism" was tedious and unproductive; and Balzac's novels achieved only a "bitter and fruitless statement of facts." [38] Devoted to a "characteristic reality" beyond simple imitation, the true artist, said Ruskin, struck the proper balance between fact and design; he not only observed the natural world but also selected and arranged his perceptions; for "the power of assembling" was indeed the essential mark "of the poet or literally of the 'Maker.' " [39] But the artist who relied on his capacity for design without reference to the facts of experience lacked the courage to face inescapable truth; he was dishonest in his disregard for reality and base in his will to pervert his medium to the ends of a "false idealism." [40] And morally, the aesthete was less to be condoned than the "photographer." The one at least made a sincere effort to record the surfaces of matter. The other deliberately avoided matter altogether.

Though willing to modify many of his individual judgments,

Ruskin was reluctant after 1855 to alter in any essential the outlines of his aesthetic theory. Instead, he turned to social criticism in the hope that, by recalling Victorian England to the ideals of a vanished culture, he might quicken the creative will that had, he thought, once inspired all noble craftsmanship. Had he opened his sympathies to the true "modern painters," to the great French schools of the sixties and seventies, he might have been able to adapt his doctrine to the aims and objectives of a new art, an art which was, in fact, deriving much from the experiments with light and color begun by his own revered Turner. Yet Ruskin could never, we may be sure, have accepted the practices or professions of Whistler or any of the English "Aesthetes" who affected Whistlerian attitudes. For Whistler had dedicated his talents to the expression of a philosophy against which Ruskin had consistently fought — to a scorn of nature, a contempt for meaningful subject matter and "painted ideas," an assertion of the artist's independence from the claims of society, and a denial of his responsibility for vital communication. The abuse of the "Nocturnes," therefore, involved issues more fundamental than the petulance with which it was uttered might suggest. And the libel suit which followed challenged more than the critic's right to speak his mind; it placed on trial Ruskin's first principles and with them the whole Victorian "morality" of art.

It was, of course, quite without premeditation that Ruskin happened to select Whistler as the particular target for his general attack on the new aestheticism. In June 1877, while in London to address the Society for the Prevention of Cruelty to Animals, he had chanced upon the Grosvenor Gallery, lately opened by Sir Coutts Lindsay, and had there lingered for a moment over the Whistler compartment, which the critic for *The Times* had found all "musical with strange Nocturnes." [41] Repelled by the disparity between workmanship and price, Ruskin thought the artist clearly guilty of "ill-educated conceit" and "wilful imposture." And when the opportunity arose, he added his comment, almost as an afterthought, to a *Fors Clavigera* letter on the commercialization of art. "I have seen, and heard, much of Cockney impudence before now," he wrote, "but never expected to hear a coxcomb ask two hundred guineas for flinging a pot of paint in the public's face." Some five years earlier he had dismissed Whistler's "Symphony in Gray and Green" for the same reason and in language scarcely less vituperative.[42] Since his censure had then passed unnoticed, he was rather startled that the painter now ventured to bring legal action against him. Yet he welcomed the prospect of defending his judgment in the light of standards to which he had always subscribed, and which now seemed more cogent than ever in opposition "to the modern schools which suffer[ed] the object of art to be ornament rather than edification."[43] "It's mere nuts and nectar to me," he told Burne-Jones, "the notion of having to answer for myself in court, and the whole thing will enable me to assert some principles of art economy which I've never got into the public's head, by writing, but may get sent all over the world vividly in a newspaper report or two."[44]

When increasing tensions, physical and mental, made it impossible for Ruskin to take the stand, Whistler was left to explain, if he would, the principles of his own "art economy." But none of the jostling Philistines who cross-examined him felt much interested in the dictates of his "Artistic Conscience," which had, he claimed, been grossly slandered. He, therefore, preferred that the court should laugh with him rather than at him. And of necessity he made himself the nonchalant hero of an inane comic opera, a hero of matchless wit and ready logic, able to maintain throughout his performance the superior deportment he had learned at West Point. The Gilbertian judge and jury, for their part, not unresponsive to his able parrying, awarded the plaintiff the verdict — and damages to the extent of one farthing; for that, as Bernard Shaw said, was all that any conscience, much less an artistic one, could be worth "in the eyes of the Law."[45] Left to pay his share of the costs, Whistler derived little satisfaction from his token victory. If the trial of 1878 had given him a remarkable fob for his watch chain, it had also left him completely insolvent. Unable to face financial ruin, he fled to Venice, where he found the dome of Ruskin's St. Mark's less lovely than the ceiling of his own Peacock Room.

Ruskin, meanwhile, suffered a more complete bankruptcy. Before the trial he had considered abandoning his Oxford professorship, by reason of prolonged ill health. After his defeat he hastened to resign for a quite different cause. Struggling painfully to be objective, he wrote to Dean Liddell, "I cannot hold a Chair from which I have no power of expressing judgment without being taxed for it by British Law." [46] The trial, he felt, had impugned his integrity as critic and so repudiated his whole life's work. It had done nothing to shake his belief that Whistler was an incompetent technician. Yet it had given a kind of public sanction to an aesthetic philosophy which contradicted every article of his faith. Before long, Oscar Wilde would acknowledge his wisdom but deny his principles; for the master, Wilde would say, who "taught us at Oxford that enthusiasm for beauty which is the secret of Hellenism, . . . would judge of a picture by the amount of moral ideas it expresses; but to us the channels by which all noble work in painting can touch, and does touch, the soul are not those of truths of life or metaphysical truths." [47] And as Wilde and Whistler, disclaiming the "truths of life," led poetry and painting towards strange ideals, Ruskin would see a rejection of his major premises, a confessed desire to free art from the social and "moral" obligations which he had deemed essential to its existence.

Like Dallas and Hay, Kingsley, Dobell, and indeed all other mid-Victorians who gave thought to the problem of beauty, Ruskin assumed that the artist was bound to communicate a vision of the full reality, which, by its very wholeness, would awaken high emotion in the sympathetic observer. With Matthew Arnold he held that "a poetry of revolt against moral ideas is a poetry of revolt against *life;* a poetry of indifference towards moral ideas is a poetry of indifference towards *life*." [48] For he sensed as deeply as Tennyson the spiritual death that would overpower the "Aesthetic Man" isolated from the world in his palace of art. He might at last, had he paused to consider, have seen the value of the French Impressionists, who worshiped nature as completely as he and who sought, with all the humility and patience he demanded, to interpret the purity of living light.[49] But he was from the beginning constitutionally unable to admit the segregation of faculties which made possible Whistler's defense of artifice as an independent entity. And he was instinctively repelled by the frame of mind that led Flaubert to desire a book without a subject, *"sans attache extérieure,"* which would support itself entirely by the internal force of its own style.[50] Such things were undreamt of in his philosophy. His whole view of God and man made him look to art for a reflection of the final harmony, for a synthesis of the total experience. Never could he regard pure design as an end in itself; technique remained always simply the means by which the artist might make permanent his passing insight into an ultimate truth.

In the Aesthetic Movement of the eighties Ruskin could have recognized much of his own hostility to the ugliness of industrial England. Yet there were other forces, quite beyond his comprehension, leading the late Victorians towards an "art for art's sake." His own basic concepts of the true and the beautiful had rested upon a sure, though never clearly articulated, faith in the reality of spirit, in the power of the human mind to trace the patterns that unified the aspirations of a diverse culture. But long before the Whistler trial, the sanctions of that faith had begun to crumble beneath the material certainties of a post-Darwinian science. No less than the "morality of art" itself, English aestheticism sprang from an intellectual milieu which made inevitable its gradual development. Far more than they realized, the haggard and lank young men who tried to make of art a new religion had been conditioned by the society against which they rebelled. And far oftener than they were willing to confess, they felt, like their portly high priest, a deep nostalgia for the "truths of life" and all the Ruskinian ideals that they had been driven to renounce.

The Fear of Art

The fleshly gentlemen have bound themselves by solemn league and covenant to extol fleshliness as the distinct and supreme end of poetic and pictorial art; to aver that poetic expression is greater than poetic thought, and by inference that the body is greater than the soul, and sound superior to sense. . . . The fleshly persons who wish to create form for its own sake are merely pronouncing their own doom.

— ROBERT BUCHANAN

At the beginning of the seventies, Robert Buchanan was dismayed to find all Victorian England beset by the demon of the leg "cutting capers without a body or a head." Wherever he turned in London, he saw the snake Sensualism coiled in readiness to spit its venom upon him. Polite society, he believed, was so far forgetting its reticences that it would admit the impolite reality of physical passion; while art, in its turn, seemed more and more prepared to ignore the conventional respectabilities that it might cater to the depraved appetites of wanton youth or furnish models for imitation to "young gentlemen with animal faculties morbidly developed by too much tobacco and too little exercise." The worst literary offenders — those indeed most hostile to Buchanan's didactic sentimentalism — constituted the Fleshly School of Poetry,[1] a group united by perverse loyalties against all that was sane and wholesome and normal and decently veiled from public view. And the grossest offender among the fleshly poets, even more debased than the infamous Swinburne, was Dante Gabriel Rossetti, "a fleshly person, with nothing particular to tell us or teach us," a man "fleshly all over, from the roots of his hair to the tip of his toes, . . . never spiritual, never tender; always self-conscious and aesthetic."

To most readers, it should have been clear enough that Buchanan's indictment of the Pre-Raphaelites and his expanded pamphlet describing the endemic "Leg-disease" were products of a mind itself diseased, obsessed with deep inhibitions, unnaturally familiar with a long tradition of scatological literature. Yet to Rossetti and Swinburne the attack seemed sufficiently serious to warrant reply in kind; for it raised objections which, if not countered, might discredit their work among those who had hitherto accepted its essential sincerity. Unlike Whistler, they were unwilling to assert their complete independence as artists from the concerns of society. However individual their techniques, however startling their subject matter, they refused to deny altogether their responsibility for "moral" communication. Despite a thorough devotion to their craft, they feared the autonomy of art; they remained as suspicious as Ruskin of a declared aestheticism. The gravity of Buchanan's charge, therefore, lay less in the prudishness with which he decried sensuous detail than in the suggestion that the fleshly poets were intent upon exalting poetic expression above poetic thought, sound above sense, and "form for its own sake" above meaningful content.

It was Buchanan's "final and revised opinion" (1887) that Rossetti had never been a fleshly poet at all, and that "those who assert that he loved [his] Art 'for its own sake,' know nothing of his method." [2] Yet his original complaint (1871) that Rossetti's work "might be dangerous to society" by reason of its "inherent quality of animalism" was shared by such orthodox critics as W. J. Courthope, who shrank from an "emasculate obscenity" and a "deification of the animal instincts." [3] In Boston, an anonymous reviewer for the *Atlantic,* wishing that the Fallen Woman (presumably Jenny) might "be at least policed out of sight," regretted that Rossetti's "imagination should be so often dominated by character and fact which are quite other than pure." [4] Though Tennyson felt the condemned "Nuptial Sleep" remarkable for its "passion and imaginative power," [5] James Russell Lowell had seen in the sonnet only "a sort of clean indecency, . . . a sort of deliberate hovering between nudity and nakedness." [6] and J. R. Dennett had detected elsewhere in the volume "something like morbidly gratified sexual sensuousness." [7] Even Browning, however, welcomed the "Fleshly School" diatribe; and encouraged perhaps by Buchanan's remark that "Jenny" resembled the verse of "an emasculated Mr. Browning," he passed his own "virile" commentary on the poem in *Fifine at the Fair* (1872), where he turned a similar dramatic situation to more robust "moral" purpose.[8]

Few later critics have been repelled by a "fleshliness" real or imaginary.[9] But the corollary charge of aestheticism has been repeated often enough to condition the poet-painter's whole reputation. Rossetti has time and again been selected — for praise or for blame — as "indisputably the representative man of the Aesthetic Movement" [10] and as probably the dominant English influence on the Decadence of the nineties. More reluctant than Buchanan to pass moral judgment, many of these critics have nonetheless found Rossetti's work overwrought, affected, lacking in spontaneity, essentially esoteric in its appeal; and, like Buchanan, they have insisted that both his poetry and his painting betray a self-conscious delight in aesthetic *décor* and a basic confusion of aesthetic media. Discounting Ruskin's high regard for the "moral" truths of his art,[11] they have found significant the fact that Oscar Wilde professed deep admiration for *The House of Life,* borrowed the lilies of the Blessed Damozel, and struck the "medieval" attitudes for which, to his own advancement, he was satirized in *Patience.* Still, if we are to understand either the true Pre-Raphaelites or the Wildean Aesthetes, we must discriminate aright between their diverse concepts of beauty. And at the outset we must seek to explain why Rossetti resisted almost every attempt to place him among the "amoral" apostles of art for art's sake, and why, like the half-"aesthetic" Walter Pater, he viewed with strange ambivalence the general drift towards aestheticism.

Dismissed by Buchanan as "an unwholesome periodical," the Pre-Raphaelite *Germ* of 1850 was designed as an avowed "protest against existing conditions in art." Yet its eager young contributors, though they adopted distinct mannerisms of style and technique to proclaim their identity as a "Brotherhood," registered no serious protest against existing standards of conduct. Their mild Bohemianism was of a piece with the early affectations of Arnold, the "Merry Matt" of Oriel whose gestures were precise and Parisian and whose hair remained "guiltless of English scissors." [12] No more than Arnold did they ask for the artist a freedom from the impulses of a living society, nor for art itself an independence from human relations. They were quite unable to imagine the picture or the poem as a self-contained entity existing in and for its own beautiful form, its line and color, its imagery and music; for all great art, they felt, was worthy only insofar as it suggested by its content some deeper "criticism of life." Far from being "aesthetic," they set out consciously to attack artifice and calculated design. Their hostility to the "Raphaelites" represented an impatience with the formalized art of all academicians, with painting and poetry which had yielded to stultifying conventions. Like Wordsworth half a century before, they pled for a simpler language of emotion. And in their various media they worked conscientiously towards a closer "truth to nature." Yet their reverence for accurate reproduction was from the first qualified by a desire that each detail fully realized might stand as a symbol of some spiritual force above sense perception.

As the movement spread beyond the first Pre-Raphaelite circle, the newly recruited "Brethren" sought more and more to transcend — by their allegories of word and paint — the mechanized drives of their industrial age. With a too-deliberate defiance, Burne-Jones at last announced, "The more materialistic Science becomes, the more angels shall I paint." [13] But the spirituality of a Giotto was not to be recovered by a mere conjuring with "medieval" motifs. Eventually the "protest" against existing formulas became itself stereotyped. Grown increasingly ornate, Pre-Raphaelite *décor* lost all vitality as it passed into the hands of artists uncertain of its original meaning, uninterested in any recognizable "nature," intent only upon some vague evocation of a world remote from the Philistine conflict. And the stained-glass attitudes of Burne-Jones's angels ultimately seemed to Wilde sufficiently void of "spiritual" suggestion to be valued solely as expressive tokens of "aesthetic" intensity. By the time that a younger generation was ready to assert the doctrine of art for art's sake, Rossetti, who had been the prime mover of the Pre-Raphaelite group, felt compelled to disparage the label by which the Aesthetes sought to praise his work. "As for all the prattle about Pre-Raphael-itism," he told Hall Caine in 1880, "I should confess to you I am weary of it, and long have been. Why should we go on talking about the visionary vanities of half-a-dozen boys? We've all grown out of them, I hope, by now." [14]

But though Rossetti dissociated himself from the "aesthetic young men" who hailed him as the harbinger of a new Art, Wilde and others could find elements in his life and work which might suggest sympathy with their ideals. To all intents and purposes, he had with-drawn from the social and economic struggles which had preoccupied almost every major mid-Victorian. Contemning "the momentary momentousness and eternal futility of many of our noisiest ques-tions," [15] he showed little interest in theological dispute, no real un-derstanding of nineteenth-century science, and no lasting concern with the political issues that had inspired an atypical half-dozen son-nets. To the outside world he seemed completely lost in the rarefied atmosphere of his shuttered studio. So apparent was his absorption in painting that Longfellow, when visiting him, failed to suspect his equal devotion to poetry, and, on leaving, asked to be remembered to his brother whose "Blessed Damozel" he greatly admired.[16] In both arts Rossetti labored to achieve a highly concentrated imagery and a symbolism rich in connotations often unfamiliar to the com-mon reader — the "reader" of pictures or of poems. And to the extent that it lacked popular appeal, his work became all the more attractive to the Aesthetes, who professed undying scorn of the commonplace.

Moreover, in his answer to Buchanan's attack, he had confessed to taking "a wider view than some poets or critics, of how much, in the material conditions absolutely given to man to deal with as distinct from his spiritual aspirations, is admissible within the limits of Art." [17] It was, therefore, not altogether unreasonable to assume that he supposed style in itself sufficient to dignify a subject matter of no "moral" consequence. If not "fleshly," his verse was undeniably sensuous; he seemed better able than any poet since Keats to identify himself with the physical reality of the object he chose to portray. His insistence that art demanded "an inner standing-point" must surely have implied a willingness to suspend judgment, to grasp his subject dramatically on its own terms. And the "negative capability" with which he intuited the dark desires of Lady Lilith or many another *femme fatale* may have indicated to some among the "aesthetic" elect that he rightly considered the body more immediate than the soul and "form for its own sake" the "supreme end" of art.

In a review of Rossetti's late verse,[18] J. A. Symonds pointed to an "arduous fullness" as the poet's chief merit and abiding weakness. The originality of his work, said Symonds, lay in its form and style rather than its thought and sentiment, and the man in Rossetti, therefore, seemed "less important than the artist." Now, had such a judgment been passed upon the "aesthetic" *Poems* of Oscar Wilde, which appeared in the same year (1881), the "aesthetic poet" might have welcomed the review as evidence that he had achieved a complete formal objectivity, an art fashioned for art's sake without emotional irrelevancies. But Rossetti was sufficiently concerned with "non-aesthetic" values to reject the criticism as rather less than "civil." [19] For he considered the artist as nothing apart from the intellect and feeling of the man; and he thought the art work meaningless which sacrificed the drama of human passion to the harmonies of pure design.

As a painter he cared more for the content of a picture than for its construction; the pattern was at best incidental to the idea that had gripped his imagination. Though a relatively unskilled draftsman, he was an accomplished colorist, deeply indebted to the medieval illuminators. Yet color served him less as an architectonic device than as a means of enriching the emotional symbolism of his canvases; his clear reds and blues and yellows evoked a "primitive" innocence or terror, the naïve ecstasy of a "Pre-Raphaelite" world. His sonnets for his own pictures emphasized the universals which the detail in color was intended to suggest. And his verses on the work of a Leonardo, a Botticelli, or a Giorgione betrayed his persistent will to decipher the allegory which lent new dimension to the masterpiece. Even in his poem on "The Card Dealer," a genre study by Theodore von Holst, where the actualism had no obvious overtone, Rossetti concentrated attention upon the central figure until her enigmatic gaze had drawn him into the very picture, and he, too, became a player in the game of chance, which was essentially Life itself and Death:

> *Whom plays she with? With thee, who lov'st*
> *Those gems upon her hand;*
> *With me who search her secret brows;*
> *With all men, bless'd or bann'd.*
> *We play together, she and we,*
> *Within a vain strange land.*

All art to Rossetti invited such participation; it opened the gate to a strange land, "a land without any order," timeless beyond the momentary momentousness of transitory experience. Finding its universals in the particulars of "nature," art offered an interpretation of the ultimate truth rather than an escape from the actual; it was nothing less than reality lifted to a new plane, a "transfigured life" shaped by the artist from all the conflicting passions of the man.

While the Lady Lilith, "subtly of herself contemplative," became Rossetti's symbol of the Body's Beauty, the figure of Beata Beatrix appeared in many guises and with many titles, throughout his work, as the object of the ideal love that would seek through the physical some final identity with the infinite, some full intimation of the transcendent spirit:

> *Shall birth and death, and all dark names that be*
> *As doors and windows bared to some loud sea,*
> *Lash deaf mine ears and blind my face with spray;*

> *And shall my sense pierce love — the last relay*
> *And ultimate outpost of eternity?*

Drawn from countless models and from pure imagination, the type of the Beloved varied little from picture to picture, from poem to poem. Her head poised upon an odd "swanlike" neck, her lips slightly parted, she peered nostalgically from a Florentine casement, from an enchanted wood, from an ivied balcony, even from the gold bar of heaven, always with the same bemused "commemorative" eyes, eyes through which the god of love would grant the lover

> *clearest call*
> *And veriest touch of powers primordial*
> *That any hour-girt life may understand.*

The experience of the higher love meant for Rossetti the perfect comprehension of all values material or spiritual; the vision, the call, the touch coalesced to seize upon a single truth. Yet even Lilith, however beset with the fleshly desires of absolute possession, represented no permanent antithesis to her passive counterpart; for in all forms of beauty, the poet found the flesh so interpenetrated with spirit that he could seldom draw sharp distinctions:

> *Lady, I fain could tell how evermore*
> *Thy soul I know not from thy body, nor*
> *Thee from myself, neither our love from God.*

Like his painting, his love poetry at its best was thus suffused with a kind of mysticism replete with religious or moral feeling.[20] Its "medieval" tone derived less from an archaic *décor* than from a deeper affinity with the spiritual world of Dante, with a philosophy that valued the body not as "greater than the soul" but always as its essential expression. It was natural then that he should have been content to be regarded as a writer "Catholic" in spirit, whose influence might control "the growing sensuousness of English poetry." [21] And it was understandable that Swinburne, who recognized Rossetti's intention, should have insisted that "in him the will and the instinct are not two forces, but one strength; are not two leaders, but one guide; there is no shortcoming, no pain or compulsion in the homage of hand to soul." [22]

Rossetti's search for the universal values which underlay each sense impression led him inevitably towards a "metaphysical" verse distasteful to all who demanded of art a literal statement of fact or a facile expression of sentiment. Buchanan complained that parts of *The House of Life* were "meaningless, but in the best manner of Carew or Dr. Donne." Heedless of the sneer, Rossetti was proud to acknowledge derivation, if not from the courtier, at least from the divine. "Do you know Donne?" he asked Hall Caine, some years after the Fleshly School controversy; "there is hardly an English poet better worth a thorough knowledge, in spite of his provoking conceits and occasional jagged jargon." [23]

Rossetti's own "conceits" consisted, like Donne's, in a curious admixture of the abstract and the concrete, and were no less deliberately evoked, or "artificially" elaborated, to fortify the emotion with a strenuous intellectual logic by which the particular experience might be related to a larger unity. From his earliest mood poems to his last sonnets, his metaphors tended to become increasingly general. The precise actualism of pieces like "My Sister's Sleep" yielded to an imagery chosen to connote mental states rather than to define physical forms, an imagery often consciously blurred and "elemental," concerned all with

> *Waters engulfing or fires that devour,*
> *Earth heaped against me, or death in the air.*

In the sonnets of his final period, he struggled for a more and more highly concentrated idiom, for images thought-laden and elliptical,[24] for a diction weighted with layer upon layer of suggestion. Not seldom baroque in its detail, his verse approached the grand style as it turned to a last analysis of the ultimate mysteries — love, death, and "the one hope," time, change, and regret — the themes of "central universal meaning" which he had defended against Buchanan as inherent in the most "arduous human tragedy" that any art could depict.

Despite a frequent impatience with Ruskin's more dogmatic pronouncements, Rossetti had no essential quarrel with the high Victorian "morality of art." Though his poetry, informed as it was with a difficult symbolism, could speak to no wide audience, he was impelled perpetually by the desire to communicate his meanings to the sympathetic few. Above all, he feared misapprehension of his motives. From the beginning he had repudiated the critic who would charge him with exalting form and undervaluing content. But after Buchanan's first assault, he became almost pathologically obsessed with the sense of being wholly misunderstood, of being rejected by respectable society, "hunted and hounded into his grave." [25] Three years before his death he opened his peculiar friendship with Hall Caine, largely because Caine, insisting upon his moral impulses, had publicly championed his "spiritual passion" [26] against those who were intent upon relegating him to a place "among the 'aesthetic' poets." To Caine he expressed irritation with a tendency "to set the manner of a work higher than its substance, to glorify style as if it were a thing apart from subject." And in almost Ruskinian terms, he cautioned the youth, "Conception, my boy, FUNDAMENTAL BRAINWORK, that is what makes the difference in all art. Work your metal as much as you like, but first take care that it is gold and worth working." [27]

If he worked and reworked his own materials, Rossetti was forever convinced of their quality and importance; he sought less to perfect a style than to give the vital conception fit embodiment. In his persistent concern for form he resembled the Dante of *La Vita Nuova*, who held himself accountable for the inner logic of each sonnet, rather than Gautier and the French Parnassians, who strove for the hard surface and sharp outline of polished marble, beautiful in itself and independent of distracting emotion. By the end of his life he felt contempt for the new aestheticism with its professed faith in art for art's sake; and he regretted that Burne-Jones had shown interest in the immature postures and pretensions of Wilde.[28] For his own part, he scorned the heresies imported from France, frequently returned to the work of Tennyson which had inspired some of his earliest drawings, and sometimes spoke of holding one day "his place among the English poets," not as the founder of a short-lived school proclaiming a narrow creed, but rather as a Victorian who gave utterance to the emotions that had enkindled "the three greatest English imaginations, . . . Shakespeare, Coleridge, and Shelley." [29]

In Rossetti's 1870 volume, Swinburne found "nothing trivial, nothing illicit, nothing unworthy the workmanship of a masterhand." *The House of Life* he described as entirely "fit for the fellowship of men's feelings; if men indeed [had] in them enough of noble fervour and loving delicacy, enough of truth and warmth in the blood and breadth of their souls, enough of brain and heart for such fellow-feeling." "The Honeysuckle" and "The Woodspurge" seemed to him "not songs, but studies of spirit and thought, concrete and perfect"; "The Burden of Nineveh" was "essentially Christian" in its "pure thought and high meditation"; and "The Portrait" was all "moral weight and beauty." But no reader in any way dissatisfied with Rossetti's subject matter could have felt the eulogy at all reassuring; for none could forget that the same Swinburne who now vouched for his friend's truth, humanity, and moral strength had himself appeared, not long since, as the author of shameless obscenities, the *enfant terrible* of Victorian verse, properly denounced by John Morley as "the libidinous laureate of a pack of satyrs." His very enthusiasms were, therefore, suspect; his praise was no recommendation. Few among his enemies were surprised that Buchanan a year later included both poets in "The Fleshly School," though a good many may have wondered why he, rather than Rossetti, had not been made the principal object of attack.

Eventually most critics came to accept *The House of Life* as fit for human fellowship. But Swinburne himself could not have expected all of his own first *Poems and Ballads* (1866) to awaken a like "fellow-feeling"; for their throbbing rhythms sang blatantly of savage desire and lurid passion, of beauty "called human in hell," of "the fire-shod feet of lust," of foaming lips and bloody fangs, of "kisses that bruise" and a thousand other "barren delights" quite alien to the average man's experience and rather too fierce for his vicarious enjoyment. Though often shot through with weird moral allegory, verses so erotic appeared to suggest a poetic ideal which sought to dispense with all ethical sanction. To some readers they seemed, in short, the earliest English expression of a deliberate art for art's sake. To others, who insisted upon a more personal interpretation, they stood as tokens of a diseased sensibility all in love with violent death; they were the first fruits of the sinister tree later known as "Decadence."

Both readings, freely confused, have persisted into the twentieth century until Swinburne, like Rossetti, has been commonly linked to the schools of Wilde and all the "aesthetic" perversities of the Victorian *fin de siècle*. Even if his style in its fluent energy finds no parallel in the preciously disciplined vignettes to which the Aesthetes were devoted, his themes remain sufficient evidence of a "decadent" will to deny all established social and moral values. Picturing Swinburne as a serious disciple of the Marquis de Sade, Signor Mario Praz detects a thorough abnormality not only in various unpublished blasphemies written for the amusement of Lord Houghton, but throughout the 1866 *Poems and Ballads*. The entire series, we are told, is "completely dominated by the figure of the bloodthirsty, implacable idol," the *femme fatale,* "a type drawn from the poet's own intimate sensual nature." And "Dolores" in itself is "a complete example of sadistic profanation." [30] Such criticism, however, demands that the dreadful verses be approached with a greater sobriety than they will endure. It is difficult to believe that Swinburne, with his keen self-awareness and lively sense of humor, could seriously have worshiped a goddess to whom he would chant:

> Could you hurt me, sweet lips, though I hurt you?
>> Men touch them, and change in a trice
> The lilies and langours of virtue
>> For the raptures and roses of vice. . . .

> Time turns the old days to derision,
>> Our loves into corpses and wives;

And marriage and death and division
  Make barren our lives. . . .

Thou wert fair in the fearless old fashion,
  And thy limbs are as melodies yet,
And move to the music of passion
  With lithe and lascivious regret.
What ailed us, O gods, to desert you
  For creeds that refuse and restrain?
Come down and redeem us from virtue
  Our Lady of Pain.

Whatever the "sensual nature" that may have imagined them, the seductions of "Dolores" seem wholly factitious and no abiding menace to our sanity. The fact that *Poems and Ballads* escaped the fate of *Les Fleurs du Mal* should itself indicate that Baudelaire's exploration of evil went far beyond a verbal lust into the very heart of man's primal guilt. T. S. Eliot remarks that, had Swinburne "known anything about Vice or Sin, he would not have had so much fun out of it." [31] And Swinburne himself, long before the "decadence," whimsically sensed his own limitation:

> *Some singers indulging in curses,*
>   *Though sinful, have splendidly sinned;*
> *But my would-be maleficent verses*
>   *Are nothing but wind.*[32]

Ruskin admired the fleshly "Faustine," defended *Atalanta in Calydon* as "the grandest thing ever done by a youth," and claimed that he would no more think of advising the author of *Poems and Ballads* than "of venturing to do it for Turner if he were alive again." [33] In even the least conventional of the verses, he saw an amazing command of language, perhaps somewhat analogous to his own, and an abundant energy awaiting only some positive direction. Swinburne, as Ruskin full well realized, had self-consciously flouted an orthodox moral code, but he had done so not to repudiate the "morality of art" and not merely to conquer for beauty new worlds of subject matter. He had created dramatic situations, in part to outrage the Philistines and pharisees who distrusted all unseemly youthful exuberance, and in part also to register his own early disillusion with "romantic" love and his first dispiriting shock at finding the powers of darkness everywhere enthroned in the citadels of respectability. But already by the time of Buchanan's attack, he had moved beyond mere negation towards a vigorous assent out of which might come some new intellectual synthesis.

Published in the year of "The Fleshly School," his *Songs before Sunrise* were far too didactic in their political bias, or at least far too assertive of a revolutionary ardor, to be mistaken for the work of an artist concerned exclusively with pure "amoral" form and careless of an "unaesthetic," struggling society. Inspired alike by the passionate republicanism of Landor and Hugo and the selfless vision of Mazzini, Swinburne straightway became the major poet of the "Party of Humanity," welcomed at last by Morley and his associates of the *Fortnightly* as a noble voice evermore reminding England "of her ancient call, . . . of her dark and perilous state now, and of her glorious destiny in the future." [34] If his will to believe had once seemed thoroughly frustrated by the godless advance of science, he now looked resolutely to Darwinian evolution as "a spiritual necessity," the essential basis for a philosophy which could reconcile him to the higher purposes of man. And his new-found faith in a primordial life-force, whatever its limitations as a substitute for the old religion, preserved him in his maturity from the despair that was slowly driving lesser poets into a remote aesthetic retreat.

Convinced by the seventies that the artist must find a significant subject matter if he were to fulfill his ultimate social function, Swinburne repudiated much of his early verse as substantially thin. Though his concern for craftsmanship persisted, he came more and more, as he grew older, to demand of poetry a "twin-born music of coequal thought and word";[35] for the content of his own first volumes had not, he felt, been invariably commensurate to his own powers of expression. With considerable objectivity, he recognized his command of a technique which could only too readily be invoked to disguise a want of theme; and through skillful self-parody he exposed the recurrent mannerism of his fluent style.

In his personal relationships as in his criticism, he made increasingly clear his hostility to a self-sufficient art for art's sake. With Simeon Solomon, who had proclaimed the artist a law unto himself, he lost all sympathy, as soon as the painter's perverse appetites became "sins against society." In the "aesthetic" professions of Oscar Wilde he showed no interest; and in sunflowers he took no intense delight. He attacked Whistler's *Ten O'Clock* (1885) for its refusal to admit the role of the intellect in art. And he looked with disdain upon the "amoral" devotees of Baudelaire, a poet with whom — he confessed some thirty-odd years after his "Ave atque Vale" (1868) — he "never really had much in common." [36] All great poetry, he said on various occasions, required some animating moral idea;[37] and even Keats in the last analysis seemed, he felt, less than wholly adequate, insofar as he was "the most exclusively aesthetic and the most absolutely non-moral of all serious writers on record." [38]

Much of Swinburne's later conservatism has been ascribed, rather vaguely, to the influence of Theodore Watts-Dunton, under whose jealous protection he passed the last three decades of his life. Yet his revolt from Victorian values was well spent long before 1879 when he reached haven in Putney. And his guardian never thereafter had any real power to alter his judgments or to bridle his vituperative verse and prose. Into his jingoistic propaganda the poet carried not a little of his old republican ardor; in tone, at least, the reactionary remained the radical. If he never achieved a theology as positive as his dogmatic imperialism, he seemed ultimately, of his own accord, at one with the high Victorians in his declared wish to live as if there were in life some moral or religious purpose.[39] And it was less remarkable than it might seem that the erstwhile hater of kings should hymn the Golden Jubilee of "a blameless queen," quite as dutifully as Tennyson and scarcely more poetically.

"The Fleshly School" disposed of William Morris as a "glibly imitative" rhymester, playing a facile Guildenstern to Swinburne's "transcendently superficial" Rosencrantz. Yet to not a few readers of 1870 it was Morris rather than Swinburne, or even Rossetti, who seemed the most representative of the new poets. *The Earthly Paradise* (1868–1870), with its heroic narrative sealed frame within frame, each at successive removes from reality, was fixing his reputation as a deliberate "escapist" [40] — by his own confession, "the idle singer of an empty day," a craftsman content to forsake the "heavy trouble" of nineteenth-century England for the adventure of a speciously medieval dreamworld, half-Norse, half-Greek.

The temper of his verse, however, had been clear as early as 1858 when he published *The Defence of Guenevere,* a volume more deeply "decadent" in its own quiet way than any work of the young Swinburne. Here in solidly objective ballads Morris had sketched the drift of ghosts through a nightmare of passion, the movement of creatures helplessly predestined, reasonless, without conscience, wholly untouched by ethical conflict. Here where raw sense experience eluded moral question and character subserved only a calculated pattern of shapes and shadows, here far more than in *The House of Life,* Buchanan might have found "form for its own sake" and the soul demonstrably less than the body. In both *The Defence* and *The Earthly Paradise,* Walter Pater saw the elements of an "aesthetic poetry" designed as art's protest against nature; for the poems carried him beyond life to a land lit by "the sorcerer's moon, large and feverish," where the coloring was "intricate and delirious, as of 'scarlet lilies,'" and "the influence of summer [was] like a poison in one's blood, with a sudden bewildered sickening of life and all things." [41] It was hardly strange, then, that Wilde, who cherished the flowers of artifice, should give Morris an ampler place than any other Victorian poet, except Oscar Wilde, in the aesthetic "Garden of Eros."

But whatever the tendencies of his own verse, Morris himself stoutly resisted the "art for art's sake" movement as its principles became more and more articulate. In the year of Ruskin's attack on Whistler, he publicly acknowledged his debt to *The Stones of Venice* and, with a quite Ruskinian vigor, denounced the art or the artist that sought a retreat from human concerns. "I believe," he declared, "that art has such sympathy with cheerful freedom, open-heartedness and reality, so much she sickens under selfishness and luxury, that she will not live thus isolated and exclusive. I will go further than this and say that on such terms I do not wish her to live. I protest that it would be a shame to an honest artist to enjoy what he had huddled up to himself of such art, as it would be for a rich man to sit and eat dainty food amongst starving soldiers in a beleaguered fort." Before he turned altogether to his socialist crusade, he made it clear that art henceforth could have no significance apart from its broader relations. "I cannot forget," he told a Birmingham assembly, "that, in my mind, it is not possible to dissociate art from morality, politics, and religion." [42] Thus, if his Guenevere had borne small resemblance to the heroine of Tennyson's *Idylls,* his ultimate philosophy of the beautiful, as it involved the true and the good, echoed not distantly the lesson of "The Palace of Art."

As a practicing poet, however, Morris remained unable to treat of the themes he felt essential to the existence of serious verse; he failed to discover for himself the means by which poetry might assert its social relations without lapsing into propagandistic doggerel. Broadly speaking, his "Fears for Art" betrayed his fear *of* art, his distrust of a technique by which he might again create a paradise of heroic fictions remote from the imminent class struggle. A superb craftsman in all the decorative arts, he lacked the imaginative intensity required of the poet who is to make of his verse a "criticism of life" rather than a pleasing ornament. Accordingly, though he saw the salient defect of his rhymes, he could advance to no greater poetic attainment. Unlike Rossetti or Swinburne, he had to rest content with the imputation that his best verse provided only a pure "aesthetic" escape from all Victorian realities. Until the end he felt himself, as artist, always the "dreamer of dreams, born out of [his] due time," sustained by his vision of some earthly future when society would have resolved its conflicts and the poet with no uneasy conscience would be free to pursue the quiet delights of his craft.

Walter Pater withheld his 1868 review of William Morris from the second edition of *Appreciations,* lest it suggest a more extravagant devotion to "aesthetic poetry" than he as a mature critic cared to admit. Nevertheless, though he might at last seem reluctant to commit himself to any single-hearted enthusiasm — might appear, in fact, quite as unwilling as Gray to "speak out" — many of the Aesthetes looked to Pater as their major prophet and apologist.

Whatever the "moral" subtleties of his later writings, Pater's first and most influential book, *Studies in the History of the Renaissance* (1873), seemed clearly to foreshadow the ideals of Wildean aestheticism. His "Leonardo" depicted the Florentine master as a morbidly self-conscious craftsman wasting "many days in curious tricks of design, seeming to lose himself in the spinning of intricate devices of line and colour." His "Winckelmann" commended the sensuous forms of a pagan beauty, exultant in an overt "fleshliness" of which Buchanan could never have approved. And his notorious "Conclusion" defended "the poetic passion, the desire of beauty, the love of art for art's sake" as the abiding source of earthly wisdom. Here, then, was sufficient sanction for the first premises of the Aesthetic Movement.

Yet Pater's "aesthetic" sensibility lay deeper than any of his explicit judgments. It was inherent in the very texture of his prose, in his fastidious regard for sentence pattern and paragraph cadence, in his apparent delight in "form for its own sake." Fashioned with a keen awareness of Flaubert's achievement,[43] his style itself, quite apart from the ideas it conveyed, aspired towards the symmetry and grace of well-wrought sculpture. So static indeed seemed its self-contained completion that Max Beerbohm was annoyed to find Pater treating English "as a dead language" and bored by "that sedulous ritual wherewith he laid out every sentence as in a shroud — hanging, like a widower, long over its marmoreal beauty or ever he could lay it at length in his book, its sepulchre." [44] But the aesthetic young men of the eighties, who were fascinated by things deathly, saw in the still perfection only the final triumph of deliberate artifice.

John Ruskin, 1857

Drawing by Dante Gabriel Rossetti, 1865

Insofar as it may be read as a fragment of autobiography, "The Child in the House" (1878) suggests, perhaps more clearly than all his other sketches, Pater's temperamental affinities to the general mood of late Victorian aestheticism. As the abnormally sensitive child, Florian Deleal recognizes in himself "the rapid growth of a certain capacity of fascination by bright colour and choice form, . . . marking early the activity in him of a more than customary sensuousness, 'the lust of the eye,' as the Preacher says, which might lead him, one day, how far!" From so Proustian a response to the visible and the tangible springs his love of the concrete impression and his impatience with all theories and abstractions, for as he dwells upon the fullness of his sense experience, he comes "more and more to be unable to care for or think of soul but as in an actual body." Yet in his passion for the material form, he is reminded perpetually that the loveliness will pass as all things decay; thus "with this desire of physical beauty mingled itself early the fear of death — the fear of death intensified by the desire of beauty" — and also the artist's half-understood death-urge, his yearning for the absolute beyond time. Driven by some overpowering nostalgia, Florian will one day visit the morgue and the cemetery in search of the "waxen resistless faces" which have escaped the ecstasies and the "pain-fugues" of living. Meanwhile, he may approach religion "with a kind of mystical appetite for sacred things" and learn to love, "for their own sakes" — almost for art's sake — "church lights, holy days, all that belonged to the comely order of the sanctuary," until "its hieratic purity and simplicity" can become "the type of something he desired always to have about him in actual life."

Throughout the child's lingering reveries we may trace not uncertainly much of the overrefined delicacy, the aloofness, the introversion, the languor bordering on neurasthenia, that helped stigmatize Pater himself as the arch-aesthete. For these indeed were the personal characteristics which inspired W. H. Mallock's satiric portrait in *The New Republic* (1877), the sharpest crystallization of public opinion concerning the essayist of the *Renaissance*. Mr. Rose, to be sure, lacked the sense with which Pater could curb his sensibility; but he reflected the critic's apparent unconcern with social problems, his distaste for intellectual argument, and his obvious interest in the strange diseases of a declining culture; and he borrowed directly from the "Conclusion" — at least as it struck Mallock — an admiration for those artists who, "resolving to make their lives consistently perfect, . . . with a steady and set purpose follow art for the sake of art, beauty for the sake of beauty, love for the sake of love, life for the sake of life." [45]

Fearing such interpretation, Pater suppressed the "Conclusion" for fifteen years after its first appearance, convinced that "it might possibly mislead some of the young men into whose hands it might fall." For it was clear long before the eighties that not all readers would understand aright its counsels of perfection. Few could see only Browning's acceptance of "life in the living" in the dictum that "not the fruit of experience, but experience itself, is the end." And many an "aesthetic" youth might find sanction for his own "intensity" in the new golden rule of conduct: "To burn always with this hard, gemlike flame, to maintain this ecstasy, is success in life." Nor could the lover of beautiful things, weary of too much thought of thinking, miss the eloquent defense he might readily appropriate: "With this sense of the splendour of our experience and of its awful brevity, gathering all we are into one desperate effort to see and touch, we shall hardly have time to make theories about the things we see and touch."

But Pater himself, even in his sensitivity to shape and color and sound, had been from the outset guided by impulses which allowed him no complete sympathy with the Aesthetes and which eventually engendered in him a distrust, almost as deep as the later Swinburne's, of all the extremes of the "art for art's sake" doctrine. His very effort to retract the "Conclusion" betrayed the same sort of ethical awareness that had prompted Rossetti's reply to Buchanan, the same refusal to accept responsibility for a narrow and perhaps "subversive" philosophy of art. Any young man, he felt, who turned to the last paragraphs of the *Renaissance* for an easy rationalization of his "aesthetic" retreat had been grievously "misled." For, if "experience itself" was the end, there could be for him no full experience in a world of artifice beyond humanity. Great art "set the spirit free for a moment" by lifting it above self — not by admitting the individual to some esoteric enjoyment, but rather by carrying him to a vantage point from which he might see the essential pattern of all life, by bringing him, as it were, to "the focus where the greatest number of vital forces unite in their purest energy." All abundant living demanded a constant power of "discrimination" and a determined resistance to every "facile orthodoxy," to every dogma of philosophy or of art, that sought by formula to circumscribe man's vision. And the true "aesthetic" concentration required some permanent capacity for scientific detachment, or at least some will to suspend disbelief until the work of art had spoken on its own terms.

As critic, Pater was always far less isolated from the intellectual currents of his time than his style and subject matter might suggest. Receptive to new ideas as to new impressions, he resembled his own Sebastian van Storck who approached the renowned Spinoza with open mind, "meeting the young Jew's far-reaching thoughts halfway, to the confirmation of his own." He sought from the culture of the past intimations of "modernity" rather than aesthetic escape from the present.[46] In the Holland of Sebastian, for instance, he found "a short period of complete wellbeing, before troubles of another kind should set in," a clear enough parallel to the prosperity of high-Victorian England. And in the imperial Rome of Marius, overburdened with its civilization, threatened already with the coming of the barbarians, he saw not indistinctly a warning to the greatest of modern empires. Unlike the Aesthetes, he could regard no work of art as an object in itself, wholly cut off from the milieu that produced it. He was actually far less concerned with the description of the technical devices by which an aesthetic effect had been secured than with an analysis of the temperament of the artist and the climate of opinion which his art in subtle ways reflected. For every book or picture was to him a means of communication; and its ultimate human value lay in its power to widen man's moral sensibilities, to yield "a quickened and multiplied consciousness."

Distinguishing carefully between good art and great art,[47] he asked of the latter "something of the soul of humanity," since the highest creative energy had always, he believed, been devoted "to the increase of men's happiness, to the redemption of the oppressed, or the enlargement of our sympathies with each other, or to such presentment of new or old truth about ourselves and our relation to the world as may ennoble us and fortify us in our sojourn here, or immediately, as with Dante, to the glory of God." Greatness in art, as he conceived it, could, therefore, be attained only by a great personality, by an Epicurean of the higher kind, having no commerce with the amoral hedonism of the Aesthete, capable rather of seeing life in all its relations as a harmonious whole. The enduring poet, to be sure, achieved a firm and finished style, but style in itself could not ensure his survival. Rossetti, who developed a highly original technique, who learned to speak with a curious new-old accent, was "redeemed" from his own artifice "by a serious purpose, by that sincerity of his, which allies itself readily to a serious beauty, a sort of grandeur of literary workmanship, to a great style." [48] In the "sordid" or the brutal,[49] the "realistic" for its own sake, Pater had no interest; it was art's single function to heighten reality, to elevate, to provide, without direct didactic intent, some final guide to conduct. His aesthetic was thus in final emphasis ethical; from the idealities of art, the sensitive soul could demand and receive moral inspiration and also perhaps the religious insight, towards which Marius aspired, into a world where truth and goodness and beauty were one.

By 1882 it was clear to Buchanan that the "fleshly poets," especially Swinburne and Morris, had grown "saner, purer, and more truly impassioned in the cause of humanity," and that the late Mr. Rossetti had, after all, been quite moral in his intentions and had "never, at any rate, fed upon the poisonous honey of French art." [50] Not all writers of that year, however, seemed so earnest in their social conviction or so innocent of imported delights. For by 1882 Buchanan recognized the dominance of an "aesthetic" credo, more "dangerous to society" and less "English" in origin than any Pre-Raphaelite faith. And with his usual ability to adapt his talents to the needs of the day, he produced a novel, *The Martyrdom of Madeline,* designed as a very palpable hit at "Gautier and his school of pseudo-aesthetics, and their possible pupils in this country."

Pater, who admired the arts of France, could scarcely share Buchanan's hysteria. Yet he must have sensed within himself something of the same desire for synthesis that had made Rossetti and Swinburne distrustful of a thoroughgoing art for art's sake comparable to Gautier's and had repeatedly brought them back, sometimes almost reluctantly, to the "moral aesthetic" of Ruskin. In nineteenth-century French literature, more surely perhaps than in English, he could discern the plight of modern man unable to assimilate or interpret the new knowledge crowding in upon the consciousness, and so more and more completely lost in a universe of unfamiliar fact and half-understood conjecture. Though he sought a certain ethical integration of his own thought and sense experience, he perceived everywhere in the culture of his age the strongest inducement towards a nonmoral view of life and a narrowly specialized concept of art. At a time when the natural scientist was proclaiming his devotion to empirical discovery for its own sake and his right to dismiss moral concern as irrelevant to his research and spiritual sanction as unknowable, the artist might all too readily find in the physical world, the world of predestined matter, not the source of a Swinburnean optimism, but a mere blank denial of the human values which a less "scientific" generation had deemed essential to art. So disillusioned, he might, said Pater, quite understandably turn in upon himself, where "in the narrow cell of its own subjective experience, the action of a powerful nature would be intense, but exclusive and peculiar." Under such circumstances, "the vocation of the artist, of the student of life or books, would be realized with something — say! of fanaticism, as an end in itself, unrelated, unassociated," and his work would be inevitably distorted, "exaggerated, in matter or form, or both, as in Hugo or Baudelaire." For the health and balance of great art necessarily demanded of the artist what Pater, reverting to the language of the high Victorians, came to call "that sense of large proportion in things, that all-embracing prospect of life as a whole." [51]

X

The Revolt from Reason

They who tamper with veracity, from whatever motive, are tampering with the vital force of human progress. . . . We have to fight and do life-long battle against the forces of darkness, and anything that turns the edge of reason fatally blunts the surest and most potent of our weapons.

— JOHN MORLEY

It is far easier to laugh or weep than to think; to give either a ludicrous or sentimental turn to a great principle of morals or religion than to enter into its real meaning.

— T. H. GREEN

Let us have no more reflection, is the cry of the weary brain; let us gratify sense. . . . We have had enough of reading, writing, and thinking. Let us eat, drink, and be merry, for tomorrow we calculate again; tomorrow comes black care; tomorrow comes inky thought; tomorrow we are the slaves of awful wisdom.

— E. S. DALLAS

IN the spring of 1869 Tennyson assisted James Knowles, the journalist and architect, in the founding of a Metaphysical Society for the free discussion of the old faith and its relations to the new science.[1] Whether or not, as one less reverent member suggested, he desired to "consult the experts" about the possibility of his having "such a thing as a soul," [2] the Laureate most certainly wished to discover the means by which the intellectual leaders of his time were seeking to reconcile "advanced knowledge" with the spiritual purposes of man. And a like impulse clearly inspired many of the Metaphysicians of diverse creeds who met throughout the seventies for monthly debate. Among the orthodox, or at least the theologically minded, Manning the Romanist, Hutton the Anglican, and James Martineau the impassioned Unitarian strove most conscientiously to meet with respect the "great argument" of science. Ranged against them, Huxley the "agnostic," Clifford the "free-thinker," Tyndall with his awe of nature, Harrison with his Religion of Humanity[3] — all, for their part, confessed to the need of some moral code, an ethic to be rescued from the immoralities of ancient dogma. Few, however, achieved the compromise of Gladstone, who remained both conservative and radical; for few could match his strange "impartiality," [4] his talent for "being furiously in earnest on both sides of a question." Each member followed the logic of a differing mind with dutiful attention, only to return, perplexed but unshaken, to his own first premises of fact or faith. Tennyson had been convinced that "modern science ought at all events to have taught men to separate light from heat." Yet the light of a completely disinterested philosophy seldom illuminated the meetings. And the Society died, after ten years of heated eloquence — perhaps, as Huxley said, "of too much love," but more probably, as the poet suspected, of its failure to define the term "metaphysics." [5]

Defending "the scientific method" at a select Metaphysical symposium, or on a public lecture platform, or in the columns of the great liberal reviews, the Victorian "rationalist" had behind him the known and the knowable, the tangible evidence of the laboratory, the apparent and immediate drama of empirical research. Confident that he had found the key to all things relevant to human life, he could enter controversy with a buoyant assurance denied to those who asked some sanction beyond sense experience. His optimism knew no bounds; to the free intelligence the full truth would at last be fully revealed. Harrison, therefore, could dismiss Christianity with its "pessimism as to the essential dignity of man" as a "degrading superstition," for which he might substitute his own "rational" dogmas.[6] Morley could assail Carlyle's unreasoned emotion, to demand in its stead, as the prime need of his generation, "intellectual alertness, faith in the reasoning faculty, accessibility to new ideas."[7] And Huxley could rebuke all forms of "clericalism" as the chief impediment to free inquiry, "the deadly enemy of science" and so of all that was demonstrably true. Indeed, to his debate with Bishop Wilberforce in 1860, he had brought a moral earnestness which made the clergyman's effort to "smash Darwin" seem frivolous and vain, if not utterly depraved. He would rather, he had told the crowded Oxford Meeting, have a poor ape for an ancestor than a creature of human intellect who would deliberately employ a great gift of persuasion "to discredit and crush humble seekers after truth."[8]

If ever the theist were intent upon obscuring inescapable fact, the agnostic might thus rise in righteous scorn, convinced that he alone understood the objects of a true religion. Having destroyed false creeds and systems, "freethought" would somehow, according to Karl Pearson, be in a position to accomplish its most solemn service, "the relief of spiritual misery," albeit the misery induced by the collapse of myth and ritual.[9] For the only effectual advocates of any reform of benefit to man, wrote Harriet Martineau, "are people who follow truth wherever it leads."[10] And truth, as she conceived it, led inevitably away from the theology of her brother James into the Positivist world of Auguste Comte — a bracing but rather bleak world where she could be stringently moral, though she might at times worry a little when she "thought of the pain which her new belief in personal annihilation would carry to the heart of some friends of hers who were widows."[11] Huxley, to be sure, by the time of his *Evolution and Ethics* (1893), would come to question the possibility of grounding any ethic on the discoveries of natural science, even as he would deplore the false analogies that the Spencerians had drawn between biological and social evolution. Yet the more consistent "rationalists" of the sixties and seventies, like Professor Ptthmllnsprts in *The Water Babies,* had no doubt that they could fully describe man in "scientific" terms as a mere fact of nature, and so quite dispel his every illusion of divinity.

However low must have been his opinion of the sanguine Professor, Kingsley, "though (I trust) a Christian and a clergyman," retained the highest respect for John Stuart Mill, who was, in effect, to all Victorian liberals, the fearless apostle of pure reason. The essay *On Liberty* (1859), Kingsley felt, had made him "a clearer-headed, braver-minded man on the spot." For the erudition and intellectual integrity of its author was at once apparent, even to one who thought his view of life unfortunately circumscribed. "When I look at his cold, clear-cut face," said Kingsley, "I think there is a whole hell beneath him, of which he knows nothing, and so there may be a whole heaven above him." [12] Carlyle, whose intuitions of heaven and hell alienated him from the premises of Utilitarian rationalism, declared at the time of Mill's death in 1873 that he had never known "a finer, tenderer, more sensitive or modest soul among the sons of men." [13] Yet it was almost necessary, in the logic of events, that the young Mill should accidentally have burned in manuscript the first volume of *The French Revolution.* For Mill, more than any other Victorian thinker, was to undermine the prestige of Carlylean doctrine and lessen the authority of every other transcendental metaphysic — was, as Morley remarked, to "cut at the very root of the theological spirit." [14]

Distrustful of all overstatement, eager to qualify each proposition with the fullest possible evidence of provable fact, Mill approached psychology and ethics with the empirical bias of the laboratory scientist and with a like will to weigh and measure results in a mood of cool disinterest. His conclusions, however, were less "scientific" than he supposed. He found it difficult to discover, by the inductive method, fixed "laws" for the social sciences, comparable to the laws which governed the physical universe. He could never, even to his own satisfaction, reconcile his notion of an "unconditional sequence" of cause and effect in human affairs with his instinctive recoil from a complete determinism, his assumption of an individual free will. And he failed to account by any simple induction for the qualitative element in his moral theory. Moreover, he was guided from the first by a quite "unscientific" faith in natural goodness and a trust in the basic rationality of man, which made him quite unable to grasp the anti-intellectual implications of the new biology. But his shortcomings and errors as a systematic philosopher detracted not at all from the candor of his judgment, the force of his attacks on bigotry and prejudice, or the strength of his plea for the liberated intellect. His deepest influence arose less from an originality or coherence of thought than from a courage of outlook, an open-mindedness, an earnest optimism, and a selfless passion for social justice.

More clearly than Mill, who had been his great inspiration, John Morley recognized in the Darwinian theory a possible threat to the "voluntary activity" of man and indeed, in the increased specialization of all the physical sciences, "dangers of a new kind" to humane culture.[15] Nonetheless, he sought to propagate the "scientific attitude" with a zeal far more ardent than the stoic reserve of his master could admit. So militant was his "rationalism," yet so aflame with ethical emotion, that he seemed to Harrison a queer amalgam of Diderot and John Wesley.[16] The "agnostic" at all costs, he regretted that Mill had shown some final sympathy — in his three posthumously published *Essays on Religion* (1874) — with the "anti-naturalistic" premises of Christian doctrine and so, to some extent, with "a new and mischievous reaction towards supernaturalism."[17] In his own reverence for "free-thought," Morley could allow no concession to the willful "unreason" of the theist; for the temper of orthodox belief must necessarily, he felt, be hostile to the spirit of disinterested research. He was, therefore, unremitting in his assault on the "ecclesiastical" mind. His essay *On Compromise* (1874) stressed with firmer assurance than Mill's *Liberty* the peril of suppressing "new ideas," ideas which might, if reasonably considered, prove vital to the progress of society. And his energies as editor of the *Fortnightly* were dedicated wholly to the cause of intellectual "liberalism." All through the seventies he brought to the review's pages the signed contributions of "advanced thinkers" like Huxley, Clifford, and Tyndall, of Radicals like Henry Fawcett and Goldwin Smith, of Positivists like Harrison and Professor Beesly and Albert Crompton. Cosmopolitan in its range, though somewhat complacent in its iconoclasm, the *Fortnightly* challenged with vigor and brilliance all forms of authority which might seek to coerce the individual will. Yet it assumed too readily that the most pernicious tyrannies must arise from an established religion, reluctant to accept the miracles of science, rather than from a growing industrial system, "scientifically" indifferent to all human values. On his retirement from the editorship in 1882, Morley explained with pride that "the clergy no longer [had] the pulpit to themselves, for the new Reviews [had become] more powerful pulpits where heretics were at least as welcome as orthodox." [18] But at the same time he was driven in all honesty to ask whether the public interest in eradicating religious error had, after all, been anything more than "an elegant dabbling in infidelity." [19]

Morley himself had never preached unbelief for the mere joy of shocking the Philistine; nor had his associates decimated any active creed without serious compunction. Leslie Stephen spoke for them all in "An Agnostic's Apology" (1876), the most coherent defense of their intellectual doubt. A wide acquaintance with formal philosophy could, he argued, engender only a thorough skepticism, since every philosopher seemed intent upon flatly contradicting "the first principles of his predecessors." And a knowledge of all the natural sciences justified no certainty whatsoever about "the ultimate origin or end of our paths." The pantheist looked upon the universe "with love"; the pessimist, "with dread unqualified by love"; but the agnostic, said Stephen, found it "impossible to regard it with any but a colourless emotion." [20] Yet such neutrality had its distinct advantage; it permitted the skeptic to examine ideas with the cold objectivity that the biologist brought to a dissection. Now at last, Morley felt, men of reason could deal with beliefs from which they dissented, in the true spirit of "patient and disinterested controversy." [21]

Actually, however, few among the *Fortnightly* liberals succeeded in sustaining any real dispassion. The cause of reform, to which they were all committed, demanded in fact some standard of judgment, some criterion of right and wrong, beyond the necessary indifference of the scientist. Stephen, at any rate, could never for long remain impassive; for between man's hope and the law of nature he saw a cruel disparity, the awareness of which meant a painful disillusion. "There is," he wrote, "a deep sadness in the world. Turn and twist the thought as you may, there is no escape. . . . We are a company of ignorant beings, feeling our way through mists and darkness, learning only by incessantly-repeated blunders, obtaining a glimmering of truth by falling into every conceivable error, dimly discerning light enough for our daily needs." [22] Thus the "colourless emotion" of the agnostic might easily shade off into the gray despair of the pessimist. Yet none of the liberals, however grim his insight, lost his fundamental buoyancy of outlook. Instead, each contradicted his "rationalism" by a faith — highly irrational on his own agnostic premises — in the "sanctity" of human nature, a faith borrowed directly, though almost involuntarily, from the Christian theology he had rejected. It was, therefore, hardly remarkable that Professor Romanes, who recognized the contradiction, at last returned to orthodoxy, after first struggling in vain to show that the pure agnostic could believe Christianity false in fact but true in substance and, as a rule of conduct, pragmatically valid.[23]

Untroubled by the origins of his ethic, Tyndall declared an enlightened materialism the only adequate philosophy and proceeded to applaud "the immortal victories which science has won for the human race," in complete confidence that "the inexorable advance of man's understanding in the path of knowledge" would eventually lay bare the very heart of nature.[24] Challenging his position, James Martineau objected that, since the atom itself is a compound "which raises as many questions as it answers," it was "the strangest of illusions" to suppose "that by pulverizing the world into its least particles, and contemplating its components where they are next to nothing, we shall hit upon something ultimate beyond which there is no problem." [25] The Positivists, however, could dismiss the objection by denying that man need be concerned with any "ultimate" at all, once he had progressed from theology to metaphysics to the third — the "positive" or "scientific" — stage of his development.

In the gospel according to Comte, a mature society, one that had abandoned every futile attempt to discover final essences, would content itself with the knowledge which best served the immediate, practical demands of its life and growth. It was the business of the Positivist to ascertain by the empirical method the basic facts relevant to social action and from such facts to determine the "laws" by which all data might be related and interpreted. In practice, to be sure, many of the researchers, vaguely "positivist" in spirit, became so immersed in minute detail that they lost all power of analyzing larger problems and patterns; far too often the dogma of "scientific" dispassion led them to value only external phenomena and so to discount all subjective reality, until they came to regard history as a mere chronicle of events, rather than as the biography of ideas, the story of evolving thought.[26] Harrison, however, the most loyal of the Comtists, consistently sought some vital synthesis: "To collect facts about the past," he wrote, "and to leave the social application of this information for any one or no one to give it a philosophic meaning, is merely to encumber the future with useless rubbish." [27]

Comte himself had shown no reluctance to systematize his thought or to codify the laws which would procure discipline and order in the Positivist state. He had, in fact, freely announced his will to found a school "like Aristotle or Saint Paul, and one that will probably be more important than those two joined together." [28] And if rigid categories, inflexible imperatives, and arbitrary creeds had been enough to guarantee his school's supremacy, he would most certainly have succeeded in his design. Yet it was precisely his authoritarianism that limited his prestige and influence in England. Morley was straightway repelled by his demand for government by a small aristocracy of the intellect and his corresponding failure to consider the rights of the individual thinker. And Bagehot saw at once that even Comte would have been "hanged by his own hierarchy." [29] Though the Victorian agnostics might endorse his rejection of the supernatural, few could follow the logic by which he moved from a simple desire to work for the welfare of the race to a deification of Humanity itself as the Great Being or Goddess, a sacred entity incarnating all that was highest in man's experience. Huxley described the Religion of Humanity as "Catholicism *minus* Christianity," an attempt to rear an elaborate structure of ritual and dogma without real belief in any fundamental spiritual essence.[30] And Morley felt the new faith but further evidence that Comtism in its extreme was "hard, frigid, repulsive, and untrue." [31] Eventually even the Positivists grew restive under the constraints which their creed imposed upon them. In 1878 the Victorian converts quarreled among themselves concerning the claim of Comte's successor, Pierre Laffitte, to the leadership of the international Positivist Society. Then, after acrid debate, the more rebellious seceded to form an independent group under Richard Congreve, while the faithful, greatly weakened in power, remained to fulfill the decrees of Laffitte as transmitted through a Committee of Seven led by Frederic Harrison.[32]

"Human nature," said Harrison, "revolts against the blank of atheism, and turns away fainting from the thought of extinction." [33] Yet since his Oxford days when he had repudiated the stern Evangelical code of his boyhood, Harrison had been unable to accept any variety of theism or to discover in the natural world — which was to him the only real world — any basis for a faith in immortality. If his religion henceforth were to satisfy his free intelligence, it must, he felt, "rest on scientific proof";[34] and if it were to answer the cry of his deep moral emotion, it must furnish an ideal more certain than any that the "agnostic" scientist could postulate. Comte's "Positive Synthesis" alone seemed to meet both requirements; it professed reverence for the "scientific" method and at the same time lingered to worship "the vast and gradual evolution of human civilisation" [35] which that method, apparently, had made possible. Besides, while it could promise no survival of the individual soul, it could remind man of the lasting contribution he might make to the life of the race.

In the Religion of Humanity, therefore, Harrison saw the one means of preserving his "rationalism" and of appeasing his hunger for ethical guidance. Accordingly, to the propagation of its creed he devoted the best energies of an active brain and a rather literal imagination. In 1881 he established a school for "free," "systematic," "religious" instruction at Newton Hall in Fetter Lane,[36] where Coleridge long before had delivered his twelve lectures on Shakespeare. There, with the help of his friends, he installed appropriate fittings and decorations; "a large copy of the Sistine Madonna and busts of the great men of all ages from Moses to Bichat, whose names are in the New Calendar," adorned the walls; in the center of the floor stood the Positivist library of the two hundred and seventy volumes selected by Comte himself; and at the end of the room were an organ and a grand piano, once owned by Charles Darwin. To the hall came the converts for "Congregational worship," for the observance of the Positivist "Sacraments," or for such musical edification as a cantata based on "the great poem of 'The Dead' by George Eliot" might provide. From day to day the classes for adult education reasserted "the sense of man's dependence on the human Providence which surrounds him from the cradle to the grave"; in teaching mathematics, for instance, the Positivist lecturer, ever conscious of his religious mission, dwelt solemnly on the names of Archimedes and Pythagoras, the first-fathers of immortal principles. On special occasions, such as the anniversary of Comte's death, the leaders arranged "pilgrimages" to the homes or tombs of great men, inventors, scientists, authors, statesmen — "rational" pilgrimages, quite without "medieval folly," designed to pay due tribute to the blessed saints of humanity. To Harrison, every project or ceremony at Newton Hall was thoroughly reasonable in origin and intent, an integral part of the "Positive scheme" which sought to comprehend all human effort in a universal "religion of duty — duty as revealed by science and as idealized by the reverent soul." But to the Christian and agnostic alike, in fact to all who doubted that science could achieve any revelation whatsoever of ethical import, the faith of the Comtist seemed falsely conceived and absurdly developed; if Harrison believed his religion the highest expression of humanistic "rationalism," then the

Frontispiece to Laurence Oliphant's *Piccadilly*

"A Fairy Prince"
Drawing by Charles Conder

critique of pure reason, so far as they could see, had clearly become, by its own specious logic, the anatomy of sheer nonsense.

R. H. Hutton considered the Positivist aspiration an effort "to reconcile in man the sceptical mind and the believing heart," to combine "all the meditative ecstasy of those who wished to live in God, with the cold conviction of the student of mere phenomena that there was no God to live in." Yet the "reconciliation," if such indeed it were, had, he felt, been achieved only by the outright surrender of intellect to emotion; for "the attempt to love a *Grand Etre*, or even a *Déesse*, in the existence of which the mind does not believe, must always be a futile one, which only men of more fancy than realism, or some lesion of the brain, will be able to accomplish." To the Christian theist it seemed obvious that Comte, in his eagerness to acquire for the Religion of Humanity the consolations of the old faith, had involved himself in "all sorts of moral contradictions." In effect, Positivism had done far more to compromise the common sense which was ostensibly the basis of its creed than to destroy the theology it had discarded. At any rate, its illogicalities served only to strengthen a growing suspicion that it was the man of "science," rather than the man of faith, who had betrayed reason.[37]

With skillful dialectic, Hutton set out to expose not only the fallacies of Comtism, but the errors of every "rationalistic" attack on a supernatural metaphysic. The materialists, he argued, lacked "the verification of fact";[38] they failed to account for the breaks in their system of cause and effect or to explain the relations they assumed between the physiological and the mental; and they insisted upon the dogma of determinism, even though the free will was "a fact of experience, verified each day." Tyndall, in particular, seemed inconsistent and somewhat disingenuous in his willingness to speak "poetically" of a soul, or free moral ego, in which he could not actually believe;[39] for the concept of the soul was, to Hutton, far from an arbitrary matter, "either a most dangerous fiction or the greatest of truths." Even Mill, when he turned at last to religion, had apparently lost himself in a "purely verbal" reasoning, denied by his own tentative intuitions.[40] And Matthew Arnold, seeking to disentangle the moral from the theological content of the Bible, had virtually sacrificed his "integrity of mind"; for it was "playing fast-and-loose with language in the most ridiculous manner, to regard the long series of passionate appeals to God by his faithfulness and his mercy and his truth as mere efforts of poetry, while all the words describing the moral conceptions of man [were] interpreted with scientific strictness." [41]

Hutton himself had little sympathy with a literal or fundamentalist religion; yet he was reluctant to see faith reduced to a "Positive" knowledge or a humanistic moralism. Dissatisfied alike with the Evangelicals and the "rationalists," he was inevitably attracted to the thought of Newman, whose *Grammar of Assent* (1870) had been designed to show that "reasonable" belief need not wait upon scientific evidences. [42] Faith, as Newman understood it, was to be achieved only by the whole man — by his "illative sense," the reasoning faculty on all its levels, subconscious as well as conscious, guided by the "right state of heart," acting, as it were, "under the weight of the whole personality." Hutton, who accepted Newman's premises, could value the *Grammar* as "a long plea for cautious and deliberate yet courageous reasoning on all the various converging lines of consideration which bear on the Christian revelation." [43] Yet the skeptic, less able than Newman or Hutton to attain the "right state of heart," may well have regretted that the essay's clear and logical argument proceeded for the most part quite without concern for the main currents of contemporary thought, which seemed to be washing away the foundations of all real certitude.

On the death of Maurice in 1872, Kingsley predicted that his "master's" writings, long neglected, would seem "not only precious but luminous" to some remote generation prepared to abandon Victorian "nominalism" for a philosophy which would recognize "that substance does not mean matter, that a person is not the net result of his circumstances, and that the real is not the visible Actual, but the invisible Ideal." [44] Yet he need hardly have dipped so far into the future to discern the requisite philosophy. Had he known more of current academic opinion, he might have seen a new idealism already on its way. For two years earlier, H. H. Asquith, on coming up to Oxford, had found a growing "idealistic revolt, or reaction" slowly undermining the once almost undisputed influence of Mill.[45] And by the end of the seventies Leslie Stephen felt called upon to defend his agnostic stand against "this idealism of a newer fashion." [46]

Since the romantic period, English poets and essayists had drawn as they would upon the metaphysical stores of Germany. Yet professional philosophers, working freely within the comprehensive framework of a native empiricism, had remained largely indifferent to the schools of Kant and Hegel. Not until the natural scientists, by their own "empirical" methods, seemed to be imposing upon them a purely mechanistic view of the universe were Victorian thinkers inclined to examine with serious intent the categories of the systematic Germans. It may well have been J. H. Stirling's *Secret of Hegel* that actually first awakened a considerable interest in Continental idealism. At any rate, within the decade following the book's publication in 1865, Hegelian theory had made its distinct impress upon the speculations of such scholars as T. H. Green, F. H. Bradley, and the brothers Caird. All of these men assailed the premises of Mill's Utilitarian doctrine. All attacked not science itself but "the philosophy which claimed that science was the only kind of knowledge that ever existed or ever could exist." [47] And all sought to reassert the permanency of human values on a higher plane than scientific analysis could reach.

Green, especially, insisted upon a spiritual metaphysic which might challenge every assumption of the materialist. For man, he believed, was essentially a spiritual being, able to relate and to organize the data of sensation, able to direct and control his appetites and impulses, able to move towards a greater realization of that concept of absolute good which was the very heart of his moral self. And the end of life seemed to Green neither the pursuit of pleasure nor the worship of humanity; it was nothing less than the struggle for the perfection of the whole spirit in a coöperative society, a society dedicated to the purposes of the eternal intelligence that held all evolving nature in unity and order.

While the "rationalists," bent upon the analysis of matter, had tended to discount mind, the British idealists concentrated attention upon the mental process which constituted the dynamic world of forms behind all the appearances of fact. Like Hegel, they saw the life of the mind as the one reality, and the Absolute Idea, which was pure mind or spirit, as the highest determination achieved by the self-creating and self-subsistent God.[48] Centered as it was upon spiritual essence, their metaphysic could be turned, more readily than any other Victorian philosophy, to religious or moral account. In his *Ethical Studies* of 1876, Bradley, therefore, repudiated the naturalistic creeds of his major contemporaries with a logic somewhat more assertive than Hutton's but no less urbane and ironic. Pleasure, as the Benthamites imagined it, was, he decided, a mere abstraction and the sum of pleasures only a fiction, since the sum could never be complete as long as life lasted. Mill, however, who began by accepting pleasure as the single good, soon found his instincts telling him that he must live for others, and so concluded that the pleasure of others must be the object of living. But this, said Bradley, "is not a good theoretical deduction; . . . it is the generation of the Utilitarian monster, and of that we must say that its heart is in the right place but the brain is wanting." Yet the progeny of Positivism seemed scarcely more reasonable; for "humanity" in the abstract was but "the name of an imaginary collection," and even if "humanity" were an entity possessed of "a real self-sameness," it could not — being one finite phenomenon — serve as the object of a satisfactory religion. Nor did Arnold's theology, with its talk of a "power not ourselves that makes for righteousness," appear to Bradley other than vague and evasive. "We must not," he wrote, "be ashamed to say that we fail to understand what any one of these phrases mean and suspect ourselves once more to be on the scent of clap-trap." [49]

For the idealist, faith meant more than such nebulous emotion; it required "both the belief in the reality of an object, and the will that

that object be real." By faith the true self became "one with the divine," died unto the private will, found ultimate fulfillment in an immediate perception of the Absolute. And to faith man brought his whole being; for neither thought nor feeling nor volition could alone apprehend the reality that embraced in final harmony all the diverse aspects of the total experience.

By questioning the principles of Mill and Comte and rejecting the "poetic" religion of Arnold, the idealists were actually giving the support of a formal philosophy to some of the first tenets of an orthodox supernaturalism. Kingsley or Hutton or Newman himself might have discovered in the *Ethical Studies,* for instance, a hostility to secular creeds and a definition of faith not far removed from his own. But when Bradley turned from the attack on "rationalism" to a closer articulation of his basic premises, he was forced to enter realms of epistemology into which only the trained philosopher, familiar with the specialized language of his profession, could venture to follow him. His later work, particularly the *Appearance and Reality* of 1893, developed the concept of "mind as process" in terms which effectively destroyed the lingering notion of "mind as substance" and so prepared the path for the realists and pragmatists of the twentieth century.[50] Yet by the end of the Victorian era, philosophy, like the new theoretical physics, was no longer the property of the common man. Not entirely without dispassion could Harrison complain that truth was being obscured rather than revealed by the "Neo-Hegelian fumes" of British idealism.[51] For, in order to resolve in a new synthesis the manifold contradictions of modern thought, Green and Bradley and their followers had of necessity to sacrifice the gift of popular speech that Harrison and Morley, Huxley and Stephen had held in full measure. Though they struggled to assert an ethic for democracy, their influence was confined largely to the academic circles whence it had arisen. The average late Victorian, at all events, scarcely suspected that he might find in them a reaffirmation of the values from which an earlier Victorian culture had derived its strength.

If comparatively few young men of the seventies were touched by the new idealism, a good many nonetheless sensed the inadequacy of a "scientific rationalism," and a number, disillusioned and bewildered, openly ridiculed all the moralities formulated in the name of reason. Undoubtedly the nimblest of the younger wits, W. H. Mallock, for example, saw in parody and burlesque-romance the perfect medium for exposing the fallacies of intellectual "liberalism" without for the moment committing himself to any less absurd belief. Published in 1877, his most successful satire, *The New Republic,* was a symposium in the manner of Peacock, loosely fashioned to bring together under transparent disguises the intellectual leaders of the day — such diverse figures as Arnold, Jowett, Tyndall, Huxley, Clifford, Pater, each of whom in the course of the garrulous house party might voice his own earnest credo and in so doing inadvertently betray the folly of his conviction.[52]

Though rather less brilliant in execution, Mallock's *New Paul and Virginia; or, Positivism on an Island,* which appeared in the following year, was both more coherent in structure and more specific in its attack.[53] Professor Paul Darnley, its hero, is the distinguished Positivist who takes "nothing on trust, except the unspeakable sublimity of the human race and its august terrestrial destinies." Aboard the *Australasian,* he delivers his lay sermon discounting all theological superstitions and showing "how, viewed by modern science, all existence is a chain, with a gas at one end and no one knows what at the other; and how Humanity is a link somewhere." When the ship sinks by conforming to "the laws of matter," the Professor is left to convert to "the new Gospel" — now rather considerably limited in its application — a somewhat unwilling raft companion, the beauteous Virginia St. John, an orthodox Anglo-Catholic en route to visit her fiancé who is Bishop of the South Pacific diocese of the Chasuble Islands. Washed ashore with ample provisions, Paul and Virginia are joined ere long by an old woman, who is manifestly immoral because she is unhappy, and a curate, who, rapidly won over to Positivism, yields to certain animal impulses but prefers to call his lower nature his higher "for the sake of the associations." The sudden deaths of these intruders clearly subserve "the greatest happiness of the greatest number," and the Professor can console the lady with the thought that their removal "is part of the eternal not-ourselves that makes for righteousness — righteousness, which is, as we all know, but another name for happiness." When Virginia seems to find truer consolation in a salvaged box of sweets, Paul reminds her, "The owner of those chocolate-creams is immortal because you are eating them"; or so says "the religion of Humanity." But Virginia is to be convinced only when the Professor substitutes the language of the lover for the idiom of Harrison and Mill. Then at last together, like the owl and the pussycat, they may sing a duet by the light of the moon. Yet their chant succeeds only in attracting Mrs. Darnley and the Bishop, who have been diligently seeking their lost mates; and the embrace of the latter revives Virginia's old faith, while the sight of the former reconverts Paul to a belief in hell. For in the last analysis, Positivism can withstand neither the onslaught of passion nor the test of grim experience.

Intended to supplement his satires, Mallock's serious writings clearly indicate the mental attitude that underlay his hostility to all the "liberal" Victorian thinkers. At Oxford he had been, as he tells us, antagonized by every shade of "free thought";[54] yet he never advanced to the transcendental metaphysic of Green, which might well have provided the interplay of intellect and emotion that his spirit seemed to require. Instead, he turned virtually against the intelligence itself; what he at first conceived to be a revolt from middle-class standards soon became a completely blind reaction to the whole progress of modern knowledge. Socially, aesthetically, politically, he sought escape into a feudal past remote from the din of democracy. Thus though he saw the "absurdities" of pseudo-Gothic architecture, he praised the Gothic revival as an admirable effort to retreat from "the wintry actualities of today." [55] Even in furniture his taste was, he confessed, less artistic than political, for the kind of chair that best pleased him was "one that had been made and used before the first Reform Bill." [56] He lived all for lordly hospitality and antique manners; and he longed to inspect the old Hungarian castles when once he heard that Hungary was "the least progressive" of European countries. In a villa at Cannes among the tall cypresses and the yellow mimosa trees, he completed his expository attack on Positivism entitled *Is Life Worth Living?* (1879); and the life he described, naturally, bore no relation to the realities of industrial England. Having delighted as a schoolboy in caricaturing his "Radical" tutor, he was well prepared for the great revelation when it descended upon him. Wandering at Beaulieu "among the sleeping flowers by the light of Mediterranean moons," he was haunted by the need for a "scientific Conservatism;" [57] and thereafter the cause of reaction commanded his full resources. He wrote several "Conservative" novels which were, in effect, their own parodies. He acted as leading pamphleteer for the Liberty and Property Defence League, to safeguard the material wealth of a dwindling aristocracy. And he entered a long war against socialism in which he was eventually forced into unequal combat with the redoubtable Bernard Shaw. At the peak of his career, his lecturing carried him to New York where Mrs. Astor's "delicate presence," he said, "seemed to turn life into a picture on an old French fan," and to Cambridge where the charming professors at Harvard "had not only the accent, but also the intonation of Englishmen." [58] But whatever their final value, his activities preserved him forever from the disillusion that had inspired his best satires. For even at the end of his life, when he could no longer propagandize the virtue of reaction, he could still find an antidote to despair in the gossip of polite society or, despite the real threat of personal want, lose himself once more in the long and complex annals of the rich.

Mallock's contempt for the aspirations of the Philistines and his respect for the leisured graces of the *beau monde* were shared by the "dandies" of the Decadence, the heroes of the Wildean drama, who were less concerned than he with a "scientific Conservatism." Yet his general distrust of the free intelligence was common to a rather large group of late Victorians who felt no comparable interest in the social amenities. If the revolt from liberal thought awakened in him a nostalgia for the outward forms of a lost culture, it led others to "react" on less material planes. It helped perhaps create an audience for the anti-intellectual philosophy of Schopenhauer, at last becoming available in English translation. It was probably one of the factors driving a poet like Coventry Patmore to deny the claims of analytic science, to reject alike the microscope and telescope and beg instead

> *A mind not much to pry*
> *Beyond our royal-fair estate*
> *Betwixt these deserts blank of small and great.*[59]

And it surely encouraged a widespread quest for spiritualistic revelation, which made possible the vogue of Madame Blavatsky and the founding of the somewhat more respectable Society for Psychical Research.

The most remarkable of those who responded to the call of the occult was probably Laurence Oliphant,[60] whose satiric novel, *Piccadilly,*[61] written more than a decade before *The New Republic,* began by attacking the same fashionable society in which Mallock was to find his final refuge. Born in Capetown, Oliphant had moved freely among the great and near-great in the cosmopolitan circles of the diplomatic service. He had acted under Lord Elgin as Superintendent-General for Indian Affairs in Canada, where he had at leisure led the gayest balls of Quebec. He had been appointed, on the recommendation of Lord John Russell, as First Secretary of the Legation in Japan, and there, amid other excitements, had fought off with his hunting crop a great samurai wielding a two-edged sword. He had even entertained the volatile Prince Edward on a holiday trip down the Adriatic coast. Then suddenly, after his election in 1865 as M.P. for Stirling, he had startled his friends with his one considerable literary effort, a fierce caricature of the Vanity Fair that had so richly rewarded his nonchalance and wit.

A narrative in diary form, *Piccadilly* moves forward with the pungency of a Voltairean conte and the didacticism of *Rasselas.* Lord Frank Vanecourt, the half-mad diarist who clearly represents the author, takes what he calls a "tragic-burlesque" rather than a "serio-comic" view of life as he assails all the hypocrisies of a world Christian in name only, a world disposed to countenance both the shady speculations of Spiffy Goldtip and the spiritual compromises of Lady Broadhem, the prime example of the "worldly holy." To Lord Frank the intrigue of politics, the moral emptiness of science, the calculated duplicity of trade, and the meaningless façade of urbane manners, all seem but tokens of an imminent disintegration: "We shall fall to pieces," he remarks, "all of a sudden like old Lady Pimlico; and the wrinkles will appear before long in the national cheeks in spite of the rouge." The one escape from disaster lies, he concludes, in a determined will to "live the life," to attain the selfless charity that springs from "a divine conviction of truth imparted to the intellect through the heart, and which becomes as absolute to the internal conscience as one's existence, and as impossible of proof." Accordingly, he abandons the world that has assured his wealth and distinction and sails off with a mysterious stranger to "live the life" in an unknown America. And within the logic of the novel his act of desertion may well seem the necessary product of his rebellion.

Yet it was hardly to be assumed that Oliphant himself would feel obliged to follow literally the paths of Lord Frank. On the completion of *Piccadilly,* however, he renounced both his political career and his social position and, with quite fanatical resolve, set out to join the Brotherhood of Thomas Lake Harris in upstate New York. There, under the spell of a despotic prophet-charlatan, he endured the blissful agony of humiliation and by slow degrees mastered the rites of a perverse sexual mysticism. Then, after his inevitable break with Harris, he carried the faith to his own colony at Palestinian Haifa, whence he issued in his last years unintelligible treatises on the occult, properly considered by the worldly holies a dreadful menace to the morals of British youth.

In its eccentric detail, Oliphant's rejection of Victorian values, was, of course, far less typical than individual. But in its broader outlines, his revolt from rationalism and ultimately from reason itself was no more a distortion of a fairly representative attitude than we might expect from a determined caricaturist. If less quixotic than he and altogether saner in preserving some sense of perspective, many others throughout the seventies felt a not dissimilar impatience with contemporary thought and a like desire to escape the barren certainties of analytic science. Gerard Manley Hopkins, for instance, was finding in Catholic orthodoxy an anchor for the overpowering intensity of his emotion; yet it is perhaps significant that within the Church he was to draw less satisfaction from the intellectual synthesis of Aquinas than from the doctrine of Duns Scotus with its accent upon the unreasoning will. James Thomson, on the other hand, alienated forever from an Evangelical creed, was moving from the stringent atheism of his friend Bradlaugh to the cosmic pessimism of Leopardi, which would gloom to a darkness visible his "City of Dreadful Night" (1874). Not a few of less subtle sensibilities clung desperately to the pagan worship of physical vitality that had formed the substance of Thomson's "Sunday up the River" (1869). Popular novelists like "Ouida" provided a welcome retreat from the restive intellect by exploiting mere sensation utterly untrammeled by moral purpose; and adventurers like Richard Burton, in a series of fantastic travelogues, helped give vicarious appeasement to a longing for muscular assertion. Meanwhile, following the conspicuous precedent of the Prince of Wales — who had never been noticeably disturbed by religious or scientific controversy — the leaders of fashion were turning more and more sedulously to the pursuit of pleasure. And their hedonism, distinctly personal in direction, had little in common with Mill's search for the greatest happiness of the greatest number.

In all the arts, for better or for worse, a private impressionism, often almost as esoteric in its symbols as Oliphant's religion, began to eclipse the social concern of the high Victorians. Morley, who could hail the new "aesthetic interest" as a healthy protest against the faith of the Philistines, also saw that no specialized interest operating in isolation could further the ends of a "liberal" culture.[62] The Victorian age, he warned, would profit little by "forsaking the clerical idyll of one school, for the reactionary medievalism or paganism, intrinsically meaningless and issueless, of another." For the Aesthetes were in truth far less responsive to the argument of "rationalism" than the orthodox who feared its encroachment. And it was ultimately clear to Morley and his friends that each subjective credo which animated with its own gem-like flame the "art for art's sake" movement had arisen directly from the artist's conscious indifference to the force of general ideas.

The "Aesthetic" Eighties

What is eternal? What escapes decay?
A certain, faultless, matchless, deathless line
Curving consummate. . . .
— ARTHUR O'SHAUGHNESSY

WHILE the *Fortnightly* apologists for the "scientific method" had sought to give each new tree of knowledge its vital place in the broad landscape of ideas, the scientists themselves strove merely to cultivate their own high-walled gardens. Increasingly devoted to exclusive researches, they concentrated their energies upon specific and detailed analyses until they had become learned but narrow specialists, more and more remote from the larger issues of late Victorian culture. In 1886 Tennyson, who had once felt each material advance a token of spiritual growth, tempered the optimism, if not the rhetoric, of his first "Locksley Hall"; his imagination no longer fired by the wonders of the laboratory, he had come to see

Half the marvels of my morning, triumphs over time and space,
Staled by frequence, shrunk by usage into commonest commonplace!

And there was indeed much of the commonplace in the mechanized world of fact that preoccupied all the new "specialists" working not only in the sciences but in trade and industry, in education, even in art — working with much efficiency and little enthusiasm, weary of debate, unconcerned for the most part with first principles or general truths. If the seventies had been enlivened by bold speculation, spirited controversy, and earnest pursuit of conflicting ideals, the following decade sank into that interlude of comparative quiescence which Professor Whitehead has called "one of the dullest phases of thought since the time of the First Crusade," a respite from intellection designed only to celebrate "the triumph of the professional man." [1] Though the "dullness" was undoubtedly offset by the emergence of many a fresh and colorful personality, the eighties as a whole made no considerable effort to achieve the synthesis of "mind and soul," the complete cultural integration, towards which the major mid-Victorians had aspired. Instead, art, politics, and sociology yielded alike to "specialized" interests; the artist retreated from society, and the social worker no more asked either aesthetic or religious support for his activities.

In 1881, about a year before Oscar Wilde reached San Francisco, Henry George, traveling in the opposite direction, arrived in London to propagate the gospel of the Single Tax. No less a "specialist" in his own field than the Aesthete in his, the economist commanded attention not by a wide range of reference but by a clarity of analysis and a firm coherence of argument. More distinctly than most Englishmen, he demanded an economic approach to the economic issues of progress and poverty. Ruskin, to be sure, had long since declared "the force of mechanism and the fury of avaricious commerce" so irresistible that he must withdraw from the study of art and give himself wholly as "in a besieged city, to seek the best modes of getting bread and water for its multitudes, there remaining no question . . . of other than such grave business for the time." [2] Yet Ruskin throughout his social crusade had continued to guide himself by the same idealities to which creative minds had given artistic form; for great art remained to him the highest expression of the full life in the good society, and the artist indeed the true legislator of mankind. But Henry George and all the new reformers who drew inspiration from George's creed, or at any rate from his method, considered legislation a less imaginative, a more scientific process.[3] They learned to regard social questions as technical problems requiring technical solutions. And they strove to convince, not by passionate appeals to conscience, but by careful documentation and incontestable statistics.

Many young men of the eighties who might in less agnostic times have become fervent evangelists were attracted to the cause of social democracy. Yet nearly all preferred definite recommendations to sweeping moral indictments or Ruskinian anathemas. Even General Booth, directing the campaign of his newly organized Salvation Army, the heir to a long and popular tradition of Dissent, found it necessary to buttress his exhortation with the mortar of hard fact; and his detailed survey of darkest London, replete with percentages and tabulations, moved not a few, for whom faith was impossible, to a kind of secular charity or to immediate and practical measures which might assure at least some shadow of hope. Like George, most of the social thinkers were content to accept the inevitability of gradualness as they strove patiently to advance the proposals they had adopted. Whereas the European Marxists worked deductively in the light of a romantic idealism which had glimpsed the perfect state, the scholarly Fabians followed the inductive method of slow but certain change to a future of unknown possibilities. Over the years the British "socialists," operating on various intellectual levels, succeeded in subtly reshaping for the better a large part of the nation's industrial economy. Yet their "radical" thought, most effective when most specific, could barely touch the free creative imagination of the late Victorian artist. From their strenuous exertions arose little more of even passing literary value than several novels like Walter Besant's *All Sorts and Conditions of Men* (1882) and Bernard Shaw's *Unsocial Socialist* (1883), fictions sometimes charged with lively intellectual suggestion, but generally less than half realized in terms of character and drama. Edward Carpenter's *Toward Democracy* (1883), the most ambitious of the "socialist" poems, intended as a Whitmanesque paean to the liberal virtues, devolved only into a prosy defiance of the bourgeois respectabilities. And the numerous propagandistic verses of William Morris seldom attained even in metrics the competent facility of his less deliberate dream sagas. If Henry George was in a sense the Godwin of the period, his ordered program most certainly awakened no Shelleyan ecstasy.

As the major English novelist to begin publishing in the eighties, George Gissing understood both the purposes of the new socialism and the conditions that made necessary its work.[4] Introducing him to miseries almost subhuman, his own bitter experience had left him little sympathy with the existing economic system. In despair he had turned at one time to Comte's Religion of Humanity and, when befriended by Frederic Harrison, had even become for a while an active member of the Positivist Society. Yet his aesthetic impulses had been from the beginning at war with his social conscience. And as the acquisition of a coveted book had seemed in his most indigent days more needful to his survival than the purchase of a dinner, he came before long to feel the demands of his craft more urgent than the dissemination of any social doctrine.

It was natural then that an unresolved conflict between the artist and the reformer, or the artist and a milieu that defied reformation, should furnish the principal theme of his many volumes. In *Workers in the Dawn* (1880), for instance, Helen Norman the heroine learns from Tennyson's "Palace of Art" the emptiness of "intellectual delights" and finds in Comtism the means by which her short unhappy life may reach some measure of fulfillment; but Arthur Golding the hero, a painter unable to record the ugliness that has obscured his vision of beauty, suffers complete frustration in a grim world from which a melodramatic suicide affords the sole escape. Contributing directly to his downfall, Arthur's union with a besotted slattern, one of the many marriages in Gissing surely made in hell, serves as symbol of the tragic disparity between the artist's ideal and the sordid reality to which he is fettered.

Workers in the Dawn is, of course, in large part autobiographical, and, broadly speaking, its hero's struggle is his creator's. Similarly, in *The Unclassed* (1884), the progress of Waymark the novelist towards the scientific detachment of "art for art's sake" reflects Gissing's own effort to convince himself that "only as artistic material has human life any significance," while his final unwilling recognition of man's social responsibilities indicates the force that defeated Gissing's every attempt at a pure "aesthetic" objectivity. And in *New Grub Street* (1891), Reardon's fierce battle to maintain a literary standard has likewise its immediate personal parallel. None of the novels approaches in disinterest the clinical naturalism of *A Mummer's Wife* by George Moore, published in 1885 as a conscious tribute to the theory and practice of Zola.[5] For Gissing, always less independent than Moore of the backgrounds he was describing, could neither restrain his compassion nor withhold moral judgment. Far from doing so, he identified himself with his doomed protagonists, sensitive souls warped by circumstance, rejected by a commercial society, but finding no imaginative stimulus in a doctrinaire radicalism, prone to endless self-pity, yet forever faithful in their fashion to an incomplete aesthetic ideal.

Gissing's dread of poverty and his revulsion from the evils that were its logical consequence made impossible a sympathetic or even wholly dispassionate portrayal of urban life on its lowest levels. Yet his desire for the economic security he felt essential to the artist in no way mollified his indictment of the prosperous Philistines with their shoddy substitutes for culture. His aversion to the complacent middle class prompted such satire as his caricature of Samuel Barmby, the successful bourgeois of *In the Year of Jubilee* (1894), who, having read about *In Memoriam,* called it "one of the books that have made me what I am." Mr. Barmby's mind, we are told, "was packed with the oddest jumble of incongruities; Herbert Spencer jostled with Charles Bradlaugh, Matthew Arnold with Samuel Smiles; in one breath he lauded George Eliot, in the next he was enthusiastic over a novel by Mrs. Henry Wood." For Mr. Barmby was a typical product of the new education, not quite illiterate, but zealously ignorant of any intellectual, moral, or aesthetic criterion apart from hearsay or popular prejudice.

Such readers (the bulk, it seemed, of the new reading public), while professing a love of literature, were prepared to destroy the writer who placed any strain whatsoever upon the indolent intellect or the sluggish imagination. Though ardent devotees of fiction, they had little use for the novel of ideas or the novel, commended by the philosopher Green, that strove to assert in an age of specialists the claims of "mankind at large . . . as against the influence of class and position." [6] They were, in short, Gissing felt, inimical to all serious art and openly hostile to the Reardons, the Waymarks, the Goldings, the Gissings — to all concerned with the artist's integrity and his truth to nature. And they were encouraged in their hostility by a new journalism designed for their special consumption, shaped to satisfy the ill-formed tastes of their own social "class and position." [7] Jasper Milvain of *New Grub Street* was franker perhaps, but no more ruthless, than his living prototypes, in announcing his will to follow a journalistic career dedicated to the proposition that "to please the vulgar, you must, in one way or another, incarnate the genius of vulgarity." The popular *Chit-Chat,* encouraged by Jasper, a digest which reduced thought to anecdote and news to gossip, scarcely matched in vogue the actual *Tid-Bits* of George Newnes. And Jasper's ultimate success as publicist but dimly foreshadowed the far more spectacular triumph of Alfred Harmsworth. Yet it illustrated with sufficient clarity the unaesthetic power of the new Philistines.

In the mid-eighties, Lord Houghton on his deathbed apologized for his conduct; "I am going over to the majority," he said, "and, you know, I have always preferred the minority." [8] Yet even without his inestimable support, the aristocratic minority of his choice, itself economically moribund, continued to resist, often as stoutly as did the socialists in their very different way, all the "cultural" values of an aggressive Philistinism. If they held themselves aloof from Gissing and other artists beyond the pale, they gave at least a nonchalant assent to the protest of the Aesthetes against middle-class standards. And the Prince of Wales, though hardly a connoisseur of painting, was glad to officiate at the opening of the "aesthetic" Grosvenor Gallery in 1877, just as Albert in a rather more democratic frame of mind had presided over the Great Exhibition a generation earlier. Under the Prince's gentle leadership, high society, at the very moment of the aging Queen's greatest popularity, had entered, one might have supposed, upon a new "Regency" period.

The wit, the charm, the easy grace of the later Georgians, which had hidden away throughout the early and mid-Victorian years in tightly closed circles, emerged at last from long concealment to become the most conspicuous inheritance of Arnold's "Barbarians." When Mallock defended wealth on the ground that the sight of its enjoyment must rouse the ambitions of the poor,[9] he was actually attempting to rationalize the life of an aristocracy which, whatever its limitations, managed to preserve something of a tradition dear to his irresponsible heart. It was the literary stylist in him, rather than merely the cynic or the snob, that responded to the urbane malice of the great ladies[10] who gave balls for the express purpose of not inviting their best-loved enemies, or found delight in the terse epigrams lightly tossed into the expectant air by titled gentlemen whose only vocation was to remain eligible bachelors. He may well have seen in the verbal brilliance of the Duchess of Montrose, for example, a perfection of tone and attitude denied forever to the Philistine, the same sort of ultimate perfection that Proust, observing to better advantage, embodied in his portrait of Madame de Guermantes. For among such people, freed for a season from the cares of a mercantile professionalism, there lingered, if not a creative art, surely a true abundance of artistic materials. At any rate, from their world before it had quite passed over to the majority, Oscar Wilde and his "aesthetic" friends drew an idiom, a gesture, and a pose.

The half-conscious attempt of the aristocrat to recapture the mannered graces of a forgotten eighteenth century bore no direct relation to the efforts of Leslie Stephen, George Saintsbury, and others to achieve a critical revaluation of British thought from Locke to Hume, or to rescue from ill-deserved neglect the vigorous literature of the great Augustans. Yet it was not without its influence on the surfaces of late Victorian culture. It helped lead architects like Richard Norman Shaw from a grotesque neo-Gothic to a shapely neo-Georgian style,[11] which would eventually restore to the English country house a long-absent elegance of proportion. And it encouraged the fashionable designers of furniture and ornament — and so also their more popular imitators — to sacrifice the heaviness of mid-Victorian baroque for the lighter curve of a French rococo or even on occasion the chaste line of a "classical" mode. In effect, the revival of eighteenth-century *décor* represented an anti-Philistine reaction from the disorderly excesses of middle-class taste. And as such, it had its literary counterpart in the work of several minor poets who saw in belles-lettres from the age of Pope the ideals of aesthetic restraint, economy, and decorum that the Spasmodic School had once willfully rejected.

As the accredited master of the new *vers de société,* Austin Dobson was frankly nostalgic for the reign of good Queen Anne, when men could still

> *afford to turn a phrase,*
> *Or trim a straggling theme aright.*

Yet he sought a more obvious rigidity of form than he himself could attain within the subtle confines of the Popian couplet. He learned well the advice of Gautier, whose poetic credo he excellently translated:

> *Leave to the tiro's hand*
> *The limp and shapeless style;*
> *See that thy form demand*
> *The labor of the file.*[12]

But to an organic form, a form dictated by content, he preferred an artificial pattern so exacting that it would necessarily reduce a subject to its own dimensions. He, therefore, drew not upon the example of Gautier and the major Parnassians but upon the conventions explained by Théodore de Banville, a secondary poet who had led in the rediscovery of the "Old French" forms. So inspired, Dobson submitted with a cheerful patience and perhaps even a mild irony to the discipline of the ballade, the rondeau, the triolet, and the villanelle, intricate measures in which he moved with an apparent ease, sometimes equaled though seldom surpassed by his fellow-craftsmen, the whimsical Lang and the exuberant Henley. From such arabesques of rhyme, the reader could expect little more than a semi-serious defense of the forms themselves, a delicate evocation of a leisurely past, a quiet regret that loveliness must die, a sprightly description of a Japanese print or a Nankin plate, or a gay memory of the long intriguing afternoons when the Pompadour flirted an animated fan. But Henley, who admired the precision and objectivity of Dobson's technique, found the thinness of subject matter no cause for complaint. "In writing of this sort," he said, "there is a certain artistic good breeding whose like is not common in these days." [13] And for that in itself he was deeply grateful.

If Dobson was artistically too "well-bred" to indulge in the personal eccentricity of the Aesthetes, his verses nonetheless betrayed a quite "aesthetic" devotion to technique. Compact and highly polished, each rondeau or ballade was designed as an exquisite miniature, complete, self-contained, existing only for its own imagery and sound, its own delicate *décor*. Like the formalistic pieces that Henley called *Bric-à-brac,* almost all Dobson's poems escaped unseemly emotion and the pressures of social or ethical conflict. The products of a "specialized" craftsmanship, they represented an unobtrusive yet distinct contribution to the "art for art's sake" movement of the eighties.

Long before the coming of the Aesthetes, however, Victorian poets far more considerable than Dobson had sensed the attraction of a "pure" art independent of all moral concerns. Tennyson, half the century earlier, hearing the debate of the two voices, had, as we have seen, hearkened more than a little after the counsel of the tempter who promised the artist release from the burden of humanity. Arnold as a young man had had to resist the "aesthetic sensibility" that tortured his own Empedocles. And Rossetti until the end had feared the power of a fleshly beauty, threatening to overwhelm the wholeness of the soul. Even Browning, though never so uncertain of his poetic faith, had been able to dramatize the "aesthetic" temperament — in his study, for instance, of the duke who treasured his last duchess simply as the source of a wondrous pictorial arrangement, or, again, in his portrait of the dying bishop whose whole life had been consecrated to the cherishing of beautiful impressions: the shadow upon the grained marble, the intonation of the mass apart from its meaning, and the all-possessing aroma of "good strong thick stupefying incense-smoke."

Yet all of these poets had sooner or later come to accept the broad essentials of the Victorian "morality of art." Each had found for his verse a criterion beyond mere formal perfection — a religious, philosophic, or cultural point of reference; and each had gained accordingly in range and strength, even if he was forced to sacrifice something of his special skill as poet to do so. Convinced like Ruskin that a noble art must presuppose a worthy audience, they could not but dismiss as shallow or insincere any aesthetic doctrine which denied the artist's responsibility for serious communication. It was inevitable then that the new Aesthetes, proclaiming "art for art's sake," should seem as ridiculous to them, perhaps even as mean-spirited, as Skimpole the arch-aesthete had seemed to the Dickens of *Bleak House*. But the censure of the surviving mid-Victorians like Tennyson, who hailed art for art as "truest lord of Hell," [14] rallied rather than rebuked the "aesthetic young men" of the eighties, who, unable to comprehend the sanctions of Ruskinian art theory, professed a gay defiance of every "ethical aesthetic."

Though Oscar Wilde on his first visit to America rightly disclaimed credit for founding a new school of poetry, he identified himself too readily with the Pre-Raphaelite group, from whom he actually derived little more than a taste for the archaic.[15] Few of the Aesthetes, in fact, owed much to the essential tone of Rossetti's work, which the religious verse of Richard Watson Dixon was reproducing with a quiet fidelity.[16] Compounded of many influences, their credo reflected both a love of the languorous *Rubáiyát* and a careful misreading of Pater's unguarded "Conclusion"; but, above all, it bore the stamp of their familiarity with French aestheticism.[17] From the Parnassians they drew not only the formal emphasis that had impressed Dobson, but also an attitude towards the whole artistic process and a sense of the artist's necessary remoteness from a bourgeois public. Buchanan, whom they roused to a Philistine fury, assailed Gautier, their most obvious source of inspiration, as "that hairdresser's dummy of a stylist, with his complexion of hectic pink and waxen white, his well-oiled wig, and his incommunicable scent of the barber's shop." [18] And his attack, though it betrayed no understanding at all of the real Gautier, suggested quite accurately the manner in which the English Aesthetes, precious, affected, well-barbered, were adapting their imported creed.

In France the doctrine of art for art's sake had served during the fifties and sixties as a liberal protest against the reactionary Second Empire. In late Victorian England, on the other hand, it gained currency for the most part as a reactionary escape from a tradition of "liberal" thought. In Paris a splendid generation of painters and poets had achieved — self-consciously, perhaps, but sincerely — the status of the "Bohemian," intent upon discovering the beautiful in worlds beyond and beneath the polite façades of a commercial society; by rejecting a conventional ethic, they had succeeded in extending the depth and breadth of their art. But in "aesthetic" London of the eighties there was only, as George Moore discovered to his great delight, "a Bohemianism of titles that went back to the Conquest." [19] For the Aesthetes, eager to transcend a middle-class culture and the intellectual conflicts to which it gave rise, sought their materials not in a broader, classless humanity, but rather within the narrow limits of an urbane aristocratic circle. Moore, who naughtily declared himself repelled by the name of Shakespeare as by "all other popular names," maintained with some conviction that art must remain "the direct antithesis to democracy." [20] And Wilde, though he later exercised his talent for paradox upon a brief defense of socialism, believed beauty inseparable from the elegance of caste and art the prerogative of privilege.

Dorian Gray — or so at least Wilde informs us — was eventually to know to the full "that terrible *taedium vitae,* that comes on those to whom life denies nothing." But before dipping wearily into actual "Decadence," he had been merely the perfect example of a very intense, a super-aesthetical, young man. And as such, he had cared, he claimed, more for "the artistic temperament" than for all the expensively beautiful things at his command, "old brocades, green bronzes, lacquer-work, carved ivories, exquisite surroundings, luxury, pomp." Yet the Aesthetes in general and the early Wilde in particular seemed to feel their admiration of lovely rarities in itself a sufficient mark of temperament, a sound guarantee that they had achieved the requisite sensibility. They, therefore, professed to cherish fantastic ornament and antique bric-a-brac, as less sensitive souls had once cherished illusory ideals. They worshiped the ultimate line of the Oriental print and the absolute grace of the peacock feather; and they saw in the pale lily, the radiant sunflower, the bleeding poppy, symbols of their salvation from middle-class vulgarities. So great, especially, was their taste for things Japanese — and so considerable the vogue which it inspired — that the resourceful men of Manchester found profit in manufacturing cheap replicas, until the yet cannier gentlemen of Japan, using the replicas as models, began to mass-produce still cheaper imitations.[21]

The Aesthetes, however, could scarcely afford to acknowledge the extent of their own influence or the diffusion of their enthusiasms. For they were committed on principle to a scorn of the commonplace and a defense of a calculated artistic eccentricity. They despised the unromantic Trollope, who had left behind an autobiography, published in 1883, shamelessly recording his regular habits and scheduled labors, his distrust of original genius, and his respect for the normal emotions of the common reader. The true aesthetic spirit, as they conceived it, rejected forever a pedestrian technique; it made no concession to a conventional morality; it maintained at all costs the indispensable artifice of art. And the single duty of the artist was not to communicate his vision but to express his individuality, to enshrine in splendidly factitious forms the product of a prolonged self-indulgence in aesthetic appetites beyond the imagination and the means of the Philistine.

More interested in "aestheticizing" about beautiful objects than in creating beauty itself, the Aesthetes rapidly fell into the affectations of the self-conscious appreciator. And their postures well deserved the amusing satires of George Du Maurier, his cartoons for *Punch* of the "intense" Maudle and the susceptible Mrs. Cimabue Brown.

Yet many of them like Moore "confessed" to attitudes more outrageous than any the caricaturist had lampooned. Living in constant fear of not being misunderstood, they welcomed ridicule which might emphasize their deviations from the norm of mediocrity. They were, therefore, gratified by the attention that Gilbert and Sullivan accorded them in *Patience* (1881).[22] They rejoiced to detect in Bunthorne's costume and deportment resemblances to Wilde and in the grouping of the twenty lovesick maidens some suggestion of Burne-Jones's "Triumph of Love." They admired the black Japanese gown of the arrogant Jane, lifted, as it was, fold by fold from a Whistlerian "harmony." And they delighted in the multiple references to their favorite haunts and pastimes — to the Grosvenor Gallery and the ladies' art school in South Kensington, to their love of blue china and frail flowers, to their not-too-French French gestures and their response to the English eighteenth century. From Gilbert, at least, they had to fear no real understanding, no sharp insight into the essentials of their creed.

If *Patience* exposed to Philistine laughter their obvious mannerisms, it left untouched the first principles of art for art's sake. In *The North Wall* (1885), an early prose-satire by John Davidson, the Aesthetes might perhaps have found a somewhat subtler attack on their basic faith. Eager to live the novel he is unable to write, Davidson's hero feels forced "to execute atrocities which, committed selfishly, would brand the criminal as an unnatural monster, but which, performed for art's sake, will redound everlastingly to the credit of the artist." But even if they had come by odd chance upon this burlesque, few among the intense young men would as yet have grasped the truth of its intimation that a consistently "amoral" art must lead at last to the inverted moralities of Decadence.

In 1870 Arthur O'Shaughnessy, the unimpassioned keeper of fish in the British Museum, startled his associates by publishing the passionate *Epic of Women and Other Poems*. Yet the average reader, who knew nothing of the poet, could hardly have thought the verses themselves remarkably startling in either form or content. Frankly derivative, O'Shaughnessy's early volumes all echoed the melodies of

Swinburne transposed with delicacy and tact into the new singer's own minor key. At its weakest, his song betrayed merely the over-copiousness or the too facile diction of much mid-Victorian poetry. At its best, it reaffirmed, in complete accord with the moral aesthetic, the role of the singer in society:

> *We are the music makers,*
>   *And we are the dreamers of dreams,*
> *Wandering by lone sea-breakers,*
>   *And sitting by desolate streams —*
> *World-losers and world-forsakers,*
>   *On whom the pale moon gleams —*
> *Yet we are the movers and shakers*
>   *Of the world forever, it seems.*

But by the end of the seventies, the poet, stricken with private griefs, had so far forgotten the power of the world-shaker as to accept the disillusion of the world-loser, clinging to his art as a final refuge from intellectual conflict. And his last poems, *Songs of a Worker,* which appeared shortly after his death in 1881, betrayed a surrender to the rising Aesthetic Movement rather than the sympathy with the new socialism which their title might conceivably have suggested.

Turning from life to art and drawing upon art for his materials, O'Shaughnessy had sought to recover a lost absolute; the pure aes-thetic form alone seemed eternal, alone able to give the cold reality a vital meaning:

> *I carve the marble of pure thought until the thought takes form,*
> *Until it gleams before my soul and makes the world grow warm.*

His "Thoughts in Marble" accordingly were designed as self-subsist-ent embodiments of beauty. "My artistic object," his preface tells us, "is gained if, in them, I have kept strictly within the lines assigned to the sculptor's art, an art in which I have as yet failed to perceive either morality or immorality. They are therefore essentially thoughts in marble, or poems of form, and it would therefore be unjustifiable to look in them for a sense which is not inherent in the purest Parian." Then, as if to contradict his own intention, he denied the complete adequacy of the amoral or asocial aesthetic. "I have been represented," he added, "as saying with Baudelaire, 'Art for Art,' and laying myself open to all the unfavourable limitations which that dictum is unjustly supposed to imply. Truly, I think that a little 'Art for Art' has already done a great deal of good in England, and that a little more is needed, and would be equally beneficial. But with Victor Hugo I do not say 'Art for Art,' but 'Art for humanity,' and my meaning is that Art is good — is an incalculable gain to man; but art, in itself equally perfect, which grows with humanity and can assist humanity in growing — is still better." The confusions of his theory, however, were of small account to the Aesthetes who could respect his search for a beauty that must never die and his solemn worship of the indestructible form,

> A certain, faultless, matchless, deathless line
> Curving consummate. . . .[23]

Though at the very center of the Aesthetic Movement, Wilde himself was scarcely clearer than O'Shaughnessy in his defense of art for art's sake. As lecturer, he confounded the precepts of Gautier with unconscious memories of the Ruskinian doctrine against which he was rebelling — for he could never wholly escape the culture he had determined to reject. Thus, while in America, he asserted the artist's independence of all social concerns and all other "truths of life," and at the same time maintained that art must draw upon the full resources of modern society if it were to accomplish its beautiful mission.[24] Even in his verse he seldom achieved the objectivity of the faultless line, the pure amorality of the consummate curve. To be sure, several of his vignettes, with French titles, seemed "aesthetically" conceived and executed. "Le Réveillon" captured in a few deft strokes as much of French impressionism as Whistler had been able to adapt to his own purposes:

> The sky is laced with fitful red;
> The circling mists and shadows flee;
> The dawn is rising from the sea,
> Like a white lady from her bed.

And the "Impression du Matin" added to a similar Whistlerian harmony the barest suggestion of Baudelaire's urban nightmare,[25] which the poet several years later was to develop with more striking effect in "The Harlot's House." But most of the pieces were far closer to a recognizable Victorian tradition. Many paid the tribute of direct appropriation to makers as familiar as Tennyson, Swinburne, Rossetti, and Mrs. Browning. And — far from being amoral — a few like "Hélas" even recalled the mawkish moral posturing of the rueful Spasmodics:

> *To drift with every passion till my soul*
> *Is a stringed lute on which all winds can play,*
> *Is it for this that I have given away*
> *Mine ancient wisdom and austere control?*

All in all, the poems — on the whole, the best verse that the Aesthetes could produce — represented not so much a triumph of "aesthetic" design as Oscar Wilde's own calculated effort to persuade himself, and, of course, his disciples, that he had found, in the world of the senses, the beautiful ideal — that

> *though the gorgèd asp of passion feed*
> *On my boy's heart, yet have I burst the bars,*
> *Stood face to face with Beauty, known indeed*
> *The Love which moves the Sun and all the stars!* [26]

Unimpressed by the poetic homage of "the amiable, irresponsible, esurient Oscar," Whistler deplored the flamboyant gestures with which the school of Wilde seemed to be vulgarizing the beautiful. And in his sprightly "Ten O'Clock," delivered at Princes Hall in 1885, he passed oblique commentary upon the whole Aesthetic Movement. "Alas!" he mourned, "alas! ladies and gentlemen, Art has been maligned. . . . She is a goddess of dainty thought — reticent of habit, abjuring all obtrusiveness." Yet as man and artist Whistler himself was neither unobtrusive nor discreet. On his return from Venice in the autumn of 1880, he had appeared in Bond Street, swathed in long black coat and white peg-top trousers, with a black cane in his right hand and a white Pomeranian at his left side; he

had made himself his own most striking pen-and-ink design. Thereafter, throughout the eighties, though he affected to despise the "aesthetic" label, he strove no less self-consciously than Oscar to assume
the aspect of the complete Aesthete. And it was assuredly as such
that he at length mounted the lecture platform to endorse a resolute
art for art's sake.

Despite its scorn of the "Dilettante," the "Ten O'Clock" was intended primarily as a final repudiation of the Ruskinian aesthetic.
Ruskin was clearly the "Amateur," the "sage of the universities —
learned in many matters, and of much experience in all, save his
subject, . . . gentle priest of the Philistine withal, . . . [ambling]
pleasantly from all point and through many volumes, escaping scientific assertion." But whatever the Amateur might preach to the con-
trary, Art, said Whistler, was nothing if not the specialized activity
of the professional artist. Independent of virtue, indifferent to society,
aloof like pure science from human emotion, Art must, he felt,
remain forever "selfishly preoccupied with her own perfection only —
having no desire to teach — seeking and finding the beautiful in all
conditions and all times." And the artist, above nature and beyond
all relative truths, would continue to devote himself exclusively to
the mastery of line and color, always with the full awareness that
only his fellow artists could ever approach an understanding of his
beautiful patterns.

Whistler the craftsman carried into his painting the art-for-art ideal
which had largely eluded the practice of the "aesthetic" poets. Affix-
ing musical titles to his pictures, he sought to banish from the canvas
not only all literary association but all shadow of human thought or
feeling. His landscapes were conceived as monochromatic "harmonies," blurring natural outlines for decorative effect; and his portraits
were planned as artful "arrangements" of two-dimensional forms
related by contrasts of mass and color. None of his Thames "Nocturnes," therefore, was charged with the wonder of pulsing light
which animated Monet's visions of the Seine; and none of his
arranged ladies compared in feminine vitality with the golden girls
of Renoir or the dancers of Degas, held forever in arrested move-

ment. For Whistler deliberately strove after the static design that owed no debt to a changeful reality. Denying all motion to art, he opposed the idea of "decadence," "this teaching of decay." The artist, he insisted, had no concern with the rise or fall of civilizations; for he stood "in no relation to the moment at which he [occurred] — a monument of isolation — hinting at sadness — having no part in the progress of his fellow men." Yet the "symphonies" of line and shade that shrank from all suggestion of the dynamic life necessarily approached the stillness of death. And the philosophy of art that cut off the artist from the impulses of a living society was in itself the symptom, if not the product, of a "decadent" culture.

Whistler's art theory was to be amplified long after the eighties by such aestheticians as Clive Bell, who, demanding thoroughly dehumanized design, would concede no value to a representational art. But his actual practice as technician encouraged no immediate disciples. Within a year of the "Ten O'Clock," a group of young painters under Walter Sickert had set about organizing the New English Art Club, a society dedicated to a most un-Whistlerian "return to nature" following the example of the French Impressionists. Nor did the literary Aesthetes, who shared Whistler's devotion to artifice, cling long to an amoral art for art. Since language itself was beset forever with ethical connotation, they were forced eventually to abandon all pretence of a complete moral neutrality; while they relented not in their hostility to the Philistine ethic, they became increasingly aware that an amoral literature, if indeed it were possible at all, must betray some moral point of departure.

Nevertheless, the Aesthetic Movement left its mark on the creative activity of later decades. When the affectations of the intense young men had become as *démodé* as the costumes in *Patience,* the "aesthetic" regard for craftsmanship remained the controlling force behind many a serious and powerful work of art, from the subtle moral geometries of James to the enormous intellectual labyrinths of Joyce. And — apart from all formal concerns — there persisted the "aesthetic" concept of the artist as specialist, working with his own symbols in his own difficult medium, defiant of the wide and widening public that was ever less prepared to fathom his particular intention. Painters and poets far removed from the late Victorian conflict, the children of another lost generation, in revolt against another middle class, were to know only a more desolating sense of detachment from the life of their time. And the critic sensitive to their remarkable achievement would at last assume that a successful picture must of necessity be a public failure, or like George Orwell take for granted that "in an age like our own" a good poem can never enjoy "any genuine popularity." [27]

In the eighties, as in the years that followed, the divorce of art from society could be ascribed variously — to the masses and to mass-education, to the decline of a general culture enriched by common ideals, to the social thinkers distrustful of the aesthetic temper, and even to the artist himself, despairing of human values, disillusioned by scientific discovery, seeking escape from doubt in the dogma of self-expression. But wherever lay the blame, if blame there were, both art and society paid the price of independence. Art suffered the burden of self-consciousness and the blight of exclusive and arbitrary interpretations. And society, intent upon its own specialized pursuits, lost the vision of an integrated pattern, the meaningful experience of a "transfigured life."

XII

The Decadence and After

O wasted is that wine like blood,
Wasted the flesh that was our food!
If in the dimness without strife
I perish, life, O give me life!
— STEPHEN PHILLIPS

J'ai beau entendre parler de décadence. Je n'y crois pas. Je ne
crois pas même que nous soyons parvenus au plus haut point de
civilisation.

— ANATOLE FRANCE

As the nineteenth century drew at last to its close, many a late Victorian pulpit rang with apocalyptic warnings. To the ardent Evangelical the end of all things was at hand; the old order, it seemed, could hardly long survive the faith that had made possible its dominance. By the early nineties, one Reverend Mr. Baxter was, therefore, quite convinced that the day of final doom, fast approaching, would be presaged by the ascent to Heaven, at an appointed hour in 1896, of some one hundred and forty-four thousand selected Christians.[1] But when the hour arrived, most of the chosen, apparently, preferred to linger on earth for at least another year, that they might join in the festivities of Victoria's Diamond Jubilee. For the true-born Englishman, in fact, grown less and less responsive to every Evangelical appeal, was finding more immediate forms of emotional release in the imperial concerns of his Empress-Queen.

Ever since the collapse of British agriculture in the seventies, the middle classes, despite an ingrained insularity of outlook, had been no longer able to think wholly in terms of an island economy, self-sufficient and inviolate. Driven alike by the demands of trade and a mistrust of Continental competitors, industrial Britain had become increasingly dependent upon the resources and markets of her wide empire. From the imperial fervor of Disraeli — in its time as "realistic" as it had been visionary — there had arisen a bellicose jingoism which concealed in its foolish boast the practical purposes it was designed to serve. Clearly by the end of the eighties, the creed of the jingo had usurped much of the authority of the old religion. And the new Press, ready to exploit every popular sentiment to its own devious ends, had turned resolutely from the condition of England, which the "radicals" and the socialists were intent upon reforming, to the fortunes of Englishmen abroad, whose adventures actual or imaginary furnished the foreign correspondent sensational copy.

More guileless in their worship of things British, the poets of imperialism sought to reassert the basic values of their national heritage. In the best — at any rate — of their patriotic verses, Kipling, Henley, William Watson, even Henry Newbolt, all transcended the frantic bluster of the mere jingo. Hymning "England my mother," Watson begged a deeper reverence for the literary culture which must certainly outlive any material disasters of an ominous future, for

> *Nations are mortal,*
> *Fragile is greatness;*
> *Fortune may fly thee,*
> *Song shall not fly.*[2]

Similarly Newbolt, recalling to his countrymen the splendors of a storied past, asked earnestly, on the very eve of the African war,

England! wilt thou dare tonight
Pray that God defend the Right? [3]

And Henley, during the long-drawn conflict, came to dread that the "faith" which had guided the "master-work" of England, his England, might not necessarily "endure" forever; and repeatedly, in despair, he strove to overwhelm his own doubt with the resonance of hysteric doggerel. But his fears were by no means unique. All through the nineties there lay behind the cult of empire a half-hushed uneasiness, a sense of social decline, a foreboding of death as deep as Baxter's conviction, though far less precise in its prophecy. And it was therefore quite appropriate that Kipling, the true imperial laureate, should close the great Jubilee pageant itself with an eloquent reminder of the fate that had befallen the kindred pomps of Nineveh and Tyre.

Present in even the high imperial symphony, the note of world-fatigue dominated altogether the tenuous music of Decadence. To Wilde and his later disciples, to Beardsley and his friends of the *Yellow Book,* to the Rhymers[4] whose youth was their age, *fin de siècle* meant more than the death of a century; it connoted a time of lulled disenchantment when Joy's hand was ever at his lips bidding adieu. Aware of their attributes and proud of their title, the Decadents suffered — or affected to suffer — the ineffable weariness of strayed revelers lost in a palace of fading illusion. Dowson, the most delicate lyrist among them, described in languid couplets their common ailment, "spleen," an antique English malady which Baudelaire had refined into a quite French and thoroughly modern malaise:

> *I was not sorrowful, I could not weep,*
> *And all my memories were put to sleep.*
>
> *I watched the river grow more white and strange,*
> *All day till evening I watched it change.*
>
> *All day till evening I watched the rain*
> *Beat wearily upon the window pane.*

I was not sorrowful but only tired
Of everything that ever I desired.[5]

And Arthur Symons, more deliberately, made the sigh of a lost lover the complaint of his whole "aesthetic" generation:

Trouble has come upon us like a sudden cloud,
A sudden summer cloud with thunder in its wings.
There is an end for us of old familiar things
Now that this desolating voice has spoken aloud.[6]

So the artist, spiritually dispossessed, alienated from the life of old familiar things, might experience the defeat of desire, a private doom less remote than the larger death threatening all Victorian culture.

Yet the Decadents, for all their disillusion, were not so completely the victims of "spleen," of "that terrible *taedium vitae,*" as to approach with mere indifference the uncommon delights of art. For even to savor the weariness of self, they had had first to regard their own creative individuality as the one certain value in a disintegrating civilization. Sedulously, therefore, they strove to proclaim, by their very dress and speech and gesture, a full aesthetic autonomy. Like Dorian Gray, whose "chiselled lips curled in exquisite disdain" of all that was commonplace and vulgar, they struck the pose of the perfect dandy, self-sufficient and ironic, silhouetted in solemn black against the arc lamps of the London night, contemptuous of the busy grayness that scurried abroad in the sun. As writers and as draftsmen, they struggled to make a highly personal style the ultimate expression of their highly stylized personalities. Their prose glittered self-consciously with paradox and epigram fashioned to invert every bourgeois platitude. Their poems, moving lightly through unoriginal stanza patterns, turned a conventional poetic diction to new and sometimes startling effect. And their drawings and sketches, often as overwrought as Byzantine mosaics, imposed a kind of diseased vitality upon the fixed traditions of a fragile rococo.

In their various media they carefully emphasized rather than concealed the necessary artifice of art; and they looked not to nature but to art itself for their images and themes. Hubert Crackanthorpe, for instance, in a story "staged" like a one-act play, could describe his heroine's face as "a subtle harmony of tired colour." [7] Beardsley could declare the pretty Princess of his ballad "as lyrical and sweet / As one of Schubert's melodies." And Symons could adapt to his verse the languid swirl of a Javanese dance, or, again, repeatedly play a weary passion against the painted backdrops of the theater or the lurid *décor* of a gas-lit café as chalked by the *décadent* Toulouse-Lautrec. Wilde, with similar intent, designed his single novel to demonstrate that the natural has significance only insofar as Nature may succeed in imitating Art. Thus the sky in *Dorian* becomes "an inverted cup of blue metal," the clouds are "like ravelled skeins of glossy white silk," and the chimney smoke ascends as "a violent riband, through the nacre-coloured air"; Sybil attains "all the delicate grace" of a Tanagra figurine; and Dorian holds through the years the untarnished glory of Hallward's first impression, while his career follows the course of Huysmans' wonderful fiction, which is virtually "the story of Dorian's life, written before he had lived it."

Dedicated as a whole to a determined artificiality, the novel flaunted the faith of the English Decadence that Art must transcend the actual, must indeed represent "man's gallant protest against Nature." But the gallantry of Decadent art demanded no courage of action, no true boldness of execution; it was a passive gallantry of style, precious, effeminate, effete. At odds forever with Victorian "manliness," the Decadent hero might well like Dorian bury "his rebellious curls" in the perfume of "great cool lilac-blossoms"; for he could never, on principle, face the social realities of his time. And before he yielded quite to overpowering ennui, he might escape to a world of unnatural sensation, presided over by some malign spirit of beauty, perhaps even Conder's androgynous Fairy Prince, masked, brocaded, and sinister.

"There is no such thing," wrote Wilde, "as a moral or an immoral book. Books are well written, or badly written. That is all." [8] But the most overwritten literature of Decadence was nonetheless animated by a conscious will to explore the dark underside of experience, with which the Decadent himself associated immorality and evil. At a time when all normal objects of desire seemed weary and stale, smutched indeed by the rude hands of the Philistine, the artist might yet seek a fresh titillation, a genuine *frisson nouveau,* in the rarer enticements of sin, or at least in a lingering glance at sinful pleasures. Accordingly, like the George Moore who had penned his purple *Confessions* (1888), many a young Decadent prided himself on his love of "almost everything perverse" and his fierce "appetite for the strange, abnormal and unhealthy in art." [9] There were moments, we read, when Dorian — and so, perhaps, Dorian's creator — "looked on evil simply as a mode through which he could realise his conception of the beautiful," moments when "the coarse brawl, the loathsome den, the crude violence of disordered life, the very vileness of thief and outcast, were more vivid, in their intense actuality of impression, than all the gracious shapes of Art, the dreamy shadows of Song."

Symons, apparently, understood Dorian's impulse; for though he remained in fact a conscientious and quite respectable craftsman, he declared in verse his surrender to the "multitudinous senses," and he found inspiration for lyric and sonnet in the outcast children of passion — the fallen woman in "the villainous dancing-hall" or the distraught opium smoker, with "soul at pawn," brooding in his rat-ridden garret. Crackanthorpe, likewise, through his several slender volumes, followed at a discreet distance the careful experiments with sex of the sadistic dandy or the "morbid craving for self-inflicted torture" of the duped lover. And Richard Le Gallienne, who in soberer mood decried Decadence as "limited thinking, often insane thinking," [10] acknowledged, in a rhyme called "Beauty Accurst," the dread fascination of the lustful lady, the *femme fatale* whose kiss was death. Few of the Decadents achieved in their private lives a more than vicarious knowledge of the wickedness that flowered egregiously in their poems and stories. And very few indeed merited the humorless, hysterical indictment of Max Nordau, whose *Degeneration* (1895), purporting to explore the pathology of *fin de siècle,* discovered in the Decadent artist an insane criminal type as yet unclassified by the great criminologist Lombroso. If a mysterious Baron Corvo[11] hovered on the periphery of aesthetic London, not many young writers could even imagine the scope of his infamous adventures. Wilde himself, whose falling from grace when publicized was to shock most of his disciples, indulged but a commonplace and tawdry perversion far beneath the nameless exotic sins upon which Dorian was wont to speculate. As it appeared in artistic form, Decadent "evil" was actually for the most part, like Decadent style, an artificial growth, the calculated product of a curious sensibility; and as such it reflected not the terrors of the objective world but the spiritual isolation of the artist, striving too deliberately to transcend the moral values of a middle-class convention.

Studiously unnatural in their aesthetic emotions, the Decadents, naturally, attracted many a satirist intent upon measuring all "specialized" subject matter by the broad perspectives of humor. Himself a nonchalant dandy on intimate terms with the best of the new minor poets, Max Beerbohm, for example, smiled urbanely at their most shocking productions, "the lurid verses written by young men, who in real life, know no haunt more lurid than a literary public-house." [12] Less familiar with the objects of Decadent art, Owen Seaman rhymed off his direct reprimand "To a Boy-Poet of the Decadence," ridiculing the "dull little vices" of which the precocious worldling sang so wickedly. And G. S. Street in his prose *Autobiography of a Boy* (1894) invoked the indirection of irony to demolish the Decadent Tubby, a youth who, despite his conceit, enjoyed a certain popularity for his alleged sins and "the supposed magnificence of his debts," and who aspired as author of a "Ballad of Shameful Kisses" to be considered "a man to whom no chaste woman would be allowed to speak, an aim he would mention wistfully, in a manner inexpressibly touching, for he never achieved it." [13]

But of all the anti-Decadent wits, Robert Hichens achieved through parody the gayest and subtlest attack. In *The Green Carnation* (1894) he allowed his determined dilettantes, Mr. Amarinth and Lord Reggie Hastings, each wearing most conspicuously "the arsenic flower of an exquisite life," to expose, by their every word and sigh and gesture, absurdities of thought and sentiment no less artfully cultivated than the exotic boutonniere itself. Lord Reggie, in whom the knowing might have seen a sharp resemblance to the young Lord Alfred Douglas, defended against all rational argument the creed of the Decadent life-taster, "the philosophy to be afraid of nothing, to dare to live as one wishes to live, not as the middle-classes wish one to live; to have the courage of one's desires, instead of only the cowardice of other people's." And Mr. Amarinth, clearly a caricature of Wilde,[14] maintained a Decadent love of artifice and Whistler and his own brilliance and a loathing of the very word "natural," which meant to him "all that is middle-class, all that is of the essence of jingoism, all that is colourless, and without form, and void." Acquainted like Wilde with the principle of sensory "correspondences," Mr. Amarinth could befuddle an unaesthetic curate with his appreciation of a brown Gregorian chant — for all combinations of sounds, he explained, conveyed "a sense of colour to the mind" and Gregorians were "obviously of a rich and sombre brown, just as a Salvation Army hymn [was] a violent magenta." Or, again, recalling perhaps the preface to *Dorian,* he might exhort the simple-souled children of the village to cherish a dubious amorality: "There is nothing good and nothing evil. There is only art. Despise the normal, and flee from everything that is hallowed by custom as you would flee from the seven deadly virtues. Cling to the abnormal. . . . Forget your Catechism, and remember the words of Flaubert and of Walter Pater, and remember this, too, that the folly of self-conscious fools is the only true wisdom." Yet the burlesque, for all its cleverness, scarcely matched in sheer hilarity Wilde's own bright farce which adapted to the glory of nonsense the paradox of a Wildean Ernest and the aimless ennui of an effete Algernon. For the Decadents, in fact, required no parodist to remind them of their departures from the sober norms of reason. Quite self-conscious in their folly, they successfully anticipated all contemning laughter.

Not indeed until it was too late did Wilde himself actually realize the importance of being earnest. "I was," he wrote truly, if rather defiantly, from prison, "—I was a man who stood in symbolic relations to the art and culture of my age."[15] This much he had known almost from the beginning. Yet as artist he was never able throughout his career, except perhaps in the powerful "Ballad of Reading Gaol" (1898), to achieve the intensity, the self-effacement, the high seriousness, required to produce the "one beautiful work of art" of which he dreamed. For all his apparent egotism, he lacked an essential faith in his own creations; he failed always to sustain for long any willing suspension of disbelief. Though he felt that a great literature must be born of a passionate sensibility rather than an overcurious, analytic brain, he somehow feared his own Decadent fancy, and he perversely allowed his disillusioned intellect to mock his aesthetic emotion. His best books are, therefore, vitiated, as well as enlivened, by his own ambivalence. His plays, for example, draw heavily upon the conventions of the concealed identity, the wronged woman, the barriers of caste — in short, upon all the stock in trade of the sentimental comedy; yet their abiding life lies in the free range of an intellectual wit which impedes the action and, long before the contrived finale, almost destroys the sentiment. On occasion, to be sure, we may suspect the playwright of deliberately burlesquing the distress of his heroines;[16] but we can hardly assume that he would have us regard his most calculated pathos as completely ironic. For Wilde's intentions as dramatist are far more confused than his obvious fluency might indicate; and it is, after all, not impossible to see how, in a Soviet Russia grown conservative under the pressures of war, *An Ideal Husband* (1895) could one day be revived as a serious vindication of the stability of the cultured home.[17]

Not even in *Dorian Gray* (1890), despite its avowed amorality, are his purposes at all clearly defined. The novel, perhaps the most representative product of the Decadence in England, oscillates precariously between the two styles born of the artist's inner conflict. As a reworking of the familiar Faust theme, its allegory was fashioned to explore the terrors of evil that the soul yielding to the temptations of hedonistic desire must ultimately experience. But the overwrought prose which describes in deliberate detail all the furniture of Dorian's pleasure palace establishes no illusion of aesthetic truth; the "dreadful places near Blue Gate Fields," blurred by fog or ignorance, remain far more ludicrous than dreadful; and the whole sentimental melodrama which carries Dorian, the lovely "son of Love and Death," far from "the stainless purity of his boyish life" through "the sanguine labyrinth of passion" lacks both psychological depth and emotional conviction.

The prose, on the other hand, which enshrines the wit of Lord Henry, attains an apparently spontaneous ease and vivacity; it springs crisp and clear from Wilde's artificial second nature which became to him more natural than his original passionate impulse. As tempter, Lord Henry is detached and urbane, like the Spirit of Clough's *Dipsychus,* ironic rather than malevolent; "enthralled by the methods of natural sciences," he is the analyst of sin whose own worst vice is passivity, the rationalist whose diffident virtue hides in paradox.[18] He represents, in fact, the more reasonable Wilde who, suspicious of his own perverse sensibilities, restrained *Dorian Gray* from the complete Decadence of the Huysmans novel which inspired its most lurid pages. And his shadow falls across even the pitiful *De Profundis* (1905), where the sinner, weary of time, can scarcely make convincing the will — tragic and intense, were it wholly earnest — to seek the Spiritual New-birth of the high Victorians, to believe — in their terms — that as "the sea . . . washes away the stains and wounds of the world" so at last may Nature "cleanse me in great waters and with bitter herbs make me whole."

Though less striking than Wilde as personalities, and generally less eager to melodramatize their private emotions, the Decadents of the *Yellow Book* experienced in varying degrees the same conflict between the amoral dictates of a deliberate aesthetic creed and the unwelcome compulsions of a moral or social conscience. Symons, for instance, while probably the most serious and worshipful defender of the French literary *décadence,* could not but admit that the perfect *décadent*, Des Esseintes of Huysmans' *A Rebours*, seemed "half-pathological" in his misanthropy and altogether morbid in his quest for exotic sensation.[19] And it was hardly strange that Symons' own verse "Credo," demanding of every full life "a strenuous virtue or a strenuous sin," should echo not the inhuman music of Verlaine, whose "disembodied voice" he admired,[20] but the quite human message of "The Statue and the Bust" and indeed the whole far-from-Decadent assertion of the Browning who was his first master.

Intricate in its arabesques of line and overlaid everywhere with the suggestion of evil, Aubrey Beardsley's subtle art might appear at first glance a more complete expression of the Decadent spirit. Yet his best drawings betrayed a satiric purpose stronger than any delight in a perversely wicked *décor;* they were, in part at least, as his publisher John Lane insisted, the work of a "modern Hogarth . . . lampooning the period and its customs." [21] And among his writings, the notorious fragment *Under the Hill* (1896) was actually designed to rework with semi-ironic elaboration the legend of Tannhäuser,[22] which remained in effect the tragic moral history of all the Decadents damned by the uncontrolled senses; and the grim "Ballad of a Barber" was surely intended to convey a complete allegory of Decadence itself through the tale of the artist-barber Carrousel, whose amoral art for art's sake crumbled forever on the intrusion of insane desire.

Crackanthorpe, who lacked Beardsley's talent for satire, sought to emulate in his brief fictions the cool objectivity of Maupassant. Yet he found a soulless naturalism quite unable to satisfy his own deeper emotional impulse; and he yielded again and again, in spite of his struggle for detachment, to an ethical commentary, sometimes oblique, but always more or less incompatible with the dispassionate method. In an unguarded moment he confessed that "all great art is moral in the wider and the truer sense of the word." [23] But, failing to discover for his own art any moral sanction that he might accept with his whole intellect, he turned in despair to the Decadent "pursuit of experience," which he called, self-consciously, "the refuge of the unimaginative," [24] until eventually, defeated in all calmer efforts to escape, he plunged from a Paris bridge to his death in the cold impassive river.

Whatever his attitude towards Crackanthorpe's last defiant gesture, Lionel Johnson apparently regarded with due skepticism the suicidal gloom of many another late Victorian; for he proceeded in an amusing satire entitled "Incurable" (1896) to ridicule a typical young Decadent who resolved to "live his poetry . . . by dying, because he could not write it." [25] Still, Johnson himself had to do battle with the Dark Angel that had desecrated the bright world of art, that had turned the Muses to Furies and had made

> *all things of beauty burn*
> *With flames of evil ecstasy.*[26]

And it was only after painful contest that he could reassert his essential faith in the moral will of the artist.

Even Ernest Dowson, who was perhaps never so certain of his adversary, sensed the inadequacies of the Decadent aesthetic and the hollowness of all the self-conscious posturing that passed for Decadent intensity. For even in Dowson, who more sweetly than any of his fellow poets sang the dark disillusions of the *fin de siècle,* the spirit of Decadence was not sufficiently strong to stifle a longing for ethical direction or to mitigate greatly the sincerity of an ultimate confession:

> *we cannot understand*
> *Laughter or tears, for we have only known*
> *Surpassing vanity: vain things alone*
> *Have driven our perverse and aimless band.*[27]

Among the more serious Decadents there thus persisted some capacity for a contrition which was neither perverse nor aimless nor in fact particularly "Decadent." But there was at the same time, throughout their works and days, so marked an addiction to pose that a knowing young man like Richard Le Gallienne, suspicious of their remorse, might charge them with invoking the long-neglected soul merely to serve as "bitters to the over dulcet sins." [28] Few literary critics could see, looking beyond the artifice of Crackanthorpe or Symons or Dowson, much more than a dim shadow of the positive emotion, the "moral" intensity, the objective human drama that they had learned to expect of the great writer. And many, therefore, waited rather impatiently, after the deaths of Browning and Tennyson, for the arrival of a new major poet, capable of transcending his own self-conscious moods.

At length Le Gallienne himself, and a good many readers less susceptible than he to passing enthusiasms, came suddenly upon a slender volume which apparently bore the impress of unmistakable power, a volume which spoke, as the Decadent chapbooks did not, for "the great heart of humanity." Issued by John Lane in 1897, "Christ in Hades" struck Le Gallienne at once as a poetic achievement of signal importance, and its author, Stephen Phillips, seemed already by endowment one with the immortals. Here at last, Le Gallienne said, rang the voice of the true singer: "Poetry so full of the beauty of reality, so unweakened by rhetoric, the song of a real nightingale in love with a real rose, poetry so distinguished by the impassioned accuracy of high imagination, I know not where else to find among the poets of Mr. Phillips' generation."

No poet indeed since the days of the Spasmodic School had enjoyed a vogue at all comparable to that of Stephen Phillips, and none suffered so complete and tragic an oblivion as the extravagance of ill-considered eulogy would surely precipitate.[29] On first reading "Christ in Hades" and "Marpessa," William Archer and William Watson, Sidney Colvin and Stephen Gwynn vied one with another in the worship of the new Apollo whose glories passed description. John Churton Collins declared the poet of *Paolo and Francesca* (1899), at his most intense, the peer of Sophocles and Dante. Owen Seaman the parodist bowed reverently before a talent which he believed "something without parallel in our age." And the anonymous reviewer for *Blackwood's,* which long before had printed Aytoun's *Firmilian,* properly found a remote parallel in the fame of Alexander Smith, but "this time," he hastened to add, "the genius is no illusion."

Phillips himself was far less assured of his creative strength. Yet he had from the beginning aspired towards the ideals which his admirers were to find embodied in his work. Convinced that noble poetry — "high poetry," as he called it — must transcend all subjective impulse, must represent a complete merging of the poet's self into "visions and revelations of the Truth and the Loveliness that are of God," [30] he had consciously rejected the delicate forms of Decadent art and had sought instead to reproduce the most conspicuous achievements in the grand style, to recover, if possible, the epic manner of Milton or at least the opulence of Tennyson. His verse, accordingly, always more rhetorical than Le Gallienne supposed, rang with echoes from a literary past. Through his plays moved insubstantial shadows, drawn from the remote traditions of poetic drama, unreal creatures sonorously declaiming their tragic woe in an outmoded "poetic" idiom; and even his sad Francesca, perhaps the most vivid of all his characterizations, breathed but a borrowed vitality as the last of the pale ethereal Rossetti women. Occasionally, as in "Marpessa," he might reassert a lost faith in human values or even, as in "Christ in Hades," catch once more the heroic note of the Victorian Ulysses:

> Give me again great life! To dare, to enjoy,
> To explore, never to tire, to be alive,
> And full of blood, and young, to risk, to love!
> The bright glory of after-battle wine,
> The flushed recounting faces, the stern hum
> Of burnished armies, thrill of unknown seas!

Yet he found no real sanction for his assent to life either in himself or in the intellectual temper of his time; and his heroics were in fact little more than a deliberate protest against his own deeper despair, against the same fear of doomed beauty that haunts the Virgil of his poem, nostalgic in the underworld:

> Dear gladiator pitted against Fate,
> I fear for thee: around thee is the scent
> Of over-beautiful, quick-fading things,

The pang, the gap, the briefness, all the dew,
Tremble, and suddenness of earth: I must
Remember young men dead in their hot bloom,
The sweetness of the world edged like a sword,
The melancholy knocking of those waves,
The deep unhappiness of winds, the light
That comes on things we never more shall see.[31]

Thus, despite his impatience with the smaller instruments of verse, Phillips failed to escape the weariness that pervaded the less ambitious art of the Decadence. And his poetry, therefore, looking to the past for its inspiration but touched everywhere by the mood of the nineties, remained in the last analysis an eloquent epilogue to a dying century rather than a foretaste of the literature to come.

Aware that a new art would demand a new philosophy, John Davidson felt little of Phillips' respect for established values, social, aesthetic, or moral. Determined to "undo the past," he urged "the new men" of a troubled present to build a new faith upon the ruins of the old:

Love, and hope, and know;
Man — you must adore him.
Let the whole past go;
Think God's thought before Him. . . .
Heat the furnace hot;
Smelt the world-old thought
Into dross and dew;
Mold the earth anew.[32]

And in his own work he sought to achieve an entirely new accent through a fresh imagery and diction and a free and flexible technique. Though a member of the Rhymers' Club and an early contributor to the "Decadent" *Yellow Book,* he wittily assailed the aesthetic perversities of the Decadence in such nimble satires as *Baptist Lake* (1894) and *Earl Lavender* (1895). A few of his poems, to be sure, drew upon typically Decadent themes and materials, but only to recharge them with a vigorous and positive emotion; his "Ballad of a Nun," for example, told the tale of a recluse saved rather than damned by her one terrible excursion into the world of sinful man; and his "Ballad of Hell" portrayed the power of the undaunted human soul to resist beyond all delusions the menace of a cynical depravity. For much of his subject matter, however, he turned directly to the actualities of everyday living which the Decadents for the most part tried to dismiss and which Phillips struggled to transcend. He opened his verse to the sublime vulgarities of London, to the fevered joys of the sportive Cockney and the bitterness of the City clerk at "thirty bob a week," to the half-literate cry of the music-hall singer and the rational dream of the Fleet Street journalist able, like the poet himself, to supplicate the gods of reality:

> Save us from madness; keep us night and day,
> Sweet powers of righteousness to whom we pray.[33]

For poetry, Davidson believed, was above all "the product of originality, of a first-hand experience and observation of life, of a direct communion with men and women, with the seasons of the year, with day and night." [34]

Yet by the end of the nineties when the "new men," who had once seemed half-inclined to listen, had found newer and more intense enthusiasms, Davidson felt himself tragically isolated from the essential "communion" and deeply oppressed by a sense of betrayal, which his blatant masculinity could never thereafter conceal. The universe became to him "a golden bough of Irony, flowering with suns and systems";[35] and his disillusioned intellect was henceforth unable to accept without reservation any single creed. Still, like many a greater artist in the years to follow, he recognized the poet's need for a working mythology; and he set out accordingly, in a world of little meaning, to create for his own purposes a synthesis and a symbolism to which he might give at least an aesthetic assent. To the advancement of this "new cosmogony," designed, he said, as "a new habitation for the imagination of man," [36] he devoted his long, pretentious *Testaments* (1901–1908), involved sermons in verse extolling in Nietzschean terms the beauty of brute strength or preaching long before D. H. Lawrence the gospel of the body electric and the warm brainless blood. But the intensely personal mythos he devised remained too arbitrary and too doctrinaire to provide a sound framework for an imaginative art that, passing beyond the personal, might achieve the high illusion of objectivity. And it was with more defiance than ultimate conviction that he described his last *Testament* as the prelude to the poetry of a new age; for, even as he wrote, he was pondering his own escape from unrenewed time, the escape of the death-seeker standing, literally, as his verse had promised, "out to sea" against the flood, resolved in defeat "to win the heaven of eternal night." [87]

But long before Davidson was to martyr himself as prophet of a lost cause, another poet of the nineties, far less self-consciously the innovator, had found a surer path from Decadence towards a new literature of assent. It was William Ernest Henley who almost from the beginning directly assailed the premises of late Victorian aestheticism and until the end strove to inspire his countless protégés with his own hard-won faith in the romance of reality. In 1888, at the close of an arduous apprenticeship, Henley had published an unassuming *Book of Verses,* into which he had gathered not only his delicate *Bric-à-brac* in Old French forms (a somewhat ironic concession to a declared art for art's sake), but also many a more representative piece, from the intense yet too strident "Invictus" to the poignant elegy, "I. M. Margaritae Sororis." Though the bulk of the poems simply announced in divers keys a quite "unaesthetic" delight in the fullness of living, the remarkable sequence *In Hospital* chronicled with a strange detachment the precise process of assertion. Here, to the horror of the Aesthetes, was the record, complete in all its unlovely detail, of the soul's battle against pain and death, and of the long conquest culminating in the will, as profound as it was naïve, to accept for its own worth the essential miracle of life itself:

> *Carry me out*
> *Into the wind and the sunshine,*
> *Into the beautiful world. . . .*

Free . . . !
Dizzy, hysterical, faint,
I sit, and the carriage rolls on with me
Into the wonderful world.[38]

Amid all the denials of the Decadence, Henley struggled to maintain the same unquestioning acceptance of the world's wonder and its beauty. At times, as in *The Song of the Sword* (1892), where he sought a crude Darwinian sanction for a too boisterous activism, he might invoke heavy rhythms to persuade himself that he had put behind him forever the memory of an experience and a weakness he was unable to forget. But in the best of his verse — in such poems as the "London Voluntaries," in which he proposed, as he said, "to attempt an heroic treatment of London and things Londonian" [39] — he achieved an impressive objectivity of vision; he succeeded in identfying his own passion for life with a larger vital force, with the immediate realities of the crowded city, the sweep of the dark river, the extravagance of the yellow sun, the endless cycle of the seasons. His assent, as it animated the truest of his lyrics, carried him far from the sad disillusions of the Wildean aesthetes and the fragile craftsmanship with which they were striving to make permanent their malaise.

Throughout a turbulent journalistic career, Henley worked with all the vigor at his command to check the course of Decadence and at the same time to promote a literature unflinching in its regard for the long-neglected "truths of nature." Though not less than Davidson the child of an agnostic age, he yet discovered a "morality of art" without the absolute sanctions assumed by Ruskin and the mid-Victorians, an ethic grounded in his own intuitions of value, his personal response to the painter, poet, or novelist who saw in the human tragicomedy some pattern of ultimate meaning. As literary critic he displayed a considerable catholicity of taste. But he preferred always satire to sentiment, the crowded panorama to the painstaking portrait, a gusto of style to a subtlety of analysis. He discounted Flaubert and George Eliot to applaud Balzac and Dickens; he commended Tolstoi's magnificent perspective; and he admired beyond words the uninhibited Georgians, especially Fielding and Burns, sanguine masters who, unlike the bitter "Zolaphytes," had found "the way of realism" no highroad to despair. If his prejudice assuredly closed to him much of the poetry of tranquil meditation, his enthusiasm for the robust eighteenth century warned him against the sick introspections of a too subjective art and also made him straightway the champion of the new British "realists" already challenging Decadent artifice.

As editor of the *National Observer* (1890–1894), Henley dominated a lively band of eager apprentices, each well drilled in a crisp incisive prose, each prepared to advance the critical standards of his "unaesthetic" chieftain. Though most of the Young Men subordinated their individual talents to the larger purposes of the weekly, several achieved independent publication; and a few like Gilbert Parker, G. S. Street, Charles Whibley, and Arthur Morrison eventually attained some measure of literary repute when the last *Observer* had long since gone to press. But during the early nineties none sought a greater stimulus than Henley's approval and the knowledge that each was doing his anonymous part to sustain a vehicle which might worthily bear the signed contributions of Henley's more remarkable protégés. For in the work of the latter the Young Men could see the bright promise of an art reborn. Here were the lyrics and folk tales of the unknown Yeats, carefully edited to be sure, yet fresh in substance, direct and dramatic of idiom. Here, too, before long were the *Barrack-Room Ballads* of Kipling, boisterous songs in a Cockney vernacular, dedicated in quite Henleyan terms to "the God of Things as They are." Then, a little later, in the days of the *New Review* (1895–1898), came *The Time Machine* and *The Nigger of the Narcissus,* the appearance of which at once established H. G. Wells and Joseph Conrad as vital forces in the new fiction. By attracting and befriending writers so gifted and so various, Henley accomplished his own editorial mission. His journals, though practical failures, bravely heralded the quality and tone, the social bias, the masculinity, the imaginative range and emotional intent of the literature shortly to be called Edwardian.

Meanwhile, beyond Henley's power to edit or reject, the larger cultural context in which Yeats and Conrad, Kipling and Wells would reach their maturity was year by year assuming more distinct and intricate form. Throughout the nineties a number of artists and thinkers, dissociated for the most part from the conflicts of Decadence and Counter-decadence, were anticipating in individual ways the primary concerns, aesthetic and intellectual, of the post-Victorian world. Housman and Hardy, each after long preparation, issued first volumes of verse which subjected a personal disenchantment, sometimes deeply moving, sometimes overdeliberate, to a clipped speech rhythm that later decades would consider characteristically "modern" in its remoteness from the ornament and rhetoric of the grand style. Pinero and Jones, alike contemptuous of the Philistine theater, worked with serious purpose and technical competence to effect a "renascence of the English drama," and Bernard Shaw began a series of experiments, no less witty than garrulous, designed to prove beyond all doubt that the stage had awaited only the delayed advent of the Shavian intellect. At the same time, Shaw's friends, Sidney and Beatrice Webb, completed their detailed *History of Trade Unionism,* a triumph of Fabian research which lent the impetus of sound scholarship to the newly organized Independent Labour Party. F. H. Bradley published his *Appearance and Reality* and thereupon proceeded to survey new areas for philosophic speculation. And J. G. Frazer continued to augment the great compendium already known as *The Golden Bough,* a project which was to leave its mark upon all subsequent study of comparative religion and, incidentally, to become an almost inexhaustible source book for the central myths and symbols of a twentieth-century literature.

Few men of the nineties could match these in true originality of thought and craftsmanship. Yet many by seeking novelty, and some by discovering newness, escaped the apocalyptic vision that haunted the evangelist and enervated the Decadent. "Certainly," the more hopeful might say with Havelock Ellis, who recently had welcomed the "new" spirit — "certainly old things are passing away;

not the old ideals only, but even the regret they leave behind is dead, and we are shaping instinctively our new ideals." [40]

By 1901, when the Victorian era at long last yielded nominally to the Edwardian, the makers of the new society had already determined their "new ideals," the clear if limited objectives of their private labors. No prophet now arose, with the selfless intensity of the young Carlyle or the mature Ruskin, intent upon relating to a larger synthesis the manifold interests of a diverse culture. The Edwardians as a whole cheerfully followed their own specialized pursuits without great concern for a common ethic which could be no longer theirs. If a few like Yeats and Conrad and Henry James felt the need of fixed values, most of them saw no urgency for a "conversion" unto any moral or aesthetic absolute. For they found an immediate assent in the material prosperity of an active world advancing almost visionless towards the Armageddon of Western Europe. By the end of their period many could recognize too late the broad delusions that had underlain their highest achievement. But at the beginning nearly all attained for a time a brave irrational confidence, a credulous optimism that mocked the doubter. And even Hardy, who still asked a deeper pattern of meaning, was half disposed, as the nineteenth century moved into the twentieth, to believe that his darkling thrush, armored with joy against the bleak winter, might perhaps know some blessed Hope of which he himself remained unaware.

NOTES AND SOURCES

Notes and Sources

THE passage from John Morley's *On Compromise* in the first chapter and the several quotations in the fourth from Tennyson's *Unpublished Early Poems* have been included with the permission of the Macmillan Company of London. Excerpts in the final chapter from Dowson, Symons, Davidson, and Phillips have been reprinted by permission of Dodd, Mead and Company of New York from *The Poems of Ernest Dowson,* the *Amoris Victima* of Arthur Symons, John Davidson's *Ballads and Songs,* and *Poems* by Stephen Phillips. Charles Conder's drawing, "A Fairy Prince," has been reproduced from *The Yellow Book,* XIII (1897), 287, by special arrangement with the John Lane Company of London.

When two dates are given in parentheses following a title, the first indicates date of first publication, the second the date of the edition I have used. Dates in parentheses following individual essays or poems indicate date of composition.

CHAPTER I: "VICTORIANISM"

1. For the anecdote, see Frank Hardie, *The Political Influence of Queen Victoria* (London, 1935), p. 206.

2. The charge is stated ironically by Arnold Bennett (*The Old Wives' Tale,* chap. I), but is seriously repeated in various forms; cf. H. H. Asquith, *Some Aspects of the Victorian Age* (Oxford, 1918), p. 6, or an incidental remark by an art critic in the *New Yorker,* Jan. 26, 1946, p. 58.

3. Cf. H. V. Routh, "The true sign of the times was spiritual isolation" (*Towards the Twentieth Century,* New York, 1937, p. ix); or see W. C. Frierson, *The English Novel in Transition* (Norman, Okla., 1942), p. 36.

4. H. J. and Hugh Massingham, eds., *The Great Victorians* (Garden City, 1932), p. 11; or, for a more extravagant judgment, see E. B. Burgum, "Victorianism," *Sewanee Review,* XXXVI (1928), 282, 286.

5. Cf. Routh, *Towards the Twentieth Century,* p. 45.

6. Cf. Osbert Sitwell, *Sober Truth* (London, 1930), p. 22, or A. C. Ward, *Twentieth-Century Literature* (New York, 1940), pp. 2–3.

7. Arnold's charge freely echoed by the neo-humanists, who often dismiss Arnold himself along with his lost generation.

8. Contrast Routh, *Towards the Twentieth Century*, p. 74, with William Gaunt, *The Aesthetic Adventure* (New York, 1945), p. 237.

9. Cf. Edith Batho and Bonamy Dobrée, *The Victorians and After* (London, 1938), p. 81; contrast G. M. Trevelyan, *English Social History* (New York, 1942), p. 521: "The last thirty years of Victoria's reign . . . the real period of the 'emancipation of women' in England."

10. Cf. Batho and Dobrée, *Victorians and After*, p. 37, or Florence B. Lennon, *Victoria through the Looking-Glass* (New York, 1945), *passim*.

11. See Mario Praz, *The Romantic Agony* (London, 1933).

12. Observe the wise cautions of Trevelyan, *English Social History*, p. 509, and of G. M. Young, *Victorian England* (London, 1936), p. 150.

13. See Bonamy Dobrée, "Addison," *Essays in Biography* (London, 1925), p. 206. Addison seems to Dobrée sufficiently hypocritical to merit the title, "the first Victorian."

14. Lascelles Abercrombie, for instance, in a generally judicious estimate of Tennyson, speaks of "that false emphasis of feeling which is the peculiar vice of the Victorian age"; see *Revaluations* (London, 1931), p. 63.

15. See O. F. Christie, *The Transition from Aristocracy* (London, 1927), p. 108; here the historian indulges in generalization.

16. Lytton Strachey, still the liveliest of the iconoclasts; see esp. "A Victorian Critic" (Arnold), *Characters and Commentaries* (New York, 1933).

17. See Anna Kavan (author of the distinguished fiction, *Asylum Piece*), "Back to Victoria," *Horizon*, XIII (1946), 65.

18. See Lennon, *Victoria through the Looking-Glass*, p. 5.

19. Isabel C. Clarke, *Elizabeth Barrett Browning* (London, 1929), p. 241.

20. See William H. Swift, "Tennyson in the Twentieth Century," *Search Quarterly*, III (1933), 343; cf. also C. H. O. Scaife, *The Poetry of Alfred Tennyson* (London, 1930), p. 96.

21. See Asquith, *Aspects of Victorian Age*, p. 13.

22. Batho and Dobrée, *Victorians and After*, p. 36.

23. See Morley, *Critical Miscellanies* (London, 1923), pp. 74–75.

24. G. R. Porter, *The Progress of the Nation* (London, 1851), p. 631.

25. See Harrison, *Autobiographic Memoirs*, 2 vols. (London, 1911), II, 313.

26. Quoted by Walter Besant, *Fifty Years Ago* (New York, n.d.), p. 124.

27. Havelock Ellis, *The New Spirit* (1890), preface to the 1926 edition (Boston, 1926), p. xii.

28. Tennyson, "Locksley Hall Sixty Years After" (1886).

29. See below, Chapter VI.

30. F. W. Newman, *Causes of Atheism* (Ramsgate, 1871), p. 12.

31. Cf. R. C. K. Ensor, *England, 1870–1914* (Oxford, 1936), p. 137.

32. See Clive Bell, "Victorian Taste," in R. S. Lambert, ed., *Art in England* (Pelican Books, 1938), p. 45.

33. A comparison suggested by Oliver Elton, *A Survey of English Literature, 1780–1880*, 4 vols. (New York, 1920), III, 3.

34. Quoted by John Henry Overton, *The Church in England*, 2 vols. (London, 1897), II, 324–325.

35. See F. W. Knickerbocker, *Free Minds* (Cambridge: Harvard University Press, 1943), p. 29.

36. See Symonds, *Essays Speculative and Suggestive*, 2 vols. (London, 1890), II, 274.

CHAPTER II: THE ANTI-ROMANTICS

1. See Walter Jackson Bate's rewarding study, *From Classic to Romantic* (Cambridge: Harvard University Press, 1946).

2. See Frank P. Chambers, *The History of Taste* (New York, 1932), pp. 171–172.

3. See Bate, *Classic to Romantic*, p. 170.

4. E. T. Cook and Alexander Wedderburn, eds., *The Works of John Ruskin*, 39 vols. (London, 1903–1912), XXIII, 122.

5. Keats was rather less affected by hostile reviews than his friends supposed. The artist could expect little sympathy from the periodical critic; see William S. Ward, "Some Aspects of the Conservative Attitude towards Poetry in English Criticism, 1798–1820," *PMLA*, LX (1945), 368–398.

6. See Amy Cruse, *The Victorians and Their Reading* (Boston, 1936), p. 176.

7. See John Stuart Mill, *Autobiography* (1873; London, 1924), p. 126.

8. Quoted by Clement K. Shorter, *Victorian Literature* (New York, 1897), p. 7.

9. See Hallam Tennyson, *Alfred, Lord Tennyson, A Memoir* (hereafter *Memoir*), 2 vols. (New York, 1897), II, 288. Though Tennyson made this remark late in life, it may be taken as representative of his earlier opinion.

10. Quoted by Cruse, *Victorians and Their Reading*, p. 177.

11. See Charles Gavan Duffy, *Conversations with Carlyle* (New York, 1892), p. 55, and Charles Eliot Norton, ed., *Reminiscences by Thomas Carlyle*, 2 vols. (London, 1887), II, 298.

12. Cf. the charge of Eneas Sweetland Dallas, *The Gay Science*, 2 vols. (London, 1866), I, 50–51.

13. Matthew Arnold, *Essays Literary and Critical* (London, 1906), p. 5; cf. Arnold's more positive estimates in "Memorial Verses" and "Wordsworth" (*Essays in Criticism, Second Series*, 1888).

14. See Thomas Carlyle, *The Life of John Sterling* (London, 1907), pp. 56, 57, 59. Coleridge the thinker and prose writer excited more comment than Coleridge the poet. But many felt the verse also suffered "lack of all reality." See Clough's general opinion of Coleridge in Goldie Levy, *Arthur Hugh Clough* (London, 1938), p. 215.

15. See Dallas, *Gay Science*, I, 109, 192, and cf. I, 170, 173.

16. See below, Chapter III.

17. See Tennyson, *Memoir*, II, 287.

18. Ruskin, *Works*, XXXIV, 328.

19. Charles Kingsley, "Thoughts on Shelley and Byron," *Literary and General Lectures and Essays* (London, 1890), p. 44.

20. See Charles Eliot Norton, ed., *Two Notebooks of Thomas Carlyle* (New York, 1898), p. 71.

21. See Mill, *Autobiography*, p. 124.

22. For the opinions of Macaulay and many others, see Samuel Chew, *Byron in England* (London, 1924), pp. 220–262. On the problem of misanthropy, cf. Morley, "Byron," *Critical Miscellanies*, p. 137.

23. Robert Browning, "La Saisaiz," *Works* (New York, 1936), p. 1131.

24. Quoted by Chew, *Byron in England*, p. 256.

25. See George H. Ford's excellent study, *Keats and the Victorians* (New Haven, 1944).

26. The phrase quoted is from the 1880 essay "John Keats" (first published as an introduction to the selections from Keats in T. H. Ward's *English Poets*, vol. IV, 1880; it was later included in *Essays in Criticism, Second Series*), but Arnold's opinion of Keats was well fixed by the forties; see Howard Foster Lowry, ed., *The Letters of Matthew Arnold to Arthur Hugh Clough* (London, 1932), pp. 97, 100–101, 124.

27. For a provocative account of Shelley's reputation, see Robert M. Smith, *et al., The Shelley Legend* (New York, 1945), but check against Frederick L. Jones's searching review, *PMLA*, LXI (1946), 848–890. See also F. C. Mason, *A Study in Shelley Criticism* (Mercersburg, Pa., 1937).

28. See letter of May 1829 in Gordon N. Ray, ed., *The Letters and Private Papers of William Makepeace Thackeray*, 4 vols. (Cambridge: Harvard University Press, 1945–46), I, 74.

29. See Kingsley, *Lectures and Essays*, pp. 46–47.

30. See Taylor's 1834 preface to *Philip van Artevelde* (London, 1883), p. xv; contrast a late Victorian opinion in E. M. Forster, *Goldsworthy Lowes Dickinson* (New York, 1934), p. 37.

31. See Mason, *Shelley Criticism*, pp. 48, 66.

32. See Tennyson, *Memoir*, I, 141; II, 285.

33. See Carlyle, *Reminiscences*, II, 292–293.

34. See George L. Nesbitt, *Benthamite Reviewing: The First Twelve Years of the Westminster Review, 1824–1836* (New York, 1934). I quote from pp. 98, 100, 101.

35. See Newman, "Poetry with Reference to Aristotle's Poetics," *Essays Critical and Historical*, 2 vols. (London, 1919), I, 9–10. For a detailed account of Newman's rather ambiguous regard for "romanticism," see Charles Frederick Harrold, *John Henry Newman* (New York, 1945), pp. 246–254.

36. See preface to *Philip van Artevelde*.

37. See Lowry, *Letters of Arnold to Clough*, p. 124.

38. See Arnold's 1853 preface to *Empedocles*.

39. Arnold, "To a Gipsy Child by the Sea-shore."

40. See George Orwell, *Dickens, Dali and Others* (New York, 1946), pp. 1–75, and cf. Young, *Victorian England*, pp. 49–50.

41. See Miriam M. H. Thrall, *Rebellious Fraser's* (New York, 1934), esp. pp. 64–107.

42. See George Kitchin, *A Survey of Parody and Burlesque in English* (Edinburgh, 1931), p. 265.

43. Quoted by Cruse, *Victorians and Their Reading,* p. 408.

44. Quoted by Walter Jerrold, *Thomas Hood* (London, 1907), p. 322.

45. See "The Portrait" and "Literary Reminiscences," *The Choice Works of Thomas Hood,* 4 vols. (New York, 1857), I, 36–100.

46. See Frederick William Roe, *Thomas Carlyle as Critic of Literature* (New York, 1910), esp. pp. 72–89 on his debt to the romantics.

47. Quoted by Emery Neff, *Carlyle* (New York, 1932), p. 267.

48. See, esp., Charles Frederick Harrold, *Carlyle and German Thought* (New Haven, 1934), Hill Shine, *Carlyle and the Saint Simonians* (Baltimore, 1941), and René Wellek, "Carlyle and the Philosophy of History," *Philological Quarterly,* XXIII (1944), 55–76.

49. Quotations from Thomas Carlyle, *Works,* Centenary ed., 30 vols. (New York, 1896–1901), II, 64 ("Signs of the Times," 1829), and V, 172, 176 (*Heroes and Hero-worship,* 1841).

50. Quotations from Carlyle, *Lectures on the History of Literature* (New York, 1892), pp. 190–224.

51. See Carlyle, "The Hero as Poet," *Works,* V, 83; and, on Byron's "siren-charming," *Works,* II, 78.

52. See J. A. Froude, *Thomas Carlyle,* 2 vols. (New York, 1910), I, 304, and John Forster, *The Life of Charles Dickens,* 3 vols. (Philadelphia, 1873), II, 110.

53. See Carlyle, *Works,* V, 159, 164.

54. See Morley, *Critical Miscellanies,* p. 71.

55. See Neff, *Carlyle,* p. 247.

56. Carlyle, "Signs of the Times," *Works,* II, 80.

CHAPTER III: THE SPASMODIC SCHOOL

1. See John Nichol, ed., *The Poetical Works of Sydney Dobell,* 2 vols. (London, 1875), I, xxvii.

2. Kingsley, *Lectures and Essays,* p. 51; from an article of November 1853, the first use I have discovered of the label "spasmodic school."

3. Kingsley, "Alexander Smith and Alexander Pope," *Miscellanies,* 2 vols. (London, 1860), I, 288.

4. See Arnold's 1853 preface to *Empedocles,* which, without using the label, suggests the limitations of much "Spasmodic" verse.

5. Quoted by Cruse, *Victorians and Their Reading,* p. 180.

6. The quotations from *Festus* were transcribed from a copy once owned by Longfellow (Boston, 1845), pp. 286, 413.

7. Quotations from *The Age* are from the Boston edition (1858), pp. 56, 87, 119.

8. See R. H. Horne, "Henry Taylor and the Author of 'Festus,'" *A New Spirit of the Age,* 2 vols. (London, 1844), II, 289, 303.

9. See Horne, *Orion* (London, 1874), pp. v, xxiii. Originally published in 1843, *Orion* was to be sold for one farthing as a mark of Horne's contempt for the public regard for epic poetry.

10. See Horne, *A New Spirit*, II, 165.

11. See Marston's preface to *Gerald* (London, 1842), p. vi. The quotations which follow are from this edition.

12. See *Gerald*, p. 23n.

13. See R. H. Shepherd, ed., *Studies of Sensation and Event* (London, 1879), pp. xi, xxxix, lviii, lxviii, 96.

14. Quoted by W. Robertson Nicoll, *Gilfillan's Literary Portraits* (London, 1909), p. ix.

15. Gilfillan unlike Carlyle was a staunch supporter of European liberals like Kossuth, Mazzini, Garibaldi. On his thought in general, cf. Nicoll, *Gilfillan's Portraits*, p. vii, and R. A. and E. S. Watson, eds., *George Gilfillan, Letters and Journals* (London, 1892), p. 99.

16. See Watson, *Gilfillan*, pp. 93, 95.

17. See letters to Dobell, quoted by Watson, pp. 139, 140, 144.

18. See Watson, p. 159.

19. Quoted by Watson, p. 166.

20. See Gilfillan, "A Cluster of New Poets," *A Third Gallery of Portraits* (New York, 1855), p. 155; "Alfred Tennyson," *Tait's Edinburgh Magazine*, April 1847, p. 229; and Watson, *Gilfillan*, p. 150.

21. See *Third Gallery*, p. 163.

22. See Massey's preface to the third edition of his *Poems and Ballads* (London, 1854).

23. See *Third Gallery*, pp. 150, 151.

24. Quotations from Bigg, *Night and the Soul* (London, 1854), pp. 9–10, 12, 23.

25. See Watson, *Gilfillan*, p. 155, and Gilfillan, *Third Gallery*, p. 142.

26. See *DNB* article on Smith by Thomas Bayne.

27. The lines from *Life Drama* are from Smith's *Poems* (London, 1866), pp. 9–10, 13, 34–35, 63, 120, 210, 211.

28. Note Edward's realistic rejoinder to Walter's astral speculations (p. 131): "I think — we are two fools: let us to bed. / What care the stars for us?"

29. Quoted by Watson, *Gilfillan*, pp. 133, 139.

30. Letters quoted by Watson, pp. 137, 151.

31. See Dobell, *Thoughts on Art, Philosophy, and Religion*, John Nichol, ed. (London, 1876), p. 15.

32. For Dobell on poetic truth and metaphor, see *Thoughts on Art*, esp. pp. 17–20, 33, 51, 53, 142.

33. Gilfillan, *Third Gallery*, p. 116.

34. The quotations from *Balder* are from *Poetical Works of Dobell*, II, 151, 248, 260.

35. Aytoun had already quarreled with Gilfillan over attitudes towards the Scottish Covenanters; see Watson, *Gilfillan*, pp. 213, 389–391. There may also

have been political disagreement, since Gilfillan was associated with the liberal *Tait's Magazine* and Aytoun with the conservative *Blackwood's.*

36. See Theodore Martin, *Memoir of William Edmondstoune Aytoun* (Edinburgh, n.d.), pp. 146–147, 164.

37. Quotations from *The Book of Ballads and Firmilian* (New York, 1890), pp. 26, 101, 112.

38. See "E. J.," ed., *The Life and Letters of Sydney Dobell,* 2 vols. (London, 1878), I, 353–354.

39. Gilfillan, quoted by Nicoll, *Gilfillan's Portraits,* p. xii.

40. Quoted by Watson, *Gilfillan,* p. 414.

41. Browning in *The Ring and the Book* was able to subject criminal passion to a dispassionate analysis far beyond any attained by the Spasmodics.

42. See Edmund Gosse, "A Plea for Certain Exotic Forms of Verse," *Cornhill,* XXXVI (1877), 54–55. Gosse explicitly attacks Dobell's influence.

43. See Nicoll, *Gilfillan's Portraits,* p. xvi, and Buchanan, "Sydney Dobell and the 'Spasmodic School,'" *A Look Round Literature* (London, 1887), pp. 185–203.

44. W. H. Mallock, *Every Man His Own Poet; or, The Inspired Singer's Recipe Book* (1873; Boston, 1878), pp. 26–27.

45. See dedication to *Aurora Leigh,* and Clarke, *Elizabeth Barrett Browning,* p. 232.

46. Mrs. Browning later warned the young Lytton against "diffuseness" when writing to him of his *Lucile,* which vied with *Aurora Leigh* as the most popular verse novel of the Victorian period. See Aurelia Brooks Harlan, *Owen Meredith* (New York, 1946), p. 140.

47. Quoted by Cruse, *Victorians and Their Reading,* p. 196.

48. Regarding Tennyson and the Spasmodics, see Tennyson on Smith, *Memoir,* II, 73; and Gilfillan on Tennyson, quoted by Nicoll, *Gilfillan's Portraits,* p. xviii. See also Frederic Harrison's comment on *Maud* in his *Autobiographic Memoirs,* I, 164. Professor P. F. Baum, I believe, seriously underestimates the "Spasmodic" element in Tennyson; see his *Tennyson Sixty Years After* (Chapel Hill, 1948), pp. 309–310.

CHAPTER IV: TENNYSON — THE TWO VOICES

1. For the anecdote, see Tennyson, *Memoir,* I, 6.

2. Quoted from *Nineteenth Century,* XXXII (1892), 832. Huxley praised Tennyson as the only poet since Lucretius "who has taken the trouble to understand the work and tendency of the men of science." See Leonard Huxley, ed., *The Life and Letters of Thomas Henry Huxley,* 2 vols. (New York, 1916), II, 359.

3. Cf. Henry S. Salt, *Tennyson as a Thinker* (London, 1893), p. 16; Ford, *Keats and the Victorians,* p. 47; Batho and Dobrée, *Victorians and After,* p. 45; Baum, *Tennyson,* pp. 230–231.

4. See Harold Nicolson, *Tennyson* (Boston, 1925).

5. Hugh I'Anson Fausset, *Tennyson, a Modern Portrait* (London, 1923), p. 41.

6. See W. H. Auden, ed., *A Selection from the Poems of Alfred, Lord Tennyson* (Garden City, 1944), p. x. Auden draws freely on Nicolson. Both were anticipated by Salt; see Salt, *Tennyson as a Thinker*, pp. 9, 49, 51.

7. See Douglas Bush, *Mythology and the Romantic Tradition* (Cambridge: Harvard University Press, 1937), p. 198.

8. See Tennyson, *Memoir*, I, 4, 15, 17.

9. Quoted from Charles Tennyson, ed., *The Devil and the Lady* (London, 1930), p. viii.

10. Lines quoted from Charles Tennyson, ed., *Unpublished Early Poems* (London, 1931), pp. 32, 29.

11. Quoted by J. C. Thomson, ed., *Tennyson's Suppressed Poems* (New York, 1903), p. 16n.

12. For his early Cambridge period, see Tennyson, *Memoir*, I, 34, 35, 66–68, 76.

13. See "Sense and Conscience," *Unpublished Early Poems*, p. 44.

14. See Frances M. Brookfield, *The Cambridge "Apostles"* (New York, 1906), p. 314.

15. Stirling Maxwell's sobriquet for Milnes; see Marquess of Crewe, "Lord Houghton and his Circle," in Harley Granville-Barker, ed., *The Eighteen-Seventies* (Cambridge, 1929), p. 20.

16. Charles Buller had been admitted to their circle "solely on account of his logical mind and in spite of his lively qualities." See Brookfield, *Cambridge "Apostles,"* p. 107.

17. Quoted by Brookfield, p. 174.

18. See Arthur Waugh, *Alfred, Lord Tennyson* (New York, 1896), p. 23.

19. Tennyson, *Memoir*, I, 118.

20. See *Memoir*, I, 119. "The Palace of Art" was dedicated to Trench.

21. *Memoir*, I, 97.

22. Lines from "A Character," published in 1830.

23. See *Memoir*, I, 44.

24. See *Memoir*, I, 41.

25. Hallam, quoted from *Memoir*, I, 89.

26. Hallam, quoted from *Memoir*, I, 81.

27. Quoted by John Brown, *Arthur H. Hallam* (Edinburgh, 1862), p. 58.

28. Cf. *Memoir*, I, 193.

29. *Memoir*, I, 196.

30. Charles Kingsley denied the charge that "Locksley Hall" was "Werterian and unhealthy"; it was rather, he said, a study of "man rising out of sickness into health . . . conquering his selfish sorrow, and the moral and intellectual paralysis which it produces, by faith and hope." See Kingsley, "Tennyson," *Miscellanies*, I, 224.

31. Tennyson, *Memoir*, I, 83.

32. *Memoir*, I, 158. By the late thirties the vogue of the annuals was passing; see Besant, *Fifty Years Ago*, p. 195.

33. *Memoir*, I, 12.

34. *Memoir,* I, 507.

35. See *Memoir,* I, 145.

36. *Memoir,* I, 122.

37. Quoted by T. H. S. Escott, *Great Victorians* (London, 1916), p. 315.

38. See *Memoir,* I, 265.

39. *Edinburgh Review,* XC (1849), 432.

40. See *Memoir,* I, 223, 266.

41. Cf. D. W. T. Starnes, "The Influence of Carlyle on Tennyson," *Texas Review,* VI (1921), 316–336.

42. See *Memoir,* I, 227.

43. See *Memoir,* I, 278; cf. I, 102.

44. See *Memoir,* I, 319.

45. For the anecdote, see Anne Thackeray Ritchie, *Records of Tennyson, Ruskin, Browning* (New York, 1892), p. 52.

CHAPTER V: THE PATTERN OF CONVERSION

1. As late as 1888 the themes seemed vital to Roden Noel; cf. Noel's major poem, *A Modern Faust* (1888).

2. See *Poetical Works of Dobell,* I, xviii.

3. Browning and imperfection: Quotations from "Rabbi Ben Ezra," "The Last Ride Together," "Andrea del Sarto," "The Grammarian's Funeral," and "Abt Vogler"; see also "Old Pictures in Florence," *Pippa Passes* (where Jules learns that perfection is failure), *Luria* (esp. Act V), and "Saul." Cf. Edward Dowden, *Studies in Literature* (London, 1887), p. 219, and Joseph Warren Beach, *The Concept of Nature in Nineteenth-Century English Poetry* (New York, 1936), pp. 451–453.

4. See Bailey, *Festus,* pp. 312–313, 319.

5. See Ruskin, *Works,* X, 200, 202, 203.

6. See Alexander Smith, "Horton," *City Poems* (London, 1857), pp. 41–42.

7. Cf. Maurice on purgatory and purgation, quoted by Claude Jenkins, *Frederick Denison Maurice and the New Reformation* (London, 1938), pp. 21–22.

8. See *The Sickness unto Death,* trans. Walter Lowrie (Princeton, 1941), esp. pp. 25, 69, 93, 99.

9. See R. H. Hutton "The Metaphysics of Conversion," *Contemporary Thought and Thinkers,* 2 vols. (London, 1894), I, 372–373.

10. On Mill's mental crisis, see *Autobiography,* pp. 112–155.

11. On Newman's development, see the lyrics of 1832, esp. "Bondage," "The Scars of Sin," and "Angelic Guidance," in *Verses on Various Occasions* (London, 1890); the *Apologia,* pt. III, and pt. VII, par. 1; and cf. Harrold, *Newman,* esp. pp. 1–47.

12. See "Symbols," *Sartor Resartus,* bk. IV, chap. 3; and cf. Bate, *Classic to Romantic,* p. 180, on the empirical symbols of Schlegel.

13. Cf. Carlyle on Coleridge, who lacked the courage to cross "the howling

deserts of Infidelity . . . to the firm new lands of Faith beyond" (*Life of Sterling,* p. 62).

14. See *Sartor,* bk. IV, chap. 5, and *Lectures on the History of Literature,* p. 208.

15. The *Water Babies* has interesting "psychological" overtones; with Tom's sea journey, compare Jung on the myth of "the night journey under the sea," discussed by Maud Bodkin, *Archetypal Patterns in Poetry* (London, 1934), p. 52.

16. Hardy's treatment of the drowned lovers in *The Return of the Native* recalls David's view of Steerforth; for Eustacia in death attains a beauty beyond all her earthly loveliness, and Wildeve, washed clean of his guilt, recovers an expression of "luminous youthfulness."

17. On the regeneration theme in George Eliot, cf. Routh on the role of "spiritual awakening" in her novels (*Towards the Twentieth Century,* p. 262). The theme recurs in many other works of fiction; see, for example, *Two Years Ago* by Charles Kingsley or *Ravenshoe* by Henry Kingsley.

18. I limit my discussion of the water image in verse to four major poets, but we might well consider the role of the sea or of "living water" in much verse from Hood's "Bridge of Sighs" to Henley's "Rhymes and Rhythms." See esp. Clough, "Bethesda," "A River Pool," "O Thou of Little Faith," "The Stream of Life," and *Dipsychus* (discussed below). Cf. Hopkins, "The Wreck of the Deutschland" and "Eurydice."

19. See Lowry, *Letters of Arnold to Clough,* p. 34. Cf. Bodkin on "Sohrab and Rustum," *Archetypal Patterns,* pp. 65–66.

20. See "The Two Voices," line 389, and *In Memoriam,* XII, line 6.

21. See *In Memoriam,* CIII, and cf. "a calling of the sea," *Enoch Arden,* line 904. For other water images in *In Memoriam,* see esp. IX, X, XVI, XXXV.

22. See Ruskin, *Works,* III, 494, 573, and cf. III, 44, and XXVIII, 758. See also Ruskin's treatment of Turner's "Slave Ship," where he describes the guilty ship in the conquering sea, all in terms of an allegory of line, color, and symbol (III, 571–572).

23. See Swinburne, *Studies in Prose and Poetry* (London, 1894), p. 222.

24. Cf. James Hinton, *The Mystery of Pain* (London, 1866).

25. See R. H. Nettleship, ed., *Works of Thomas Hill Green,* 3 vols. (London, 1889), III, 36.

26. See Lowry, *Letters of Arnold to Clough,* p. 146.

27. See Newman, *Phases of Faith* (London, 1850). Newman goes on to suggest his later conversion to a kind of spiritualized naturalism.

28. See Overton, *Church in England,* II, 366–369.

29. Humbert Wolfe denies that Clough is the doubter at all and points to *Dipsychus* as evidence of "innate satirical genius"; but to defend his thesis he is forced to dismiss the bulk of Clough's work. See Wolfe, "Arthur Hugh Clough," in John Drinkwater, ed., *The Eighteen Sixties* (New York, 1932), pp. 20–50.

30. On Clough's fluctuation, cf. Lowry, *Letters of Arnold to Clough,* p. 146: "You are too content to *fluctuate.*"

CHAPTER VI: GOD AND MAMMON

1. See Cruse, *Victorians and Their Reading*, p. 118.

2. Walter Besant tells us that in the thirties the copyrights of the sermons of Robert Hall and Charles Simeon sold for four and five thousand pounds, respectively; see Besant, *Fifty Years Ago*, p. 192.

3. Jakob Burckhardt, *Reflections on History*, trans. "M. D. H." (London, 1943), p. 22.

4. See Hood's "Ode to Rae Wilson, Esquire," *Choice Works*, III(1), 197–213.

5. Ruskin, *Works*, XVIII, 448, and XXIX, 134; see also XXVIII, 516.

6. Kingsley, "God and Mammon," *Westminster Sermons* (London, 1874), pp. 293–294.

7. Mrs. Gore, *Men of Capital*, 3 vols. (London, 1846), I, iii, v.

8. Kingsley, *Yeast* (1848; New York, n.d.), p. 48.

9. See John Lawrence Hammond, *The Town Labourer, 1760–1832* (London, 1920), p. 145.

10. For a useful rapid survey, see Guy Chapman, "The Economic Background," in Batho and Dobrée, *Victorians and After*, pp. 132–146.

11. William Gilbert, *De Profundis* (1864; London, 1866), p. 444.

12. Quoted from *Eliza Cook's Journal* by G. M. Young, *Victorian England*, p. 55.

13. The phrase, "survival of the fittest," often attributed to Darwin, was first used by Spencer, while "the struggle for existence" was the coinage of Alfred Russel Wallace.

14. For Macaulay on the Reform Bill, see Christie, *Transition from Aristocracy*, p. 66.

15. The most stimulating treatment of Protestantism and the mercantile system remains R. H. Tawney's *Religion and the Rise of Capitalism* (London, 1926).

16. See R. B. Schlatter, *The Social Ideas of Religious Leaders, 1660–1688* (London, 1940), pp. 190–191.

17. See Knickerbocker, *Free Minds*, p. 8, and cf. Elie Halévy, *A History of the English People in 1815* (London, 1924), bk. III, chap. 1.

18. Kingsley, "Letters to the Chartists," *Politics for the People* (London), May 27, 1848, p. 58, and June 17, 1848, pp. 136–137.

19. See Christie, *Transition from Aristocracy*, pp. 75–76.

20. See Maurice J. Quinlan, *Victorian Prelude* (New York, 1941), chap. 11.

21. Quoted by J. G. Lockhart, *Life of Sir Walter Scott* (London, 1893), p. 466.

22. See Porter, *Progress of the Nation*, p. 676.

23. From the 1850 preface to *Pendennis*.

24. Cf. Michael Sadleir, *Anthony Trollope* (Boston, 1927), p. 21.

25. Cf. A. C. Bradley on the Victorian family, quoted by Knickerbocker, *Free Minds*, p. 11; see also Trevelyan, *English Social History*, p. 545.

26. See C. L. Graves, "*Punch* in the 'Sixties," *Eighteen Sixties*, p. 167.

27. Morley, *Critical Miscellanies*, p. 104.

28. Morley, "Lancashire," *Fortnightly Review*, XXX (1878), 5.

29. See Porter, *Progress of the Nation*, pp. 679–680.

30. Cf. Knickerbocker, *Free Minds*, p. 77, and Trevelyan, *English Social History*, pp. 563–564.

31. Morley, *On Compromise* (1873; London, 1928), p. 95.

32. Kingsley, *Yeast*, p. 9.

33. Cf. E. L. Woodward, *The Age of Reform* (Oxford, 1939), pp. 490–491, and Harrold, *Newman*, p. 24.

34. On Maurice and his work, see, esp., Frederick Maurice, ed., *The Life of Frederick Denison Maurice*, 2 vols. (New York, 1884), and C. E. Raven, *Christian Socialism* (London, 1920). On the political conservatism of the group, see *Life of Maurice*, I, 485–486, II, 7, 41, and cf. C. W. Stubbs, *Charles Kingsley and the Christian Socialist Movement* (London, 1899), pp. 25–29.

35. Cf. Harrison, *Autobiographic Memoirs*, I, 151: "We all loved and honoured Maurice for his moral qualities and truly Christian sympathies." Yet Harrison attacked his theology. Cf. the attitude of J. S. Mill (*Autobiography*, p. 130), who nonetheless believed Maurice "decidedly superior" to Coleridge in mental power.

36. See *Life of Maurice*, I, 479.

37. Kingsley, *Yeast*, p. 14.

38. See Overton, *Church in England*, II, 391.

CHAPTER VII: VICTORIAN TASTE

1. William Whewell, "The General Bearing of the Great Exhibition on the Progress of Art and Science," in *Lectures on the Results of the Great Exhibition of 1851* (London, 1852), pp. 12, 18–19.

2. See Mrs. Kingsley, ed., *Charles Kingsley, His Letters and Memories of His Life* (New York, 1877), p. 140.

3. Stanza added to "To the Queen," dedication to *In Memoriam*, 1851; the lines were later dropped. See also *Memoir*, I, 340.

4. See Ruskin, *Works*, X, 114; XII, 419–420.

5. See Walter Curt Behrendt, *Modern Building* (New York, 1937), pp. 42–43; and Christopher Hobhouse, *1851 and the Crystal Palace* (New York, 1937).

6. Whewell in *Lectures on the Great Exhibition*, p. 5.

7. See *Official Descriptive and Illustrated Catalogue*, 3 vols. (London, 1852), II, 730.

8. See Rita Wellman, *Victoria Royal* (New York, 1939), pp. 55–58. Miss Wellman's general account of the Exhibition is both amusing and informative.

9. See Sigfried Giedion, "Railroad Comfort and Patent Furniture," *Technology Review*, XLVII (1944–45), 97–98, 137–138.

10. On the Fourdinois sideboard, see *Exhibition of the Works of Industry of All Nations, 1851: Reports by the Juries* (London, 1852), pp. 545, 722–723.

11. See *Exhibition of Works of Industry*, p. 708.

12. Jones, "Colour in the Decorative Arts," in *Lectures on the Great Exhibition*, 2d ser. (London, 1853), p. 256.

13. *Spectator*, XXIV (1851), 663.

14. Bailey, *The Age*, p. 28.

15. Harrison, *Autobiographic Memoirs*, I, 88–89.

16. Kingsley, *Plays and Puritans* (London, 1873), p. 4.

17. Quoted by W. P. Frith, *My Autobiography and Reminiscences*, 2 vols. (New York, 1888), I, 223.

18. See Ruth Webb Lee, *Victorian Glass: Specialties of the Nineteenth Century* (Northborough, Mass., 1944).

19. See Frith, *Autobiography*, I, 202–203.

20. Newman, 1867 dedication, *Verses on Various Occasions*, pp. vi–vii.

21. See his "Tennyson, Swinburne, Meredith — and the Theatre," *Eighteen Seventies*, pp. 161–191.

22. See *Art Journal*, I (1849), 159; the art critic called the piece "in all respects so worthy a specimen of his Royal Highness's taste and skill in designing." For my illustration (which unfortunately does not show the dead hare) I am indebted to Professor John F. Kienitz of the University of Wisconsin.

23. On imitation and the use of metal, see M. Digby Wyatt, "An Attempt to define the Principles which should determine Form in the Decorative Arts," *Lectures on the Great Exhibition*, 2d ser., pp. 233, 240.

24. See *The Science of Taste* "by G.–L." (London, 1879), p. 105.

25. See *Exhibition of Works of Industry*, p. 722.

26. See *Science of Taste*, pp. 90, 100, 141.

27. Cf. William C. Holdsworth, *Charles Dickens as a Legal Historian* (New Haven, 1928), esp. pp. 79–81.

28. See John Mason Brown, "Children of Skelt," *Saturday Review of Literature*, vol. XXX, no. 1 (1947), p. 23.

29. See Dobell, *Thoughts on Art*, p. 83.

30. See Tennyson, *Memoir*, I, 259. But wherever the image occurred to Tennyson, the reviewer might have replied, it was still "artificial" in inspiration.

31. Anecdote from Ritchie, *Tennyson, Ruskin, Browning*, p. 48.

32. See George Eliot, "False Testimonials," *Impressions of Theophrastus Such* (1879; New York, n.d.), p. 155.

33. See Frith, *Autobiography*, I, 201; on his own respect for detail, cf. I, 213–214.

34. See Richard D. Buck, "A Note on the Methods and Materials of the Pre-Raphaelite Painters," *The Pre-Raphaelites* (catalogue, 1946, Fogg Museum of Art, Harvard University), pp. 14–18.

35. See Sir Algernon West, *Recollections, 1832–1886* (London, n.d.), p. 169.

36. See Frith, *Autobiography*, I, 149. Sir Charles Landseer was a brother of the more popular Sir Edwin.

37. See Kingsley, "The National Gallery," *Politics for the People*, May 20, 1848, pp. 39–40.

38. Cf. *Science of Taste*, pp. 81–89.

39. *Lectures on the Great Exhibition*, 2d ser., p. 291.

40. See Chambers, *History of Taste*, p. 225.

41. See Sir Reginald Blomfield, *Richard Norman Shaw, R. A.* (London, 1940), p. 15.

42. On Eastlake, see Wellman, *Victoria Royal*, pp. 83–91.

43. See Behrendt, *Modern Building*, pp. 54–56.

44. See John Gloag, *English Furniture* (London, 1934), p. 134.

CHAPTER VIII: THE MORAL AESTHETIC

1. Dobell, *Thoughts on Art*, p. 74.

2. On Kingsley's view of art, see esp. *Politics for the People*, May 6, 1848, p. 6.

3. J. G. Macvicar, *The Philosophy of the Beautiful* (Edinburgh, 1855), pp. 20, 24, 172. Macvicar was associated with the Edinburgh aestheticians, but was not actually a member of the Aesthetic Society.

4. D. R. Hay, *The Science of Beauty, as Developed in Nature and Applied in Art* (Edinburgh, 1856).

5. John Addington Symonds, *The Principles of Beauty* (London, 1857); quotations from pp. xi, xii, 49, 58.

6. See his *Poetics, an Essay on Poetry* (1852). On *Dallas*, see esp. G. C. Boase's *DNB* article and John Drinkwater's essay, "Eneas Sweetland Dallas," *Eighteen Sixties*, pp. 201–223.

7. Dallas, *Gay Science*, II, 105.

8. For Dallas on the "Hidden Soul," see *Gay Science*, I, 194, 196, 199, 207, 216.

9. With Dallas's distinction between logical and poetical comparisons (*Gay Science*, I, 269–272), cf. the quite similar argument of William James, *The Principles of Psychology*, 2 vols. (New York, 1890), II, 325–371.

10. See *Gay Science*, I, 274.

11. See *Gay Science*, II, 114, 116, 118.

12. For Dallas on art and morality, see *Gay Science*, II, 151, 160, 165, 195, 206.

13. For Dallas on popular taste, see *Gay Science*, I, 127–128, 129, 130; II, 305.

14. Ruskin, *Works*, XXXV, 226.

15. See esp. R. H. Wilenski, *John Ruskin* (London, 1933), David Larg, *John Ruskin* (London, 1932), Amabel Williams-Ellis, *The Exquisite Tragedy* (New York, 1929), Admiral Sir William James, *The Order of Release* (London, 1947), and Peter Quennell, "Ruskin and the Women," *Atlantic*, CLXXIX (1947), 37–45.

16. See Ruskin, *Works*, XVIII, 69–75, and XXVII, 342–345.

17. *Works*, XVII, 345.

18. *Works*, XXXIV, 344.

19. See 1874 preface to the *Stones of Venice*, *Works*, IX, 11.

20. *Works,* XVII, 415.

21. See Wilenski, *Ruskin,* p. 138.

22. See Arthur Pope, preface to Fogg Museum catalogue, *Pre-Raphaelites,* pp. 4–5.

23. See Wilenski, *Ruskin,* p. 39.

24. Quoted by W. G. Collingwood, *The Life and Work of John Ruskin,* 2 vols. (Boston, 1893), I, 225.

25. See Frederic Harrison, *John Ruskin* (New York, 1902), pp. 157–158.

26. Cf. J. A. Spender, *New Lamps and Ancient Lights* (London, 1940), p. 144.

27. See T. Ashcroft, *English Art and English Society* (London, 1936), p. 156, and Henry Ladd's useful study of Ruskin's aesthetic, *The Victorian Morality of Art* (New York, 1932), pp. 339–341.

28. For Ruskin on the artist's "morality," see esp. *The Two Paths* and "The Relation of Art to Morals," *Works,* XVI, XX. I quote from XX, 77, 79, 83. See also Ladd's general criticism and G. F. Carritt, *The Theory of Beauty* (New York, 1914), pp. 47–73.

29. Ruskin, *Works,* XXXIII, 173.

30. *Works,* III, 110.

31. *Works,* III, 92; cf. V, 19, 66.

32. *Works,* XXII, 302; cf. XXII, 125, XXVII, 146.

33. *Works,* III, 87.

34. *Works,* III, 91.

35. See Ladd's able discussion of the "ideas," *Victorian Morality of Art,* pp. 173–187.

36. See Ruskin, *Works,* IV, 146–147.

37. Cf. Bernard Shaw, *Ruskin's Politics* (London, 1921), p. 7.

38. For Ruskin on "imitation" and "realism," see *Works,* III, 12; V, 232; XXIX, 161; XXXIV, 377.

39. *Works,* V, 29.

40. See *Works,* V, 70–101.

41. Quoted by E. R. and J. Pennell, *The Life of James McNeill Whistler* (Philadelphia, 1919), p. 154.

42. For Ruskin's attacks on Whistler, see *Works,* XXIII, 49; XXIX, 160.

43. From "My Own Article on Whistler," *Works,* XXIX, 586.

44. *Works,* XXXVII, 225.

45. Quoted by Sir John Lavery, *The Life of a Painter* (Boston, 1940), p. 114.

46. Ruskin, *Works,* XXIX, xxv.

47. See Oscar Wilde, *Miscellanies* (London, 1908), pp. 30–31.

48. Arnold, *Essays in Criticism,* 2d ser. (London, 1935), p. 102.

49. With Ruskin's view of nature and his idea of purity, compare the opinions of Monet, Sisley, and Pissarro; see Robert Goldwater and Marco Treves, eds., *Artists on Art* (New York, 1945), pp. 309, 313, 319.

50. See Gustave Flaubert, *Correspondance,* 2 vols. (Paris, 1889), II, 71.

1. See Robert Buchanan, "The Fleshly School of Poetry," *Contemporary Review,* XXVIII (1871), 334–350, and *The Fleshly School of Poetry and Other Phenomena of the Day* (London, 1872).

2. See Buchanan's letter to the *Academy,* XXII (1882), 11, and "A Note on Dante Rossetti," *Look Round Literature,* p. 155; and cf. the two dedications to his novel, *God and the Man* (London, 1881, 1882).

3. For Courthope on Rossetti, see *Quarterly Review,* CXXXII (1872), 59–84. For a general survey of critical opinion, see S. N. Ghose, *Dante Gabriel Rossetti and Contemporary Criticism, 1849–1882* (Strassburg, 1929), a useful though often inaccurate compendium.

4. *Atlantic,* XXVI (1870), 116.

5. See Tennyson, *Memoir,* II, 505, but for a contradictory judgment ascribed by Buchanan to Tennyson, see Harriet Jay, *Robert Buchanan* (London, 1903), p. 162.

6. Unsigned review in *Nation,* XI (1870), 29, identified by Rossetti; see Ghose, *Rossetti and Criticism,* p. 135.

7. Dennett in *North American Review,* CXI (1870), 478.

8. See W. C. DeVane, "The Harlot and the Thoughtful Young Man," *Studies in Philology,* XXIX (1932), 463–484. See also the private (and therefore perhaps suspect) printing for T. J. Wise of Browning's *Critical Comments on Swinburne and Rossetti* (London, 1919), p. 10.

9. Rossetti has even been admired for an alleged "fleshliness"; see, for example, R. L. Mégroz, *Dante Gabriel Rossetti* (London, 1928), pp. 192, 195.

10. Lord David Cecil, "Rossetti," in Massingham, *Great Victorians,* p. 406. Cf. E. B. Burgum, "Rossetti and the Ivory Tower," *Sewanee Review,* XXVII (1929), 431–446. For earlier opinion linking Rossetti with the Aesthetes, see Walter Hamilton, *The Aesthetic Movement in England* (London, 1882), p. 123, and Arthur Symons, "A Note on Rossetti," *North American Review,* CCIV (1916), 128–134. On Rossetti's relationship to the Decadence, see Holbrook Jackson, *The Eighteen Nineties* (New York, 1914), p. 69; Osbert Burdett, *The Beardsley Period* (New York, 1925), p. 33; B. Ifor Evans, *English Poetry in the Later Nineteenth Century* (London, 1933), p. 24; Louise Rosenblatt, *L'Idée de l'art pour l'art* (Paris, 1931), pp. 104, 107, 141; and A. J. Farmer, *Le Mouvement esthétique et décadent en Angleterre* (Paris, 1931), pp. 16, 19.

11. Ruskin, *Works,* XIV, 168, and XXXIII, 269.

12. Clough, quoted by Lowry, *Letters of Arnold to Clough,* p. 25.

13. Quoted by Wellman, *Victoria Royal,* p. 296.

14. Quoted by Caine, *My Story* (New York, 1909), p. 115.

15. Quoted by Caine, *My Story,* p. 138.

16. For the anecdote, see Caine, pp. 177–178.

17. Rossetti, "The Stealthy School of Criticism," *Athenaeum,* 1871 (2), p. 793.

18. *Macmillan's Magazine,* XLV (1881), 326.

19. See W. M. Rossetti, ed., *Dante Gabriel Rossetti: His Family-Letters,* 2 vols. (Boston, 1895), II, 312.

20. In Watts-Dunton's novel, *Aylwin,* D'Arcy, obviously Rossetti, explains why he is a "mystic." See *Aylwin* (New York, 1899), p. 216. Cf. Watts-Dunton's article, "The Truth about Rossetti," *Nineteenth Century,* XIII (1883), 404–423.

21. See J. C. Earle, "Dante Gabriel Rosetti" [*sic*], *Catholic World,* XIX (1874), 271; and cf. Rossetti's opinion of the review ("about the best written on the book"), *Family-Letters,* II, 312.

22. Swinburne, "The Poems of Dante Gabriel Rossetti" (1870), in Edmund Gosse and T. J. Wise, eds., *Complete Works of Algernon Charles Swinburne,* 20 vols. (London, 1925–1927), XV, 45.

23. Quoted by Nicoll, *Gilfillan's Portraits,* p. xvii.

24. Note, for example, the concentration achieved by revising the last line of the octave of "Lost Days" from the 1870 reading, "The throats of men in Hell who thirst alway," to the final version, "The undying throats of Hell, athirst alway," where the synedoche heightens the impression of eternality by blurring the visual image. See Paull F. Baum's excellent edition, *The House of Life* (Cambridge: Harvard University Press, 1928), pp. 198–199. I cannot, however, agree with Professor Baum that the change is not an improvement.

25. See Caine, *My Story,* p. 122.

26. Caine, p. 57.

27. Quoted by Caine, p. 137.

28. See Gaunt, *Aesthetic Adventure,* p. 124.

29. Quoted by Caine, *My Story,* p. 141. See also p. 232.

30. Praz, *Romantic Agony,* pp. 220, 228, 231.

31. Eliot, *Essays Ancient and Modern* (New York, 1936), p. 66.

32. Swinburne, quoted by Georges Lafourcade, *Swinburne* (New York, 1932), p. 228.

33. Quoted by Cruse, *Victorians and Their Reading,* pp. 372, 375.

34. From a *Fortnightly* review by Sheldon Amos, quoted by Edwin M. Everett, *The Party of Humanity: The Fortnightly Review and Its Contributors* (Chapel Hill, 1939), p. 244.

35. Swinburne, *Under the Microscope* (Portland, Me., 1899), p. 23.

36. See the private printing for T. J. Wise of *Letters from Algernon Charles Swinburne to Sir Richard F. Burton and Other Correspondents* (London, 1912), p. 27 — letters which, despite Wise's ambiguous reputation, I assume are genuine.

37. Cf. his attack on the "morality" of *Idylls of the King* in *Under the Microscope,* pp. 34–35. See also Ruth C. Child, "Swinburne as a Social Critic," *PMLA,* LII (1937), 869–876.

38. Quoted by Ford, *Keats and the Victorians,* p. 167.

39. See *Current Literature,* XLVII (1909), 179–182.

40. See Oscar Maurer, Jr., "William Morris and the Poetry of Escape," in Herbert Davis, ed., *Nineteenth-Century Studies* (Ithaca, 1940), pp. 247–276.

41. Pater, "Mr. Morris's Poetry," *Westminster Review,* XL (1868), 145,

reprinted under the title "Aesthetic Poetry" in *Appreciations* (1889), but withdrawn by Pater from subsequent editions.

42. *Hopes and Fears for Art,* in May Morris, ed., *The Collected Works of William Morris,* 24 vols. (London, 1914), XXII, 25–26, 47.

43. In 1860 Pater had exercised his prose by translating passages from *Madame Bovary;* see Gaunt, *Aesthetic Adventure,* p. 57. But his style may also have been influenced by Swinburne's prose and by Rossetti's "Hand and Soul"; see T. Earle Welby, *Revaluations* (London, 1931), p. 201.

44. Beerbohm, "Be It Coziness," *The Pageant,* 1896, p. 230.

45. Mallock, *The New Republic* (1877; London, n.d.), p. 263.

46. Cf. Helen H. Young, *The Writings of Walter Pater* (Lancaster, Pa., 1933), pp. 6–7.

47. For the distinction, see Pater, "Style" (1888), *Appreciations* (London, 1931), p. 36.

48. *Appreciations,* p. 219.

49. Cf. Pater on the brothers Goncourt, in Arthur Symons, *Figures of Several Centuries* (London, 1917), p. 334.

50. Buchanan in *Academy,* XXII (1882), 11–12. For a final recognition of Swinburne, see Buchanan's *Look Round Literature,* p. 385.

51. For Pater on subjectivity and artistic disproportion, see his "Prosper Merimée" (1890), *Miscellaneous Studies* (New York, 1895), pp. 2–3.

CHAPTER X: THE REVOLT FROM REASON

1. See Alan Willard Brown, *The Metaphysical Society: Victorian Minds in Crisis* (New York, 1947).

2. Tennyson, quoted by James Sully, *My Life and Friends* (London, 1918), pp. 199, 201.

3. See Harrison, *Autobiographic Memoirs,* II, 86–87.

4. Defined by Lord Houghton; see Marquess of Crewe, "Lord Houghton," *Eighteen-Seventies,* p. 10.

5. Tennyson, *Memoir,* II, 168, 170.

6. See R. H. Hutton, "The Magnanimity of Unbelief," *Contemporary Thought,* I, 300.

7. Morley, *Critical Miscellanies,* p. 78.

8. See Huxley, *Life and Letters,* I, 193, 198–199; see also II, 249, 402.

9. Karl Pearson, *The Ethic of Freethought* (1883; London, 1901), p. 9.

10. Harriet Martineau, quoted by Morley, *On Compromise,* p. 161n.

11. See Hutton, *Contemporary Thought,* I, 298.

12. Quoted by Mrs. Kingsley, *Kingsley, Letters and Memories,* pp. 297, 401.

13. Quoted by Everett, *Party of Humanity,* p. 291.

14. Quoted by Everett, p. 283.

15. See Warren Staebler, *The Liberal Mind of John Morley* (Princeton, 1943), p. 90.

16. See Staebler, p. 44.

17. Morley, quoted by Everett, *Party of Humanity,* p. 297.

18. Morley, quoted by Everett, p. 329.

19. Morley, quoted by Staebler, *Liberal Mind of Morley,* p. 91.

20. Leslie Stephen, *An Agnostic's Apology and Other Essays* (London, 1893), pp. 15, 18.

21. Morley, *On Compromise,* p. 131.

22. Stephen, *Apology,* pp. 36, 39–40.

23. See George John Romanes, *Thoughts on Religion* (London, 1895), esp. pp. 102–103, 155–157.

24. John Tyndall, *The Advancement of Science* (New York, 1874), pp. 86–87.

25. James Martineau, *Modern Materialism: Its Attitude towards Theology* (New York, 1876), pp. 118, 121.

26. Cf. R. G. Collingwood on the Positivist view of history, *The Idea of History* (Oxford, 1946), pp. 126–127.

27. Harrison, *Autobiographic Memoirs,* II, 96; cf. II, 323.

28. Comte, quoted by Hutton, *Contemporary Thought,* I, 304.

29. Quoted by Jacques Barzun, "The Critic as Statesman," *Atlantic,* CLXXVIII (1946), 131.

30. See Huxley, *Life and Letters,* I, 322.

31. Quoted by Staebler, *Liberal Mind of Morley,* p. 90.

32. See Harrison, *Autobiographic Memoirs,* II, 258–259.

33. Harrison, I, 214.

34. Harrison, I, 247.

35. Harrison, II, 276.

36. On Newton Hall and its services, see Harrison, II, 257–281. Harrison describes the principal "human sacraments" suggested by Comte: Presentation (to correspond to Christian Baptism), Initiation (like Confirmation), Admission (to mark a man's "coming of age), Destination (to celebrate the adoption of a career, Marriage, and Burial; see II, 278–279, 285–286.

37. For Hutton on Comte's religion, see *Contemporary Thought,* I, 307, 308–309.

38. See Gaylord C. LeRoy, "Richard Holt Hutton," *PMLA,* LVI (1941), 817–818.

39. Hutton, *Contemporary Thought,* I, 244.

40. Hutton, I, 200–203.

41. Hutton, I, 217. Cf. T. S. Eliot on Arnold, "Arnold and Pater," *Selected Essays* (New York, 1932), p. 349: "The effect of Arnold's religious campaign is to divorce Religion from Thought."

42. On the *Grammar of Assent,* see Wilfred Ward, *The Life of John Henry Newman,* 2 vols. (New York, 1912), II, 246; for an excellent analysis of Newman's faith, see Harrold, *Newman,* pp. 118–162.

43. Hutton, *Cardinal Newman* (Boston, 1891), p. 238.

44. Kingsley, "Frederick Denison Maurice, In Memoriam," *Literary and General Lectures and Essays,* pp. 340–341.

45. See Asquith, *Aspects of Victorian Age,* pp. 17–19.

46. Stephen, quoted by Young, *Writings of Pater,* p. 14.

47. Collingwood, *Idea of History,* p. 134.

48. See R. G. Collingwood, *The Idea of Nature* (Oxford, 1945), p. 122.

49. F. H. Bradley, *Ethical Studies* (London, 1876), pp. 85–86, 104, 283, 291, 305–307. Cf. T. S. Eliot's comment on Bradley's view of Arnold, "Francis Herbert Bradley," *Selected Essays,* pp. 364–367.

50. On Bradley's influence, see Charles W. Morris, *Six Theories of Mind* (Chicago, 1932), pp. 47, 76, 77.

51. Harrison, *Autobiographic Memoirs,* I, 136. Pater, more sympathetic than Harrison, lacked the intellectual equipment to follow the Oxford idealists; see Young, *Writings of Pater,* p. 74.

52. Ruskin as Mr. Herbert alone escapes complete absurdity; see W. H. Mallock, *Memoirs of Life and Literature* (New York, 1920), pp. 88–89; cf. Amy Belle Adams, *The Novels of William Hurrell Mallock* (Orono, Me., 1934), p. 37.

53. Mallock's appendix to the *New Paul and Virginia* cites eleven direct parallels to the writings of Tyndall, nine to Harrison, five to Huxley, and three to Clifford — mostly passages which speak of Humanity in emotionally connotative terms or otherwise seek to make a new religion of "rationalism."

54. See Mallock, *Memoirs,* pp. 84–91.

55. See *Memoirs,* p. 260.

56. See *Memoirs,* p. 160.

57. See *Memoirs,* pp. 213–214.

58. See *Memoirs,* pp. 308–328.

59. From Patmore's "The Two Deserts," published in 1868.

60. On Oliphant, see Margaret Oliphant, *Memoir of the Life of Laurence Oliphant,* 2 vols. (Edinburgh, 1891), and Herbert W. Schneider and George Lawton, *A Prophet and a Pilgrim . . . Thomas Lake Harris and Laurence Oliphant* (New York, 1942).

61. The satire was first published in 1865 in *Blackwood's;* first edition as book, London, 1870; first American edition, New York, 1930, with preface by Michael Sadleir.

62. See Everett, *Party of Humanity,* p. 243, and Morley, "Byron" (1870), *Critical Miscellanies,* p. 129.

CHAPTER XI: THE "AESTHETIC" EIGHTIES

1. A. N. Whitehead, *Science and the Modern World* (New York, 1946), p. 149.

2. Ruskin, "The Study of Architecture" (1865), *Works,* XIX, 38. Cf. Morris, above, p. 177.

3. The best survey and evaluation of social thought in the period is Helen Merrell Lynd's *England in the Eighteen Eighties* (New York, 1945).

4. Gissing's first published novel, *Workers in the Dawn,* appeared in 1880. His earlier work consisted of a few stories and sketches published in the *Chicago Tribune* and other American papers.

5. See William York Tindall, *Forces in Modern British Literature, 1885–1946* (New York, 1947), pp. 152–153.

6. *Works of T. H. Green,* III, 41.

7. For a succinct account of the new journalism, see R. C. K. Ensor, *England, 1870–1914* (Oxford, 1936), pp. 310–316.

8. Quoted by Marquess of Crewe, "Lord Houghton," *Eighteen-Seventies,* p. 20.

9. On Mallock's view of poverty and his general debt to the classical economists, see Lynd, *England in the Eighteen Eighties,* pp. 74–76.

10. For Mallock's opinions of the "great ladies," see his *Memoirs,* pp. 97–103. Cf. E. F. Benson, *As We Were* (London, 1930), chap. IX.

11. See Blomfield, *Shaw,* pp. 20–30.

12. Lines from Dobson's "On the Hurry of This Time" (1882) and "Ars Victrix" (1876; "imitated from Théophile Gautier").

13. Henley, "Dobson," *Works of William Ernest Henley,* 5 vols. (London, 1921), IV, 111. For criticism or illustration of the Old French forms, see Gleeson White, ed., *Ballades and Rondeaus* (London, 1887), Helen Louise Cohen, *Lyric Forms from France* (New York, 1922), and J. H. Buckley, *William Ernest Henley* (Princeton, 1945), pp. 81–90.

14. See Tennyson, *Memoir,* II, 92.

15. See Stuart Mason, *Bibliography of Oscar Wilde* (London, 1914), p. 326.

16. Cf. Elton, *Survey of English Literature,* IV, 107.

17. Published in 1882, Walter Hamilton's *Aesthetic Movement in England* indicates the confusion of opinion concerning derivations. Hamilton classes as Aesthetes Browning, Whitman, and Ruskin, as well as Wilde.

18. Buchanan, *Look Round Literature,* p. 197.

19. George Moore, *Confessions of a Young Man* (1888; New York, n.d.), p. 214.

20. Moore, *Confessions,* p. 101.

21. Cf. Wellman, *Victoria Royal,* pp. 94–96.

22. On *Patience,* see Cruse, *Victorians and Their Reading,* p. 387; Isaac Goldberg, *The Story of Gilbert and Sullivan* (New York, 1928), pp. 252, 261; T. F. Dunhill, *Sullivan's Comic Operas* (New York, 1928), pp. 85–86.

23. O'Shaughnessy quoted: Lines from his "Ode" (1874), "Song of a Fellow-worker" (1881), "The Line of Beauty" (1881); prose statement from his preface to his *Songs of a Worker* (London, 1881), pp. vii–viii.

24. See H. A. Needham, *Le Développement de l'esthétique sociologique . . . au XIXe siècle* (Paris, 1926), pp. 205–206.

25. See Tindall's comment, *Forces in Modern British Literature,* p. 239.

26. Wilde, "Apologia" (1881).

27. Orwell, *Dickens, Dali and Others,* p. 157.

CHAPTER XII: THE DECADENCE AND AFTER

1. See Grant Richards, *Memories of a Misspent Youth* (New York, 1933), p. 112.

2. William Watson, "England My Mother" (1892).

3. Henry Newbolt, "The Vigil" (1898).

4. The Rhymers' Club, which was founded in 1891 and met for several

years at the Cheshire Cheese in London, included among its members W. B. Yeats, Ernest Dowson, Lionel Johnson, John Davidson, Ernest Rhys, Richard Le Gallienne, and Arthur Symons. The Rhymers read their own lyrics aloud, discussed poetry in general, and issued two anthologies (1892, 1894) of original verse, traditional in form, mildly "aesthetic" or "Decadent" in tone. See Yeats, *Autobiography* (New York, 1938), and Graham Hough, *The Last Romantics* (London, 1949), pp. 204–212.

5. Dowson, "Spleen" (1896).

6. Symons, "The Pause" (1897).

7. Hubert Crackanthorpe, *Sentimental Studies* (New York, 1895), p. 238; cf. p. 94: "It was a stage-phrase, . . . a stage-situation."

8. Preface to *The Picture of Dorian Gray.*

9. Moore, *Confessions,* pp. 40, 60.

10. See Richard Le Gallienne, *Retrospective Reviews,* 2 vols. (London, 1896), I, 25.

11. On Corvo, as Frederick Rolfe styled himself, see A. J. A. Symons, *The Quest for Corvo* (London, 1934).

12. Beerbohm, "Be It Coziness," *Pageant,* p. 233.

13. G. S. Street, preface to *The Autobiography of a Boy* (London, 1894), reprinted from Henley's "Counter-decadent" *National Observer.*

14. Speaking directly of Wilde, Reggie comments on *Dorian Gray* as basically inconsistent: "After Dorian's act of cruelty, the picture ought to have grown more sweet, more saintly, more angelic in expression." See Robert Hichens; *The Green Carnation* (London, 1894), p. 59.

15. Wilde, *De Profundis* (New York, 1910), p. 36.

16. On this sort of parody in Wilde's plays, see Richard Aldington, ed., *The Portable Oscar Wilde* (New York, 1946), p. 38.

17. See Edgar Snow, *The Pattern of Soviet Power* (New York, 1945), p. 15.

18. Cf. the scene at the dinner party (*Dorian Gray,* chap. III), where Lord Henry's paradox rebukes the sentimental reformers and suggests a rational solution to the miseries of the working class.

19. Symons, "Huysmans," *Figures of Several Centuries,* pp. 282–283.

20. Symons, "The Decadent Movement in Literature," *Harper's New Monthly Magazine,* XXXVII (1893), 867.

21. Quoted by J. Lewis May, *John Lane and the Nineties* (London, 1936), p. 84.

22. The legend embodies many a *fin de siècle* motif. Dorian Gray, significantly, sees in the prelude of Wagner's *Tannhäuser* "a presentation of the tragedy of his own soul."

23. Crackanthorpe, "Reticence in Literature," *Yellow Book,* II (1894), 264.

24. Crackanthorpe, quoted by Richard Le Gallienne, "Hubert Crackanthorpe," *Sleeping Beauty and Other Prose Fancies* (London, 1900), p. 209.

25. Lionel Johnson, "Incurable," *Pageant,* 1896, p. 133.

26. Johnson, "The Dark Angel" (1893).

27. Dowson, "A Last Word" (1899).

28. See Le Gallienne, "The Décadent to His Soul" (1892).

29. On the vogue of Phillips, see Le Gallienne, "Mr Stephen Phillips's Poems," *Sleeping Beauty,* pp. 170–180; see also comments by various critics printed as appendix to Phillips' *Poems* (London, 1900). After the poet's death, John Lane could recall a time when each Phillips volume sold by subscription ten thousand copies before publication; see May, *John Lane,* p. 107.

30. Phillips, quoted by Coulson Kernahan, "When Stephen Phillips Read," *In Good Company* (London, 1917), p. 143.

31. Phillips, "Christ in Hades" (1897).

32. John Davidson, "To the New Men" (1894).

33. Davidson, "St Swithin's Day," *Fleet Street Eclogues* (1896).

34. Davidson, *The Man Forbid and Other Essays* (Boston, 1910), p. 67.

35. *The Man Forbid,* p. 136.

36. Quoted by Donald Davidson, ed., *British Poetry of the Eighteen-Nineties* (New York, 1937), p. 155.

37. See Davidson, *The Testament of John Davidson* (1908).

38. Henley, "Discharged," *In Hospital* (1888).

39. Quoted from an unpublished letter of April 1891 to Austin Dobson, in the possession of Mr. Alban Dobson; transcribed by my friend, Mr. James K. Robinson.

40. Ellis, *New Spirit,* p. 33.

Index